Israel Pocket Library

GEOGRAPHY

Herman Rooks

KETER BOOKS

This book is compiled from material originally published in the *Encyclopaedia Judaica*

P.O. Box 7145, Jerusalem, Israel

Cat. No. 25061

ISBN 0 7065 1320 7

Printed in Israel

CONTENTS

CONTRIBUTORS

Dr. Abraham J. Brawer; Geographer and historian, Tel Aviv

Prof. Michael Avi-Yonah; Professor of Archaeology and of the History of Art, the Hebrew University of Jerusalem

Prof. Isaac Schattner; Emeritus Associate Professor of Geography, the Hebrew University of Jerusalem

Prof. Dov Ashbel; Emeritus Associate Professor of Meteorology, the Hebrew University of Jerusalem

Prof. Leo Picard; Emeritus Professor of Geology, the Hebrew University of Jerusalem

Prof. Jehuda Feliks; Professor of Botany, Bar Ilan University, Ramat Gan

Yaacov Yannai; Commissioner General of the National Parks Authority, Tel Aviv

Maj. Gen. (Res.) Abraham Yoffe; Director of the Israel Nature Reserves Authority, Tel Aviv

1 NAMES

The name Ereẓ Israel (Heb. "the Land of Israel") designates the land which, according to the Bible, was promised as an inheritance to the Israelite tribes. In the course of time it came to be regarded first by the Jews and then also by the Christians as the national homeland of the Jews and as the Holy Land. The concept of *ha-Areẓ* ("the land") had apparently become permanently rooted in the consciousness of the Jewish people by the end of the Second Temple period, at which time the term Ereẓ Israel also became fixed and its usage widespread. Prior to this there was no name in existence, or at any rate in general use, to denote the land in its entirety. At different periods there were names that designated parts of the country, either alone or together with an adjacent territory; in some periods it was regarded as part of a wider geographical unit.

During the Egyptian Middle Empire and the beginning of the New Empire (up to the 19th Dynasty), Ereẓ Israel together with part of Syria (and the Lebanon) was called Retenu (Rtnw). In the New Empire period, especially from the 19th Dynasty (14th–13th centuries B.C.E.) onward, Ereẓ Israel and (central-southern) Syria were referred to as Ḫurru (Ḫù-rú) chiefly as an ethnic term, after the Horites who inhabited the country, especially Syria. The term *pa-Ḫurru* ("[Land of] the Hori[tes]") is still found as late as 238 B.C.E. (Ptolemaic period) in the Greek text of the Canopus inscription as the synonym for "Syria." An additional name employed from the late 14th to the 12th century B.C.E. is Pꜣ-Knʿn. Two other important designations of pre-Israelite Ereẓ Israel are *Ereẓ ha-Emori* (Land of the Amorites) and *Ereẓ Kena'an* (Land of Canaan).

With the Israelite conquest began an entirely new period in the history of Ereẓ Israel, as is expressed in its names. An early term with a widespread usage is *Ereẓ ha-Ivrim* ("land of the Hebrews"—Gen. 40:15). Even later writers, especially Josephus and Pausanias (second century C.E.), sometimes employ this term. After the Israelite conquest, the name Canaan became merely an historical concept but many generations passed before the term Ereẓ Israel became standard usage. The expressions *"ereẓ bene Israel"* ("land of the children of Israel") in Joshua 11:22 and Ereẓ Israel in I Samuel 13:19 refer only to the area inhabited by the Israelites and not to the country as a single geographical entity within its natural boundaries.

Saul, David, and Solomon reigned over the kingdom of Israel, but it is doubtful whether their dominions had an official designation. The biblical references to Ereẓ Israel in the days of David (I Chron. 22:2; II Chron. 2:16) apparently reflect the later period of their composition. After the first split of the united monarchy early in David's reign, "Judah and Israel" sometimes appear side by side to indicate the territory of all the Israelite tribes, but this expression is also considered an anticipation (Josh. 11:21; II Sam. 3:10; 5:5; I Kings 4:20; 5:5). With the final division of the kingdom the name Israel was restricted to the area of the kingdom of Ephraim while the kingdom of the Davidic dynasty was known as the land of Judah. The land of Israel mentioned in II Kings 5:2 refers to the kingdom of all the tribes. In Ezekiel, Gilead and Judah in one reference are explicitly excluded from the territory of Ereẓ Israel; in another Jerusalem, though in Judah, is included in Ereẓ Israel (27:17; 40:2; 47:18).

The shortened form *ha-Areẓ* is already found in Leviticus 19:23; Joshua 11:23; 12:1; Ezekiel 45:1; Ruth 1:1; but the Mishnah, which also uses it, is the first to employ the term Ereẓ Israel to denote the "land of the children of

Mer-ne-ptah stele, with first-known mention of "Israel," 1230 B.C.E.
From W. Flinders Petrie, *Six Temples at Thebes.* →

3

Israel." After the Assyrian Exile, when the remnants of the people in the country centered in Judah, the name Jew (*Yehudi*) became a synonym for Israelite and Hebrew (Jer. 34:9). In the post-Exilic period, Judah (*Yehud* in

Jar handle stamped with the name Y[E]H[U]D from Tell en-Nasbeh, Persian period (fifth–fourth century B.C.E.). Jerusalem, Israel Department of Antiquities.

Aramaic) was the official name of the autonomous area of Jewish settlement and later of the Hasmonean and Herodian kingdoms, even though these extended over a much larger area than that of Judah in the First Temple period. The name *Yehud* was used by the Persian authorities in their Aramaic documents and it also appears on coins struck by the province; it was continued by the Greeks (*Iouda, Ioudaia*) and the Romans (Judaea). After the Bar Kokhba War (132–135), the Romans changed its name to Palaestina so as to emphasize that the rebellious Jewish nation had lost its right in its homeland. Coins from the

Coin bearing words "Shekel Yisrael," struck in Jerusalem, 68 C.E., during the revolt against Rome. Jerusalem, Israel Department of Antiquities.

Hasmonean period do not mention Israel but only *Ḥever ha-Yehudim* ("Council of the Jews"), which perhaps designates the governing body of the nation and not the territory. On the other hand, coins issued during the Jewish and Bar Kokhba Wars bore the inscription Israel (e.g., "*Shekel Yisrael,*" "*Le-Ḥer[ut] Yisrael*") but whether this referred to the people or the country is unknown. The name Judah in its broader meaning disappeared almost entirely from Hebrew literature and the Aramaic language and in the end it was replaced by the terms Ereẓ Israel and the Aramaic Ar'a de-Yisra'el and the name Ereẓ Israel entered all the languages spoken by Jews throughout the Diaspora.

Judaea Capta coin from the Roman period (after 70 C.E.). Jerusalem, Israel Museum.

The name " Palestine" was originally an adjective derived from Philistia *(Peleshet).* It is first mentioned by Herodotus 1.105 in the form *Συρία ἡ Παλαιστίνη* i.e., "the Philistine Syria"; it was subsequently shortened, the adjective "Palaistinei" becoming a proper noun. It was revived by the emperor Hadrian, who applied it to the whole country in order to eradicate the name Judea and from Byzantine times became the accepted name of Ereẓ Israel in non-Jewish languages. The Crusaders used the name Palestine but the name was only used officially again between the two World Wars. On May 14, 1948, the Jewish-held part of Western Palestine was given the name the "State of Israel" in the declaration of independence promulgated by the People's Council. Transjordan, together with Arab-inhabited parts of Western Palestine, later became the Hashemite Kingdom of Jordan, and a strip on the southwestern coast, occupied by Egypt, became known as the Gaza Strip.

2 BOUNDARIES

ACCORDING TO BIBLE AND TALMUD. The classical Jewish sources distinguish between three borders of Ereẓ Israel: (1) "the boundary of the Patriarchs," based on Genesis 15:18–21: "from the river of Egypt (the Nile) unto the great river, the river Euphrates . . ."; (2) "the boundary of those coming out of Egypt," based on Deuteronomy 1:7–8; 11:24; Joshua 1:4; 13:2–5, which was interpreted as extending from Mt. Amanus to the Brook of Egypt (Wadi el-Arish; Tosef., Ter. 2:12; Tosef., Ḥal. 2:11; Git. 8a, et al.); and (3) "the boundary of those returning from Babylonia," within which the halakhic rules for Ereẓ Israel applied, i.e., this is the actual area of Jewish settlement in talmudic times (Tosef., Shev. 4:11; Sif. Deut. 51; TJ, Shev. 6:1, 36c). Excluding the gentile coastal cities, the border extended from the coast of Galilee to Ijon, continued to the Hauran in the east, followed the desert road down to Rabbath-Ammon and Petra, and returned to the coast along the Roman *limes*. The biblical expression "from Dan even to Beer-Sheba" is used in II Samuel 24:2 and I Kings 5:5 to designate Ereẓ Israel in its limited sense corresponding to the area "from the valley of Arnon unto mount Hermon" in the lands beyond the Jordan (Josh. 12:1).

NATURAL FEATURES IN HISTORICAL SOURCES. The ancient texts do not mention all of the country's natural geographical features. Those found include Mt. Lebanon (Deut. 11:24; Josh. 1:4) and Mt. Hermon (also called Sirion and Senir; Deut. 3:9) in the north and the principal rivers of the Coastal Plain, Litas (Egyptian *Ntn*, cf. Theophanes, *Chronography*, 6235), Belus (Jos., Wars, 2:189), Kishon (Judg. 5:21; I Kings 18:40), Chorseus

(Ptolemy, *Geography*, 5:14, 3), Shihor-Libnath (Josh. 19:26), and Jarkon (Josh. 19:46). In the central mountain range, termed the "hill country of Naphtali" (Josh. 20:7), Mts. Tabor and Moreh are prominent landmarks (Josh. 19:22; Judg. 7:1). South of the Jezreel Valley (Judg. 6:33), also known as the "Great Plain" (I Macc. 12:49), are Mt. Carmel, the *rosh kadosh* ("sacred promontory," as it is already called in inscriptions of Thutmosis III, c. 1469 B.C.E.) in the west, and Mt. Gilboa in the east (I Sam. 28:4). These mountains are outcrops of Mt. Ephraim (Josh. 17:15) whose most outstanding peaks are Mts. Gerizim and Ebal (Deut. 11:29). Baal-Hazor (II Sam. 13:23) marks the beginning of the Judean mountains, where the famous Mount of Olives stands (Zech. 14:4). The Sharon and the Shephelah extend to the west of the central mountain range which ends in the Negev (Isa. 65:10; Josh. 9:1; Deut. 1:7). The four main rivers of Ereẓ Israel east of the Jordan are the Hieromices (Yarmuk; Pliny, *Natural History*, 5:16, 74), Jabbok (Josh. 212:2), Arnon (Deut. 2:24), and the Zered (Num. 21:12), of which the latter two empty into the Dead Sea. The Jordan itself flows through Lake Semechonitis (Lake Ḥuleh, Jos., Wars, 4:3) and Lake Gennesareth or Chinnereth (Num. 34:11—modern Lake Kinneret) and completes its course in the Salt Sea (Num. 34:3, now known as the Dead Sea) which is also called Lake Asphaltitis (Pliny, *Natural History*, 5:12, 72; Jos., Wars, 4:476). The term Arabah is applied to the whole of the Jordan Valley and the area south of the Dead Sea (Deut. 1:7; 34:1–3). The latter area is also called the Valley of Salt (II Sam. 8:13). To the east beyond the Jordan are the mountains of Bashan (Ps. 68:16), Gilead (Gen. 31:25), Seir (Gen. 14:6), and the most prominent—Mt. Nebo (or Pisgah, Deut. 32:48–50; 34:1) from which Moses beheld the Promised Land.

HISTORICAL BOUNDARIES AND SUBDIVISIONS. The earliest complete description of the boundaries of Ereẓ Israel is contained in Numbers 34. This is regarded by scholars as a definition of the limits of the Egyptian province of Canaan as established in the peace treaty between Ramses II and the Hittites (c. 1270 B.C.E.). The province of Canaan included the entire area west of the Jordan, Phoenicia up to Mt. Hor north of Byblos, and the Bashan, Hauran, and Hermon areas. No subdivisions of this area are known—the system of Canaanite city-states did not lend itself to any clear administrative organization. The next detailed account of the borders appears in Joshua 13–19. The date of this source and of the various fragments of lists from which it was compiled is disputed by scholars. It is nevertheless evident from the list of unconquered Canaanite cities in Judges 1:21–35 that the ideal and actual limits of Israelite power did not coincide. The theoretical boundaries extended from Sidon in the north and Lebo-Hamath in the northeast to the Brook of Egypt and the Negev in the south and included east of the Jordan the Bashan and Hauran, and Gilead and Moab down to the Arnon. In actual fact, however, the area occupied by the Israelite tribes before the time of David was limited to the mountains of Galilee and Ephraim, Judah to the southern end of the Dead Sea, and most of the area between the Yarmuk and the Arnon, excluding Ammon. In the Coastal Plain Israelite control was tenuous and Canaanite enclaves in the Jezreel Valley and around Jerusalem virtually cut Israelite territory into three separate parts. South of Jaffa the entire Coastal Plain remained the domain of the Philistines who threatened to encroach on the territory held by the Israelites.

The lands of the tribes were divided as follows: the Bilhah tribes, Dan and Naphtali, held E. Galilee (Dan being a latecomer to the area after an unsuccessful attempt to take possession of part of the Shephelah W. of Jerusalem); three tribes of the Leah-Zilpah group, Issachar, Asher, and Zebulun, settled W. and S. Galilee; the central group of tribes, the House of Joseph (Ephraim and Manasseh) together with the allied Benjamite tribe—all three of the Rachel group—occupied the hill country from Jerusalem to the Jezreel Valley, with Manasseh overspilling into Issachar and east of the Jordan (Josh. 17:11; Judg. 1:27; Num.

32:33); the southern group included the Leah tribes of Judah, centered upon Hebron, and the weak tribe of Simeon on the borders of the Negev; Reuben, Gad, and half of Manasseh occupied the lands east of the Jordan with Reuben subject to Gad as was Simeon to Judah.

From the time of King David onward, the ideal borders of Ereẓ Israel came much closer to realization. David closed the gaps dividing the tribes by conquering Jerusalem, the Jezreel Valley, and the coastal area between Jaffa and Acre. Jerusalem, originally within Benjamin, was made a royal domain outside the tribal system. David, moreover, subdued all the lands up to Lebo-Hamath, annexed Ammon, Moab, and Edom (thereby reaching the Arabah and the Red Sea) and dominated the kings of Hamath and the Philistines by means of vassal treaties. David's kingdom thus extended from the Brook of Egypt to Tiphsah on the Euphrates, although not all of his domain was regarded as Ereẓ Israel proper. He established a network of levitical cities to serve as administrative centers uniting the kingdom. Solomon reorganized the kingdom into 12 districts (excluding Judah), unequal in size, but equal in economic importance. Each district was to supply his court with its needs during one month of the year. Some of these districts were identical with the old tribal areas while others were new units. According to I Kings 4:7–19 the districts included: (1) Mount Ephraim; (2) Makaz (from Beth-Shemesh to the coast); (3) Hepher (the Sharon coast); (4) Dor and its region; (5) Jezreel Valley; (6) northern Gilead; (7) southern Gilead (Mahanaim); (8) Naphtali; (9) Asher; (10) Issachar; (11) Benjamin; (12) Gad. Judah's exclusion from this tax-paying area was one of the causes of the subsequent split of the monarchy. As to the external boundaries of the kingdom, Solomon gained Gezer, but lost Cabul to Hiram of Tyre as well as Aram-Damascus, which deprived him of access to the Euphrates.

With the division of the monarchy under Rehoboam, the northern kingdom of Israel consisted of Ephraim, Galilee, Gilead, and the rest of Israelite territory east of the Jordan.

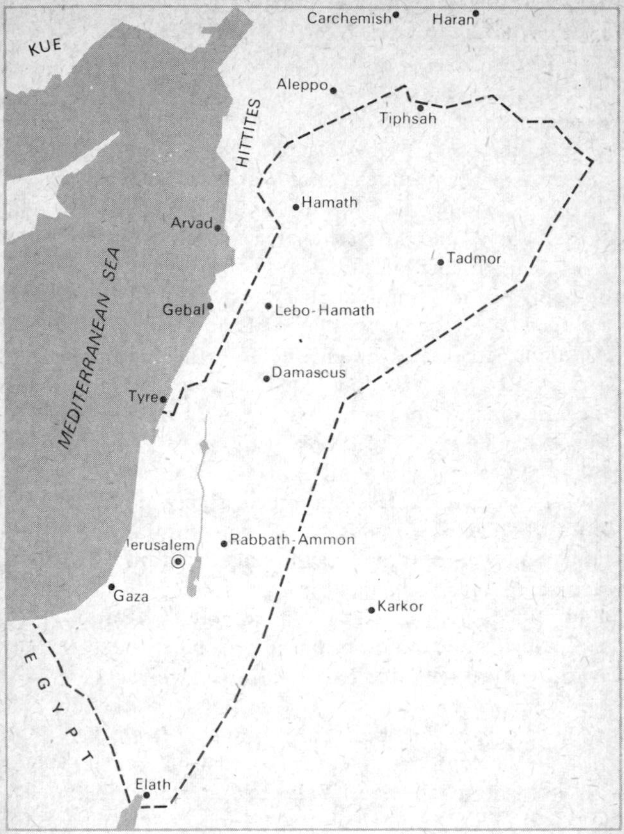

The limits of the kingdom of David and Solomon (10th century B.C.E.). After Y. Aharoni, *Carta's Atlas of the Bible.*

The southern kingdom of Judah retained Benjamin. The subject areas of Ammon, Moab, and Edom soon liberated themselves from the overlordship of weakened Israel and Judah. Apart from some futile attempts by Abijah of Judah to advance into Israel (c. 911 B.C.E.) and of Baasha of Israel to push the frontier closer to Jerusalem, the boundaries of the two kingdoms remained fairly stable. Their external borders, however, changed according to the vicissitudes of their power. On the northern front the house of Omri, and of Ahab in particular, waged several wars with Aram-Damascus and in the end lost Ramoth-Gilead (c. 850 B.C.E.). With the weakening of Aram under Assyrian pressure, Jehoash and Jeroboam II (c. 790–770) advanced to Damascus and Lebo-Hamath, almost restoring the boundaries of David. Moab was definitely lost to Mesha in approximately 855 B.C.E. In Judah, Asa or Jehoshaphat (c. 860 B.C.E.) advanced to Elath, which, together with Edom, was later lost but reconquered in the days of Uzziah (c. 750 B.C.E.) who also extended the frontier of the Judahite monarchy in the direction of Philistia (II Chron. 26:6). As to the internal administration of the two kingdoms, the capital of Israel was first at Shechem, then—perhaps already under Jeroboam in the tenth century B.C.E.—at Tirzah, and from the time of Omri (882–871 B.C.E.) at Samaria. Ostraca found at Samaria provide information on the division of the kingdom into districts in the eighth century B.C.E. The division of the Judahite monarchy into 12 districts is preserved in Joshua 15:21–62; 18:25–28. From the eighth century onward, the Assyrians began reducing the boundaries of Israel. In 732 B.C.E. Tiglath-Pileser III captured Galilee and Gilead, leaving only Samaria to Israel. In the conquered territory he established the Assyrian provinces of Megiddo, Dor, Karnaim, Hauran, and Gilead. Sargon II (722–705 B.C.E.) conquered the rest of the Northern Kingdom (721 B.C.E.) and Philistia and organized them into two additional provinces: Samaria and Ashdod. Assyria's decline in the seventh century enabled Josiah of Judah (639–609 B.C.E.) once again to extend the rule of the Davidic dynasty over most of Samaria and Galilee, but the Babylonian conquest in 587 B.C.E. brought about the final downfall of Judah. They diminished its borders and established an additional province in Edom south of Judah.

After the establishment of Persian rule (539 B.C.E.) all of Ereẓ Israel was included in its fifth satrapy called 'Abar-

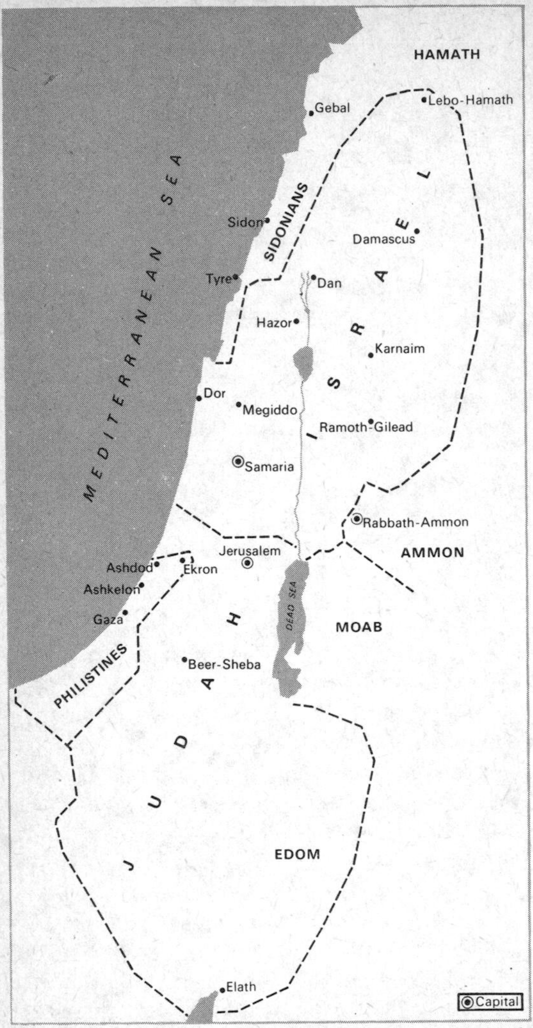

The borders of the kingdoms of Israel and Judah in the time of Jeroboam II and Uzziah, mid-eighth century B.C.E. After Y. Aharoni, *Carta's Atlas of the Bible*.

naharah ("beyond the river," i.e., the Euphrates). Its satrap residing at Damascus had under his control the various provinces as inherited from the Assyrians and Babylonians. The province of Judah (officially called Yehud) extended from Beth-El in the north to Beth-Zur in the south and from Emmaus and Keilah in the west to the Jordan in the east. The province was subdivided into six districts (called *pelekh* in Hebrew) each with a capital and subcapital. These included Jerusalem with Netophah as its subcapital in the center of Judah; Beth-Cherem (Ein Kerem) in the west (Y. Aharoni identifies Beth-Cherem with Netophah = Ramat Raḥel) with Zanoah as its subcapital, Keilah with Adullam in the southwest; Beth-Zur with Tekoa in the south; Jericho with Hassenaah in the east; Mizpah (Tell en-Nasbeh) with Gibeon in the north. The Persians continued the Babylonian provinces but added the province of Ammon which was administered by the Jewish Tobiad family. The coastal area was divided between the Phoenician cities Tyre and Sidon.

The Hellenistic conquest (332 B.C.E.) did not alter the country's internal subdivision for the time being. The Ptolemies, kings of Egypt, who ruled the whole of Ereẓ Israel from 301 to 198 B.C.E., granted autonomy to the coastal cities and gave Greek names to various cities (e.g., Acre became Ptolemais, Rabbath-Ammon became Philadelphia, etc.). The Tobiads were restricted to the western part of their district. All of Ereẓ Israel was administered from Alexandria. When Antiochus III conquered Ereẓ Israel, he established larger units, eparchies, each of which included several smaller Ptolemaic districts or hyparchies. Thus Samaria now ruled over Judea and Galilee and Perea of the Tobiads. Idumea remained a separate district, the coastal cities were joined into one district, and Paralia and all the lands east of the Jordan were combined into Galaaditis, except for Perea. The Seleucids, who were energetic Hellenizers, particularly Antiochus IV (175–164 B.C.E.), founded many Greek poleis, such as Scythopolis (Beth-Shean), Pella, Gerasa, Gadara, and Hippus. Samaria had been a Macedonian colony since the time of Alexander.

The main events in the period between the outbreak of the Hasmonean revolt (167 B.C.E.) and the death of Alexander Yannai (76 B.C.E.) were the expansion of the Jewish state, paralleled by the disintegration of Seleucid rule. In 147 B.C.E. Jonathan, the first ruler of the Hasmonean dynasty, received Ekron and the three districts of Lydda, Arimathea, and Aphaerema. Some time before 144 B.C.E. he was also ceded Perea. His brother Simeon (142–135 B.C.E.) annexed Jaffa and Gezer and Simeon's son John Hyrcanus I (135–104 B.C.E.) extended his sway over Idumea, Samaria, Scythopolis, and the inner Carmel, as well as Heshbon and Medeba east of the Jordan. Judah Aristobulus I, the son of Hyrcanus, who barely reigned one year, added Galilee. The last of the conquering Hasmoneans, Alexander Yannai (103–76 B.C.E.), captured the whole coast from Rhinocorura (El-Arish) on the Brook of Egypt to the Carmel promontory, all of Western Gilead from Paneas (Banias) to Gerasa, and all the lands around the Dead Sea. Only Acre-Ptolemais, Philadelphia, and Ascalon remained outside his rule, the last with Yannai's consent. In their internal organization of the state, the Hasmoneans preserved the basic subdivision—toparchy—of which there were 24, corresponding to the 24 *ma'amadot* (literally, "place of standing") of the Temple service. They also followed Ptolemaic practice by establishing a larger administrative unit called *meris*, and divided the country into five of them: Galilee, Samaria, Judea, Idumea, and Perea.

Roman intervention under Pompey put an end to the expansion of the Hasmonean state. Under Pompey's settlement of 63 B.C.E. the Jewish state was reduced to Judea, including Idumea and Perea, and to Galilee. The Greek cities conquered by the Hasmoneans were "freed." Those cities along the coast were placed under the supervision of the Roman governor of Syria and those east of the Jordan were united into a league of ten cities, known as the Decapolis. The Samaritans regained their independence, the Itureans obtained the Gaulan and Paneas, and the Nabateans, the Negev and the lands around the Dead Sea. Pompey's harsh arrangements were somewhat alleviated by Julius Caesar, who in 47 B.C.E. restored Jaffa and the Plain of Jezreel to Judea. When Herod replaced the Hasmonean dynasty in 40 B.C.E. he was given, in addition to the lands held by Mattathias Antigonus, the last Hasmonean ruler, the region of Marisa (destroyed by the Parthians in 40

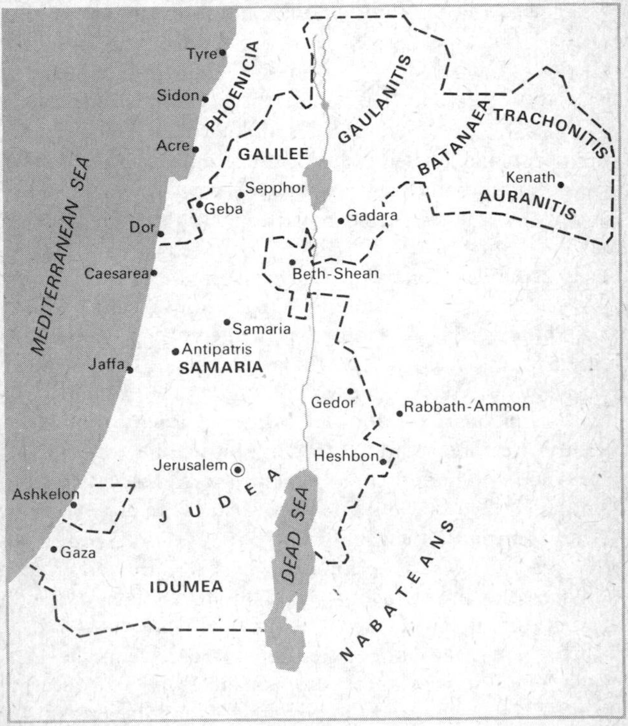

The borders of the kingdom of Herod (37–4 B.C.E.). After M. Avi-Yonah, *Carta's Atlas of the Period of the Second Temple, the Mishnah and the Talmud.*

B.C.E.) and the lands of the Samaritans. In 30 B.C.E. Augustus granted him the coastal area from Gaza to Caesarea (originally called Straton's Tower) as well as Samaria (renamed Sebaste), Gadara, and Hippus in the interior. In 23 B.C.E. Herod received Batanea (Bashan), Trachonitis, and the Hauran, and in 20 B.C.E. Augustus finally added Paneas and the Gaulan. Herod's kingdom was administered on a dual basis: the Greek cities were more or less autonomous, while the remainder, the "King's country," was ruled directly by royal officials. Herod retained the division into *merides* and toparchies. Two lists of his toparchies have been preserved: one by Pliny (*Natural History,* 5:15, 70) who enumerates them as follows: (1) Jericho; (2) Emmaus; (3) Lydda; (4) Joppa (Jaffa); (5) Acrabitene; (6) Gophna; (7) Thamna; (8) Betholeptephene (Beit Nattif); (9) Orine (Jerusalem); (10) Herodium. To this list Josephus adds Idumea, En-Gedi, and Jamnia (Wars, 3:54–55). After Herod's death (4 B.C.E.) his kingdom was divided among his three sons. Archelaus received Judea, Idumea, Samaria, and Caesarea; Herod Antipas received Galilee and Perea; Philip received Caesarea Philippi and the lands east of the Jordan. The Greek cities were placed under the governor of Syria. When Archelaus was deposed in 6 C.E. his lands were administered by a Roman procurator. This was the situation in Jesus' time. After the death of Philip, his nephew Agrippa I received his inheritance, to which were added the lands of Antipas in 39 C.E., and in 41 C.E. also those of Archelaus. When Agrippa I died in 44 C.E. part of his kingdom was reserved for his son Agrippa II (Philip's share and eastern Galilee) but most of it was administered by Roman procurators up to the Jewish War (66–73).

After the siege and destruction of Jerusalem, the Provincia Judaea was under the rule of Roman governors. In 106 Trajan annexed the Nabatean kingdom, transforming it into the Provincia Arabia. Urbanization progressed rapidly in the following centuries. Vespasian turned the lands of the Samaritans into the city of Neapolis; Hadrian set up Aelia Capitolina on the ruins of Jerusalem; Septimius Severus turned Lydda into Diospolis and Bet Guvrin into Eleutheropolis until finally only Upper Galilee, the Gaulan and Bashan, and the Jordan Valley remained non-urban areas. Under Diocletian (284) the southern part of the Roman province of Arabia was attached to that of Palaestina which was partitioned in Byzantine times. In 358 the Negev and southern Transjordan were detached and formed into Palaestina Salutaris. In c. 400 the remainder was subdivided into Palaestina Prima (its capital at Caesarea) and Palaestina Secunda (its capital at Scythopolis) and the third province, Palaestina Salutaris, was now called Palaestina Tertia; its governor resided in Petra.

This threefold division continued under the Arabs: Palaestina Prima became Jund Filasṭīn, Palaestina Secunda, Jund al-Urdunn, and Palaestina Tertia was abandoned to the Bedouins. The province of Filasṭīn was administered from the new city of Ramleh and Urdunn from Tiberias. The Crusaders (end of the 11th century) first established themselves on the coast and to the west of the Jordan; at the zenith of their power their kingdom included all of Ereẓ Israel west of the Jordan to Deir el-Balah, the Jordan Valley, and the Seir Mountains down to Elath. Their feudal administration was centered on a royal domain around Jerusalem with royal vassals in the rest of the country: the principality of Galilee, the seigniories of Jaffa and Ashkelon, Caesarea, St. Jean d'Acre (Acre), Naples (Nablus), St. Abraham (Hebron), Toron (northern Galilee), and Outre Jourdain. After the debacle at the hands of Saladin in 1187, Richard the Lion-Hearted in 1192 reconstituted the Crusader kingdom along the coast from Jaffa to Tyre and included western Galilee. In 1228 Frederick II added a corridor to Jerusalem and Bethlehem and Richard of Cornwall (1240/41) added the area southward to Ashkelon and Beit Guvrin and eastward to the Jordan near Jericho and in Galilee. From 1250 the kingdom gradually shrank under Mamluk attacks.

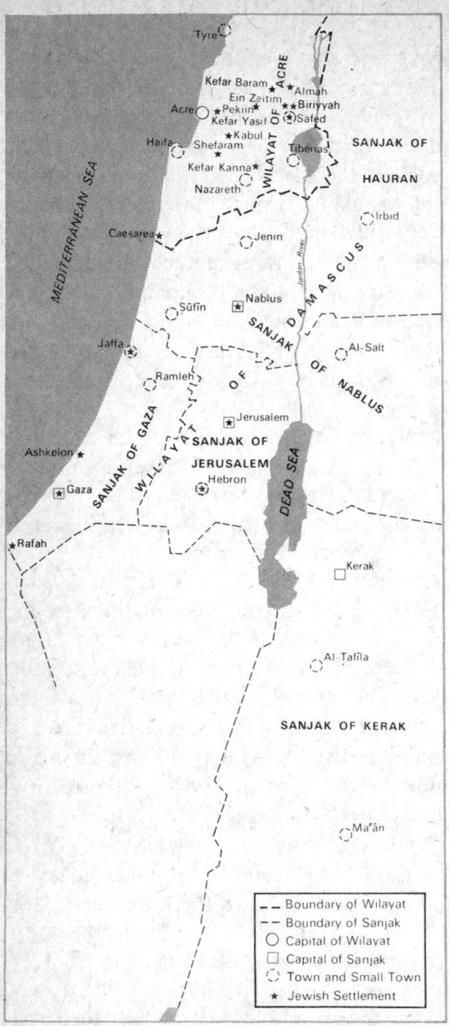

The Land of Israel under Ottoman rule, 17th century C.E. After *Atlas of Israel*, Survey of Israel, 1970.

The Mamluks (1250–1516) divided Ereẓ Israel into a number of "mamlakas": Ghazza (coast); Safed (Galilee); Dimashq (Damascus; Samaria, Judea, northern Transjordan); and el-Kerak (southern Transjordan).

Under the Turks (1516–1917), a wali at Acre ruled from the Carmel to Galilee, while his colleagues at Esh-Sham (Damascus) held the rest of Ereẓ Israel, which was subdivided into the sanjaks of Nablus (including Al-Salt), Al-Quds (Jerusalem), Gaza, Hauran, and Kerak. From 1874 Jerusalem with southern Judea was administered directly from Constantinople as a separate sanjak or *mutessarifliq*. The Turks reestablished their rule over the Negev, but in 1906 the British forced them to cede the Sinai Peninsula to Egypt.

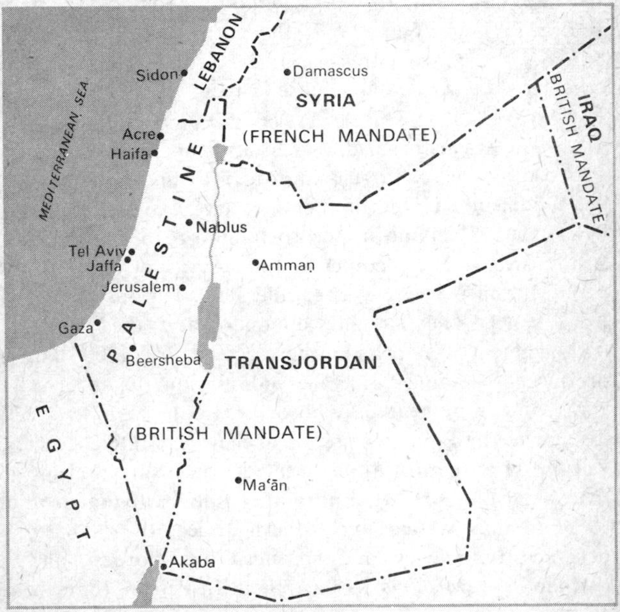

The British Mandate, 1922.

The Mandatory area (from which Transjordan was detached in 1922) extended from Dan (Metullah) to Elath, and from the Mediterranean coast up to Ras en-Naqura to the Jordan. Northern Transjordan was at first part of the French Mandate and then of Syria. During the 30 years of the British Mandate, the subdivision of the country varied from six districts to two (with a separate Jerusalem division). In 1946 at the end of the Mandate there were six: Galilee, Haifa, Samaria, Jerusalem, Gaza, and "Lydda," so called because although it contained the largest city in Ereẓ Israel—Tel Aviv—the Mandatory officials refused to honor it with the name of a district.

From 1949 to 1967 the State of Israel was bounded by the lines of the Armistice Agreements, leaving to Jordan the districts of Jenin, Nablus, Ramallah, and Hebron, as well as the lands east of the Jordan. Egypt occupied the Gaza Strip. In the Six-Day War, 1967, the entire area west of the Jordan, the Gaza Strip, and the Golan Heights were conquered by the Israel Defense Forces.

ETHNOGRAPHY: The earliest inhabitants of Ereẓ Israel of whom there is historical documentation are the West Semitic tribes known as Amurru (Amorites). In the Bible they are subdivided into a large number of groups, known collectively as Canaanites, a name properly belonging to the Phoenicians. In the Bronze Age, peoples of Indo-Aryan origin (Hittites and Mitanni) became the rulers of various cities in Ereẓ Israel. The Israelite conquest and the Philistine entrenchment on the southern coast (c. 1200 B.C.E.) produced a change in the population balance. The Canaanites were gradually absorbed by the Semitic Israelites, while the Philistines retained their separate character. The Assyrian deportations created a new mixed element, the Samaritans, in Mt. Ephraim. Under Babylonian rule, the Edomites settled in southern Judea, the Nabateans occupied the Negev and southern Transjordan, and a remnant of Jews clung to Jerusalem. In Persian times Jews returned from captivity in Babylonia and the Phoenicians and some Greek settlers inhabited the coast. Hellenistic rule brought an influx of Greeks as officials, soldiers, merchants, and estate owners and the coastal areas and part of the inland cities became Hellenized. At that time there was an overspill of Jews northward into Samaria and eastward into Perea. The Hasmoneans made the Idumeans (Edomites) and the Galileans assimilate with the Jews. During Herod's rule Jewish settlements in northern Transjordan expanded, while a sprinkling of Romans and Greeks settled in Judea and Galilee. After the Bar Kokhba War, the Jews were expelled from Judea and replaced by Syrian and Arab colonists; Galilee, however, remained Jewish up to the end of Byzantine times.

Arabs gradually began to infiltrate into Ereẓ Israel in the late Byzantine period, even before the Arab conquest. After their conquest the Christians in the country slowly became Islamized. The crusader period brought an incursion of West Europeans, mainly French, Normans, and Italians, but, lacking extensive agricultural settlements, they were unable to root themselves in the country and withdrew after the crusader collapse. From the ninth century onward, Seljuk, Kurdish, and Turkish mercenaries settled in the country, remaining its rulers until the 19th century. European colonization was resumed on a small scale by the German Templars, and many other Europeans settled in the cities for religious or commercial reasons. The Jews, who had clung throughout the Middle Ages to the "Four Holy Cities" (Jerusalem, Safed, Tiberias, and Hebron) and were reinforced from time to time by newcomers from Europe, began to expand their settlement from 1878 onward, assisted first by the Rothschilds and later by the Zionist Organization. From a population of 80,000 in 1918 they increased to over 2 million in 1972.

3 PHYSIOGRAPHY

Introduction. *Despite its historical origin and usage, the name Ereẓ Israel (Land of Israel) may very appropriately be applied to designate a major regional entity within the Fertile Crescent, wedged between the Mediterranean on the west and the Syrian and Arabian Deserts on the east and southeast. Throughout historical and very likely also prehistorical times, this area served as a bridge between adjacent African and Asian regions. It is adequately defined by "natural boundaries," i.e., major physiographical features beyond which relief configuration or climatic conditions and associated surface phenomena change markedly, as postulated by regional geography for the concept of a major unit of the earth's surface. The region is distinctively delimited on the west by the vast expanse of the Levantine Basin of the Mediterranean. Moreover, along this particular section of the coastline there are no islands, which could complicate proper delineation. Similarly, the Gulf of Eilat, by which Ereẓ Israel has access to the Indian Ocean, clearly demarcates the maximum extension toward the south. On the east, northeast, southeast, and southwest, Ereẓ Israel is bounded by extensive tracts of the great global, subtropical desert belt (Syrian Desert, Arabian Desert, and Sinai Desert). The marginal areas of this desert belt, in which the climatic conditions undergo a change from semiarid to fully arid, form the historical border zone of Ereẓ Israel as well. In the Sinai Peninsula, the Negev plains continue without interruption up to the Wadi

* Official transliteration of place-names can be found in *The New Israel Atlas*; 1969.

el-Arish, the Brook of Egypt according to the tradition. To the east, an adequate, though not continuous, delineation is afforded by a watershed zone between rivers west and east of it. Although it is not a prominent relief feature, this zone also denotes a sort of a border between the semiarid and Mediterranean areas to the west and the arid ones to the east. The northern boundaries of Ereẓ Israel are fairly well defined. There the valley of Qasimiye—the lower course of the Leontes (Litani) River—and, further east, the towering Hermon Massif form a marked natural boundary between Ereẓ Israel and the Lebano-Syrian region.

Ereẓ Israel, however, is not considered a regional entity merely because of its natural confines. These are mainly concomitant consequences of the fact that the area is morphogenetically a very consistent surface unit in almost all its physiographical aspects. The area is decidedly influenced by a singular major phenomenon: the Jordan-Dead Sea-Arabah Rift Valley, which also forms the meridional axis of Ereẓ Israel along its entire length. The morphogenetic impact of the Rift Valley is outwardly expressed by the main drainage pattern of the region. About 70% of Ereẓ Israel's rivers (and far more of its overall runoff, if the quantities of the inflow are considered) discharge into the Rift Valley, in relation to which the areas with river outlets into the Mediterranean form a sort of foreland. From the hydrographical point of view alone, Ereẓ Israel thus represents primarily the catchment area of the Rift Valley, which, within this region, is characterized by some unique topographical features. It is the deepest continental depression on the earth and contains an inland sea (the Dead Sea) whose level is about 1,300 ft. (400 m.) lower than that of the Mediterranean, with one of the highest mineral contents of any body of water in the world. Its second large body of water is Lake Kinneret, which is the lowest freshwater body on the earth's surface, about 660 ft. (200 m.) below sea level. The two bodies of water are connected by a river (Jordan River) whose bed, accordingly, is the lowest in the world. This hydrographical condition, namely the predominance of the endoreic area (i.e., an area without outlet into an ocean or a major body of water connected with it), is only one of the many influences exerted by the formation of the Rift Valley upon almost all of the surface configuration of Ereẓ Israel.

From the anthropogeographical point of view, however, the Rift Valley has proven a rather disuniting element. Due to its relative depth, and still more to the height and steepness of the mountain slopes ascending from it to highlands more than 3,300 ft. (1,000 m.) above its floor, enclosing it wall-like with a single wider breach giving access to it only from the west, the Rift Valley was throughout history one of the main factors for the division of the region into two parts, very infrequently—and then only partially—united into a single state. The Rift Valley is thus the prime cause of Ereẓ Israel's subdivision into two main parts: a western one—Mediterranean-oriented Cisjordan (referred to as western Palestine in political and historical geography)—and an eastern one—Transjordan (eastern Palestine). The first may be regarded from the geographic point of view as the mainland, the second as the backland of the entire region.

Situated between the Mediterranean on the west and an almost continuous desert belt on the south and east, and being long and relatively narrow—about 280 mi. (450 km.) in length and about 110 mi. (180 km.) at maximum width—Ereẓ Israel also morphogenetically represents a transition zone. It contains almost all the major relief elements characteristic of the adjacent countries, although generally on a much smaller scale and in somewhat subdued form: coastal plains; mountain ranges, partly continuing the systems of folds fully developed and culminating in Lebanon-Syria and Asia Minor; plateaus, much smaller and more discontinuous here than in the neighboring countries; and basins of all kinds, most of which are greatly affected by and subordinated to the dominant relief feature—the Rift Valley. The same is true of lithological conditions. Outcrops of most kinds of rocks, from basement (magmatic, metamorphic) to sedimentary ones of most recent ages, form its bedrock. Volcanic rocks (basalts, tuffs) are also widely distributed there, as are evaporites (i.e., sediments mainly generated by deposition in outletless inland seas given to intensive evaporation and thus to concentration and consequent consolidation of their solutional contents).

Located between the Mediterranean and the deserts, Ereẓ Israel exhibits complex climatic gradations and transitions ranging from conditions mainly influenced by the sea and manifested primarily by the amount of precipitation to those which already show all the characteristics of a fully desert region—manifested, inter alia, by the relatively extensive surfaces composed of evaporites. A most important characteristic of the region, and particularly of Cisjordan, is therefore the proximity of greatly differing landscapes within relatively small areas resulting mainly from the structural, lithological, and climatic conditions changing over very small distances. The region's very mosaic-like quality is also crucially important as a physiographical background to its history, illuminating, for example, the tendency to regional particularism throughout the area.

The Coastal Plains. THE COASTAL ZONE. Ereẓ Israel is bordered on the west by the Mediterranean Sea. The length of its coastline is about 170 mi. (270 km.) from the mouth of Wadi el-Arish to that of the Qasimiye River. From the morphogenetic and typological points of view, the coast of Ereẓ Israel represents a transition between the coasts of Egypt and Sinai, which are mainly deltaic, and the Lebano-Syrian coast, whose configuration is primarily determined by faulting. The coast of Ereẓ Israel is fairly smooth, without any islands representing detached parts of the mainland. A shelf zone, relatively wide at the southern portion and progressively narrower toward the north, extends along the coast up to about 500 ft. (150 m.) in depth. The coastal zone (i.e., the areas adjacent to the coastline that are directly influenced by the sea) consists of two main parts: a rather uniform southern part, extending from the mouth of the Wadi el-Arish to Tel Aviv-Jaffa, and a northern one that extends up to the mouth of the Qasimiye River. The northern part is far more complex in its origin and consequently in its outline. The southern part of the coastline is almost straight, and its course accords with that of the series of anticlines that form the mountainous backbone of Cisjordan. Sandy beaches, attaining several hundreds of meters in width, extend along the coastline, broken only at the alluvia-filled valley-exits of the rivers discharging into the Mediterranean. Breaks also occur at four other spots: Deir al-Balah, a portion of the coast south of Gaza, Ashkelon, and Mīnat Rūbīn (south of the mouth of the valley of the River Sorek), where coastal cliffs border almost immediately on the sea. The beaches are covered almost exclusively by quartz sands brought from the Nile delta and from the coast of Sinai by currents running close to the shore. Inland, the beach zone is delimited mainly by low ridges composed of sand grains cemented by calcareous material—a rock type called *kurkar* in the vernacular—and passes into areas covered by shifting dunes. The sands of these dunes are mainly of marine origin, i.e., they were brought to the coast by shore currents and waves and then transported inland by winds. The width of the sand-dune belt varies considerably; it attains its maximum—about 4.5 mi. (7 km.)—in the vicinity of Rishon le-Zion.

The northern coastal zone is rather different, in some aspects even opposite, in configuration. It is no longer straight throughout, but indented at some sections by small embayments, several of which form coves (for example at Dor and Athlit). Off-branchings of the inland mountains, the Carmel and the Ḥanitah Range (Rosh ha-Nikrah), border immediately upon the sea, forming high and steep headlands north of which the coastline recesses to form wide embayments. Only the first of these, at Haifa, represents a true bay, extending southeast for about 4 mi. (6 km.) and even forming a small secondary bay at its northern extremity at Acre. The rest of the northern coastline is bordered along its entire length by cliffs of *kurkar*. These cliffs are high as far north as Athlit—attaining a maximum height of about 130 ft. (40 m.) in the vicinity of Netanyah—and then become progressively lower. A very discontinuous small abrasion platform, i.e., a rocky, narrow shore-plane generated by progressive down-and-back erosion of the cliff faces, extends along the greater part of the coast. Waves undercut the cliffs at their bases, and as the cliffs are worn back, their bases form a progressively widening plane. The seaward parts of the platform, subject to the continuous and generally very intensive impact of the waves, in turn gradually become destroyed, with only small isolated remains—reefs—evidencing the earlier extension of the coast 1.2–1.8 mi. (2–3 km.) west of its present course. Beaches are very poorly developed along this northern portion of the coast zone. They exist mostly around coastal indentations or along the bases of cliffs, where they are somewhat protected against the onslaught of waves by an outlying strip of reefs close to the shore or tiers of

Part of the wave-cut, intensively rilled and pitted abrasion platform in the vicinity of Netanyah. Courtesy J.N.F.

beachrock (i.e., coarse sands, pebbles, and shells cemented into rocks). Areas of sand dunes are small and can be found only where the valleys of rivers discharging into the Mediterranean breach the cliffs, creating sufficiently wide gaps for the landward intrusion of wind-borne sands accumulating on the shore. Thus only at the bay of Haifa are beach and dune areas fully developed.

THE COASTAL PLAINS. In the narrow sense, the Coastal Plains are lowlands covered mainly by alluvial soils that extend from the coastal dune areas and the coastal cliff zone, respectively, to the bases of the inland mountains. The plains exhibit a large number of minor relief features, particularly isolated hillocks or those forming small ridges composed of *kurkar,* and a fairly well-developed drainage net, which is more dense toward the north and sometimes exhibits minute gorge-like valleys where traversing the *kurkar* ridges. The ridges extend without a major break from the mouth of Wadi el-Arish to the headland of the Carmel, and from there to the Rosh ha-Nikrah promontory, recurring on a very small scale as far as the valley of the Qasimiye River. From the earliest times the Coastal Plains were one of the most densely populated and intensively cultivated parts of the country, although secondary in historical importance to the mountainous interior regions. They may be rather arbitrarily subdivided into seven units: the Southern Plains (frequently referred to as the Negev Plains); the Judean Plain (including the Philistine Plain as its southern part); the Sharon; the Carmel Coast Plain (usually referred to only as Carmel Coast); the Haifa (Zebulun) Plain; the Galilean Plain (Acre Plain); the Tyre Plain, north of the cape of Rosh ha-Nikrah. Each of the last three units is usually referred to in Hebrew as *emek*, i.e., valley or narrow lowland, because of their limited width.

The Southern Coastal Plains. These plains are separated from the Mediterranean by a relatively narrow belt of sand dunes, 2 mi. (3 km.) wide on the average. Their most important characteristics are determined by climatic conditions. They receive the smallest amount of precipitation in comparison with the other units of the Coastal Plains—El-Arish, approximately 8 in. (200 mm.); Gaza, somewhat less than 16 in. (400 mm.). Due to its proximity to the desert areas, the soils of this plain are composed predominantly of wind-borne loess, probably redistributed by surface flow, and exhibit many intermixing gradations with sands in the southern parts of the plains and with the red-sand soils (called *ḥamra* in the vernacular) at its northern limits. Only two main ephemeral streams (Naḥal Besor and Naḥal Shikmah), about 12 mi. (20 km.) apart at their debouchures into the Mediterranean, traverse the region. Naḥal Besor and its tributaries have turned part of the loess zone into spectacular "badlands," i.e., intensively dissected surfaces that form a microrelief landscape of miniature hillocks and gullies of the most variegated shapes.

Three major topographical zones may be distinguished more or less parallel to the coast. East of the coastal sands, where some dunes attain heights of several tens of meters, a relatively low zone extends, delimited to some extent by discontinuous *kurkar* ridges. This zone forms a gradual ascent to a hillock region in the east and to relatively large areas covered by inland sands of eolian origin in the southeast. Because of its narrowness, elongated shape, and low topography (in comparison with the bordering zones), this area is frequently referred to in the regional geography of Ereẓ Israel as the *marzevah* ("corridor"). This is also a major topographical feature on the plains farther north and had a decisive influence in the past on the sites of settlements and communication lines (Via Maris).

Judean Plain. Rather wide in its southern part—about 15 mi. (25 km.)—the Judean Plain narrows progressively toward the north—about 10 mi. (17 km.), a characteristic common to all the plain regions described below. The plain is separated from the sea by a dune belt, which attains its maximum width—about 4 mi. (7 km.) —here. The "corridor" between the sand zone and the base of the hill country to the east of the plain (the "Shephelah") is more distinct and forms a fairly uniform surface with far fewer and smaller remains of *kurkar* ridges than are found in the Negev Plain. Climatic conditions are fully Mediterranean—16–20 in. (400–500 mm.) annual average precipitation—and are reflected in the soil cover—loess in the southernmost part and *ḥamra* covering almost the whole remaining area with rather large enclaves of heavy soils of alluvial and swamp origin. The genesis of the latter types of soil is connected with the greater number of rivers draining the plain. Although only four of these rivers reach the sea, their courses are frequently deflected to run meridionally by the extension, width, and continuity of the dune belts.

Sharon Plain. Lengthwise, the Sharon Plain extends from the Yarkon, the largest river in Cisjordan discharging into the Mediterranean, up to the Zikhron Ya'akov spur of Mount Carmel. Its width varies considerably, generally narrowing northward to a minimum of about $2\frac{1}{2}$ mi. (4 km.). It also exhibits a distinct meridional zonation, far more pronounced than that of the Judean Plain. Dune areas between the sea and the plain proper, as mentioned before, are rather sporadic there, narrow and short, and restricted to the cliffless parts of the coast, i.e., to the vicinity of the river exits into the sea. Elsewhere, the plain begins immediately behind the zone of the cliffs, which attain considerable height and are continuous, thus preventing the ingress and accumulation of sand farther inland. More or less parallel to the sea cliffs appear two major, though discontinuous, closely spaced *kurkar* ridges which indicate the former coastline. Between them are situated elongated and narrow lowlands, of which only the eastern one attains a width of about 2 mi. (3 km.), whereas the western one is much narrower. East from the *kurkar* ridge zone the "corridor" extends up to the outliers of the Samarian Highland. In contrast to the two above-mentioned intermediate areas between the *kurkar* ridges, with their prevailing *ḥamra* cover, the soil of the "corridor" is mainly alluvial. The amount of precipitation is approximately 4 in. (100 mm.) greater than in the Judean Plain, exceeding an annual average of 24 in. (600 mm.) in some places. This was one of the main preconditions for the large forested areas characteristic of the Sharon in the past. The river network is relatively dense, with far more rivers discharging into the sea than on the Judean Plain. The exits of the rivers here have also been largely blocked both by the dune areas and the *kurkar* ridges. Consequently, large tracts of the Sharon became swampy, particularly in the environs of Ḥaderah and the Ḥefer Plain (the latter was drained by Jewish settlers only in the 1930s).

Carmel Coast Plain. About 22 mi. (35 km.) long, 2–2.5 mi. (3–4 km.) wide at its southern end and a few hundred meters wide at its northern limit, the Carmel Coast Plain ends prominently at the Carmel Headland. The shape of this land unit would fully justify the omission of the term "plain" or even "valley" in its usual meaning. Like the Sharon, a considerable part of this plain consists of *kurkar* ridges, the westernmost of which is almost entirely transformed by marine erosion and ingression into reefs and abrasion platforms and is mainly characterized by

Wind-rippled sand dunes in the Ḥefer Plain, part of the Sharon Plain. Courtesy J.N.F., Jerusalem.

several kinds of indentations, including some coves and minute headlands. The other two ranges of *kurkar* ridges are still preserved, particularly in the southern portion, and greatly impede the passage of the numerous streamlets descending from the Carmel, so that in the past artificial outlets had to be cut into the ridges. Another characteristic of this plain is the relative scarcity of *ḥamra* in comparison with the alluvial soils that are derived mainly from Mount Carmel by erosion and river deposition.

Haifa Bay Plain. Tectonically, this plain represents the westernmost component of the Beth-Shean-Harod-Jezreel Valley system that traverses the entire width of Cisjordan from the Jordan Rift Valley to the Mediterranean. Flanked on the southeast by the high and steep slopes of the Carmel, it exhibits several features absent from the adjacent parts of the coastal plain north and south of it. Along the coast a relatively wide and continuous beach reappears, followed by a belt of sand dunes about a mile wide; no cliff formations are interposed between the plain and the sea. Farther inland it borders the relatively low and gently sloping Yodefat Hills—outliers of the Lower Galilee Mountains. The eastern part of the plain is covered by heavy alluvial soils, partly in consequence of the extensive swamps that existed here in the past. The southern portion of the plain is drained by the sluggishly meandering Kishon River; the northern part is drained by the Na'aman River, fed by springs and extensive swamps behind the sand area. For several kilometers the Na'aman flows parallel to the coastline and along the inland margin of the dune belt.

Acre-Tyre Plain (Galilean Coastal Plain). The coastal plain north of Acre terminates abruptly in the promontory of Rosh ha-Nikrah. It bears some resemblance to the Sharon and still more to the coastal plain of the Carmel. Here the coast is bordered by cliffs (albeit inconsiderable in height) accompanied by an extensive abrasion platform, disjointed parts of which can be discerned in the form of reefs at a distance of 1.2–1.8 mi. (2–3 km.) from the coastline. There are several very small indentations in the coast, which is subject to strong marine erosion. The paucity and smallness of beaches and their predominant cover of coarse sands are also the result of wave erosion. No larger dune-sand accumulations intervene between the coast and the plain, and there are only few and small remnants of *kurkar* ridges. The narrow plain—4 mi. (7 km.) maximum width—is bordered on the east by interfluves, i.e., mountain spurs created by the numerous rivers from the Upper Galilee Mountains discharging into the Mediterranean. These rivers also supply the bulk of the heavy soil material that forms the cover of the plain almost exclusively. The promontory of Rosh ha-Nikrah (the biblical "Tyrian Ladder"), the seaward scarp of an Upper Galilean mountain range along which the present-day border between the State of Israel and Lebanon runs, sharply delimits the Acre Plain. The headland, of a type frequently encountered along the Lebano-Syrian coast and bordering immediately on the sea for a length of about 7 mi. (12 km.), consists of calcareous rock, and its base contains deep sea caves cut in by wave erosion. Beyond the promontory the coastline curves gently in and out, and along it extend beaches and even a continuous, although very small, dune belt. Of specific interest here is Tyre, formerly situated on a reef island but now connected to the mainland as if by a tombolo. This transformation was caused by the accumulations of sand at the dam constructed during the siege of this harbor town by Alexander the Great, and it is one of the countless instances of major landscape transformations effected by man in the Middle East. The coastal plain east of the sand zone is narrower than the Acre Plain and irregularly confined by the east-west-oriented spurs of the Lebanese-Galilee Mountains. It is traversed by a relatively great number of ephemeral rivers which are the main suppliers of the predominantly alluvial soil cover of the plain.

The Western Mountain Zone. Often referred to metaphorically as the backbone of Cisjordan, the Western Mountain Zone extends from Eilat in the south to the Valley of

Qasimiye along the entire length of the region. Within the Levant, it tectonically represents the southernmost outliers of the great Alpine orogenic system and accordingly consists mainly of rather simple and short fold structures generally of medium height. The latter characteristic is also reflected in the term "Hills" (Judean Hills, Samarian Hills, etc.), which is frequently used in this region. In addition to folding, the formation of these mountains was strongly affected by faulting, particularly in the vicinity of the Rift Valley and in Galilee. Despite its moderate elevation above sea level and in relation to the lower surroundings (valleys and basin floors), the relief of this mountainous region, which occupies more than two-thirds of the Cisjordan area, is very pronounced. Steep slopes often appear as major and minor scarp and cliff faces, and surface roughness even on moderate slopes is frequently accentuated, particularly in the southern part of the Mountain Zone, by the almost complete absence of soil and vegetation cover. In the central and northern parts, large tracts were once covered by forests (now largely reduced to sporadic maquis and garigue—brush-and-thorn vegetation), and the slopes were terraced, creating a main area of cultivation. These terraces, now largely disused and in disrepair, form one of the most conspicuous external features of the slopes. The slopes that were not terraced and the mostly flat or gently domed summit surfaces are covered by coarse detritus of different sizes or are pitted by mostly small and shallow depressions, as a result of strong weathering (especially solutional) of the bare surfaces (which are composed mainly of limestone).

The bold relief of the Cisjordan mountains is mainly a result of deep incisions by the watercourses, which created valleys that frequently take the form of gorges or even canyons. In the other types of valleys as well, most of the slopes are very steep, and often no valley floors developed along the river beds. The relatively high frequency of intramontane basins of all sizes is another very important characteristic of the overall relief that contributes greatly to the multiformity and mosaic-like composition of the mountainous region. The extremely variegated pattern of the mountainous zone, resulting in a large number of small regions—and thus contributing to the particularist tendencies of its inhabitants throughout history—was brought about by the complexity of its tectonic, lithological, and climatic conditions. Tectonically, the most characteristic aspect of Cisjordan—in sharp contrast to Transjordan—is the most intensive intermixing of major features originating through up and downfolding, mostly with subsequent forms produced by faulting. In the southern and central parts of the Mountain Zone the first group of processes determined—mainly in the form of anti- and synclines—the build-up, extension, and course of the principal ranges, whereas the latter played a decisive role in their disruption. Particularly in the northern part, faulting and associated features virtually obliterate the former structures, creating a relief mainly characterized by intramontane tectonic valleys and ranges, the extent and orientation of which is determined by these valleys. The role of some major subsidence regions (Rift Valley, Beth-Shean-Harod-Jezreel Valley and Haifa Bay) in relation to general exterior configuration has already been pointed out. Fault zones and lines also exert decisive influence upon the drainage system of a greater part of Cisjordan.

The lithology of the Cisjordan Mountain Zone is rather diversified, considering the small size of the area. Most of the mountains consist of calcareous rocks, with only small areas of outcropping sandstones, magmatic, metamorphic, and volcanic rocks. Due to the great differences in their composition (limestone, dolomites, chalk, calcareous marls, etc.) and frequent intercalations—each responding rather dissimilarly to denudational processes—these calcareous formations greatly contribute to the diversification of the landscape, determining major and minor morphological features specific to the predominant bedrock. The influence of climatic factors, mainly the amount and type of precipitation, is even greater. The southern part of the Cisjordan Mountain Zone, although consisting predominantly of the same types of rock as the central and northern parts, differs greatly from the latter in its morphological physiognomy. Weathering processes are dissimilar here in degree and even to some extent in kind. For example, farther north solutional processes exert the greatest influence upon the surface configuration by creating karstic features that dominate the landscape, particularly in Galilee. These processes are almost entirely lacking in the southern highlands. Runoff is much greater and consequently erosion is much more intensive here than in regions receiving much larger amounts of precipitation. The eastern flank of the central area is semiarid and arid (the Judean Desert), due to its location leeward of the Judean Mountains, with the precipitation caused by the moisture-bearing winds from the Mediterranean consequently decreased. This area also exhibits a specific set of morphological features, in many respects similar to those of the Negev, which is also mainly affected by climatic conditions.

Mainly in accordance with the three criteria mentioned above (tectonic, lithological, and climatic conditions), the mountain region of Cisjordan can be subdivided into the following major physiographical units: the Negev Highlands, the Central Mountain Massif, and the Galilean Mountains. Each of these units comprises several subregions determined by geological, tectonic, lithological, climatic, and consequently morphological conditions. Each is very different from the others in the overall character of its landscape. The width of the Mountain Zone varies proportionately with that of Cisjordan as a whole (i.e., the distance from the Mediterranean coast to the Rift Valley), decreasing from about 50 mi. (80 km.) in the Negev Highlands to about 22 mi. (35 km.) in Galilee.

Negev Highlands. In many respects, these highlands represent a direct continuation of the plateau and mountainous regions of the Sinai Peninsula, exhibiting great similarity of tectonic, lithological, and climatic conditions and, consequently, relief. The similarities are most evident in the southern part of the Highlands, the Eilat Mountains, which extend from the Gulf of Eilat to Bikat Sayyarim and Bikat Uvdah in the north. Here, though confined to a comparatively small area, are found ranges and blocks composed of magmatic and metamorphic rocks that build up the larger part of the southern apex of the Sinai Peninsula and are not found in any other region of Cisjordan, with the exception of Makhtesh Ramon. Similarly, outcrops of Nubian Sandstone, exposed only on the floors and the foot of the slopes of the *makhteshim* (see below), are relatively widely distributed here as surface rocks. These types of rock are in very close contact with calcareous ones, creating relief forms of singular diversity and even contrast. The extremely variegated composition of the crystalline rocks makes them particularly susceptible to granular weathering, exfoliation, and sheeting. These processes result in steep, serrated, and crenulated ridges (Jehoshafat, Shelomo, Roded, Sheḥoret), separated from one another by steep fault-conditioned valleys. Even more spectacular are the relief features that developed from Nubian Sandstone. Columnar jointing—of which the Solomon Pillars in the Timna region, about 15 mi. (25 km.) north of Eilat, are but one outstanding example. Column relicts in the form of mushroom rocks, castellated rocks, rocking stones, and intensive alveolation, producing cave-like tafoni and canyons—deeply incised in the multicolored sandstone by the extremely strong erosive action of the many river courses (the Red Canyon, Naḥal Amram etc.) carrying only flash floods once or twice within a year—give rise to landscapes even far more diversified in ever-changing micro-features than those which developed in the crystalline bedrock. In sharp contrast to these landforms are those which developed on other bedrock, limestone in particular. The relief in limestone is generally far more uniform and massive and is mainly characterized by flat-topped ranges and small plateau-like elevations covered by angular gravels. The latter are produced by weathering, which imparts to the surfaces covered by them the appearance of typical *hamada* (block-strewn desert surfaces).

A canyon in the Eilat Mountains, incised in Nubian Sandstone, formed by one of the tributaries of Naḥal Timna. Photo Zvi Ron, Haifa.

The Paran Plateau. This area comprises mainly the Cisjordan catchment area of the Paran River, a major tributary of the Arabah, which is the collecting stream of the Rift Valley south of the Dead Sea. The headrivers of the Paran drain the parts of the Sinai adjacent to the Eilat

The canyon of the Amaẓyahu River, cut into the bedrock of the Lashon formation. Photo A. Strajmayster, Jerusalem.

Mountains in a relatively dense network of wide channels filled with sand and pebbles. The highest elevations of the Paran Plateau—some of which form mountain blocks or ridges—are on its northeastern side—Har Nes, 3,329 ft. (1,015 m.); Har Saggi, 3,229 ft. (1,006 m.). In the eastward direction, elevations become lower and surfaces generally more uniform. In strong contrast to the variegated lithology of the Eilat Mountains, the tableland here is built up almost exclusively of calcareous strata: limestones interbedded with chalk, marls, and thin layers of chert. The surface of the plateau features the widest areas of "desert pavement" found in Cisjordan, i.e., areas covered by angular gravels *(hamada)* or rounder pebble-like debris (a desert surface type morphologically known as "serir"). At the southern periphery of the plateau, Bikat Sayyarim and the far larger Bikat Uvdah represent typical intramontane desert basins covered and filled by sands. They are subject to occasional flooding and drain—albeit through very indistinct channel beds—into the Ḥiyyon

Typical Arabah landscape, showing the exit of the Ḥiyyon River into the Rift Valley. Courtesy J.N.F., Jerusalem.

River, a major tributary of the Arabah River, running about 12 mi. (20 km.) south of the Paran. To the northeast the tableland is delimited by the gravel-covered Ha-Meshar Basin, which, from the hydrographical point of view, belongs to the Central Negev region.

The Central Negev Highlands. The anticline of Ramon is essentially the only major structure of the Central Negev Highlands. This upfold extends approximately 43 mi. (70 km.) in length from the biblical Kadesh-Barnea in the Sinai almost to the very escarpments bordering the western side of the Arabah Rift. It is not only the highest portion of the Negev Highlands—Har Ramon, 3,395 ft. (1,035 m.)—but also structurally and morphologically the most complex. This is very evident in one of the most pronounced occurrences of relief inversion, i.e., the conversion of a major structural element into a morphologically "negative," i.e., reverse, form. Here the anticline was transformed, chiefly by erosion, into a wide, elongated, valley-like basin, about 28 mi. (45 km.) in length, enclosed by almost perpendicular slopes, some of them about 1,000 ft. (300 m.) high. This specific form, which also occurs in some anticlines of northern Sinai and in the northern part of the Negev Highlands, is referred to in Hebrew as *makhtesh* ("mortar" or "mixing-bowl"), which in the geomorphology of arid regions is now becoming a general term to denote affinite landforms. The greatest influence upon the formation, lithology, and configuration of Makhtesh Ramon was exerted by faulting along its southern flank. Accordingly, magmatic-volcanic rocks are exposed here. Wherever the enclosure is composed of these rocks, it assumes the form of a serrated range, resembling those in the crystalline Eilat Mountains and strongly contrasting with the other enclosured portions of the *makhtesh*, which consist of Nubian Sandstones in the lower and hard limestone in the upper parts of their slopes. The floor of Makhtesh Ramon, covered mainly by detritus of Nubian Sandstone, reveals many small elevations, preponderantly in the form of flat-topped basalt-covered remains of former surface levels.

Western portion of Makhtesh Ramon, the strongly dissected, hummocky floor enclosed by precipitous slopes of Nubian Sandstone capped by Cretaceous limestone. Courtesy J.N.F., Jerusalem.

The *makhtesh* is drained by the multichanneled Ramon River, which breaches the eastern enclosure in a narrow steep gorge to join the Arabah River system. To the northwest of the *makhtesh*, its foreland forms a rather level, or gently undulating, tableland up to its very rim; only at the periphery of the plateau does the relief become mountainous (Har Loẓ, Har Ḥorshah, Rekhes-Nafḥa).

The Northern Negev Highlands. On the northeast, the Central Negev Highlands are separated from the Northern Highlands by the wide, deeply incised Valley of the Zin River. This tectonically conditioned valley begins as a wide erosive cirque, the southwestern side of which forms precipitous, almost perpendicular, scarps. At a small distance from the northern side of the valley two *makhteshim* are situated: Ha-Makhtesh ha-Gadol (the "Big Makhtesh") and Ha-Makhtesh ha-Katan (the "Little Makhtesh"). They differ from Makhtesh Ramon not only by their smaller size and almost regular oval shape, but also in structure, lithology, and consequently morphology. Not affected by faulting, they represent upfolds turned into deep valley-basins, on the floors of which older sedimentary strata became exposed through erosion by the watercourses draining them. Their almost perpendicularly sloping walls of Nubian Sandstone are overlaid by much more resistant limestones and dolomites. The Ḥatirah and Ḥaẓevah Rivers, running parallel to the long axes of Ha-Makhtesh ha-Gadol and Ha-Makhtesh ha-Katan, respectively, breach their eastern walls in impressive gorges to join the Zin River. Toward the west and northwest elevations become progressively lower, although there are several upfolds rising above their surroundings as short ridges with moderate slopes, frequently worn down to isolated table-hills. In the west the plateau margins are partly covered by relatively large areas of sand dunes (Ḥaluẓah, Agur), which form a transition zone to the Plain of the Negev. On the northern side, the highlands terminate in the wide Beersheba Basin and its much narrower eastern continuation, the Valley of Arad. Structurally, and in particular climatically, these two intramontane depressions form a marked border zone between the arid Negev Highlands and the mountains north of it, where Mediterranean conditions prevail. In the Beersheba Basin, the mean annual precipitation is 10 in. (250 mm.), a quantity indicating the transition from semiarid to subhumid conditions. The thick loess cover and the amount of precipitation together give rise to the most convenient conditions for agriculture within the Negev. The main drainage artery of this part of the Negev is the Beersheba River (a tributary of the Besor River), and several of its confluents originate in the Hebron Mountains, although its almost annually recurring floodings are mainly caused by the tributaries crossing the relatively impervious loess areas.

THE CENTRAL MOUNTAIN MASSIF. This range extends from the Beersheba Basin up to the Beth-Shean-Harod-Jezreel Valley sequence in the north. It represents the most compact and continuous mountain region of Cisjordan. Its basic structures are relatively large, meridionally trending anticlinoria, i.e., systems usually composed of one major upfold flanked by downfolds and smaller anticlines. Faulting does not exert a great influence upon the configuration of the southern part of the area; its effect is far stronger in the northern portion, though not yet as decisive in determining the landscape as in Galilee. According to climatic, lithological, and hypsographical conditions, this area can be subdivided into several major units. The most important difference exists between the western part, which is fully exposed to the climatic influences of the Mediterranean, and the eastern flank descending into the Dead Sea and Jordan Valley. The landscape of the eastern portion, which is leeward of the precipitation-bearing winds, is consequently semi-desertic and desertic in character (Judean Desert). The difference is accentuated by lithological variance. The western flank is built predominantly of limestone and dolomite strata, whereas in the eastern one chalks and marls prevail. To the west a subregion of different lithology and elevation is

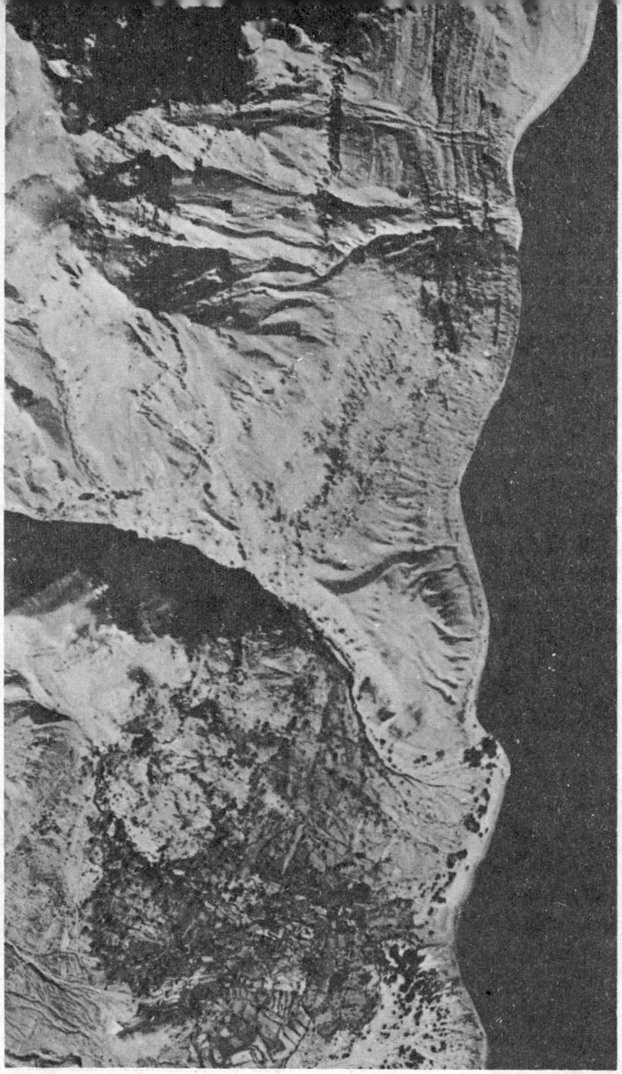

Aerial photograph of cliffs bordering the western shore of the Dead Sea in the vicinity of Masada, dissected by several canyon exits with fan outbuilds into the sea. Courtesy Israel Air Force.

interposed between the southern part of the Central Mountain Massif and the Coastal Plains. Considerably lower and built mainly of chalky rock, it is a hill region gradually rising toward the massif but separated from it in a very pronounced manner by a series of valleys running parallel to the foot of the massif. Toward the north, two major protrusions of the massif can be regarded as distinct mountain regions: a smaller one—the Gilboa—separating the valleys of Harod and Jezreel, and another, much larger and more complex in structure—the Carmel, in the broad sense—which, as already mentioned, delimits the southern Coastal Plains. According to the criteria enumerated above, the Central Mountain Massif can be subdivided into the following regions: Judean Mountains, comprising the Mediterranean southern portion of the massif; Judean Desert; Shephelah (the hill region to the west of the Judean Mountains); Samarian Highlands (the northern part of the massif) and its two subunits, Gilboa and Carmel.

The Judean Mountains. The core region of Cisjordan, the Judean Mountains consist structurally of two consecutive large anticlinoria, whose axes—in contrast to the upfolds in the Negev, which trend mainly southwest-northeast—run almost meridionally. Built up of limestone and dolomite strata with chalky and marly intercalations (the latter very important as groundwater horizons), the mountains' main topographical features are an almost continuous watershed zone (rather uniform in height and delimiting them toward the Judean Desert) and the many interfluves (i.e., ridge-like mountainous spurs separated by deeply incised valleys) extending mainly westward. The watershed zone is generally flat and widens considerably in many places. Its topography thus provided suitable conditions for defense and the development of communications by means of a highway between the cities that were built in this area from earliest times.

Not far from this divide, watercourses begin to incise progressively deeper valleys, the steep slopes of which almost fully converge at the narrow rocky river beds:

Terracing in the Judean Mountains, mainly in a state of disrepair. Courtesy J.N.F., Jerusalem.

generally there are no accompanying floodplains. The slopes rising from the valley floors are, for the most part, intensively terraced and end in almost flat or only slightly domed tops separated by wide gentle saddles. Both the mountain tops and the slopes (where not terraced) are densely covered by block detritus, deeply corroded by solutional processes, which also produced the many rounded depressions, holes, and cavities in the slope surfaces as well as many caverns and caves. The prevalent terra rossa is mainly another product of this weathering process, here strongly effective due to the considerable amounts of precipitation—about 20 in. (500 mm.) on the annual average. From the orographic point of view, three parts of the Judean Mountains, very unequal in size, are distinguished: Hebron Mountains, Jerusalem Mountains, Beth-El (Ramallah) Mountains.

The Hebron Mountains extend from the Beersheba Basin up to the Wadi Arṭās in the north (a valley belonging to the drainage area of the Dead Sea), the site of the Solomon Pools. They rise steeply from the Beersheba Basin (one of the southward protrusions of these mountains separates the latter from the Arad Basin) to heights of about 2,600 ft. (800 m.), culminating in summits near Ḥalḥul (north of Hebron) that rise to 3,300 ft. (1,000 m.). The Hebron Mountains are also the largest constituent of the Judean Mountains, with an area greatly exceeding the total of the two other subunits. From the morphological point of view, the southern portion of the Hebron Mountains can be subdivided into two main parts, separated by the relatively wide, mostly flat-floored, and not very deeply incised valley of the Hebron River, a tributary of the Beersheba River, which runs for about 18 mi. (30 km.) almost parallel to the meridional axis of the mountains. The mountains here thus consist of two main ridges. An eastern, higher one is called the Eshtemoa (Samūʿ) Range after one of the villages, the name and site of which have remained virtually unchanged since biblical times. Along this ridge extends the divide between the dry valleys (except at times of flood) descending into the Dead Sea Rift and the southern and western ones that drain into the Mediterranean. The western ridge is named after the village of Adoraim (Dūrā), also mentioned in the Bible. The highway connecting Beersheba with the townships and villages of the watershed zone runs along this ridge. Also characteristic of the Hebron Mountains are several topographic depressions, the largest of which, the valley of Berachah, is distinguished by an abundant spring. The waters of this spring, together with those of others issuing in the vicinity, feed the Solomon Pools, which were the most important source of water for Jerusalem in the past. Near Hebron the two ridges merge to form a single watershed zone that continues along the entire length of the Judean Mountains, Climatically, the Hebron Mountains represent a transition zone from semiarid to Mediterranean conditions. Whereas at al-Ẓāhiriyya, the southernmost village along the main highway, the annual precipitation is only about 12 in. (300 mm.), it increases to 20 in. (500 mm.) in Hebron, and 28 in. (700 mm.) in the region of the highest elevations, where snowfall is frequent. Accordingly, the larger part of the soil cover (where preserved) in the Hebron Mountains is terra rossa.

The Jerusalem Mountains are about 500 ft. (150 m.) lower on the average than the Hebron and Beth-El Mountains—highest elevation, al-Nabī Samwīl, 2,870 ft. (875 m.)—and form a wide saddle-like region between these sections. This topographical feature somewhat facilitates the ascent from the Coastal Plains to the watershed region, with its settlements and highway, and the descent into the Rift Valley, in particular to Jericho, the most important township of the Valley region throughout history. The Jerusalem Mountains are also intensively dissected into interfluvial ridges. One of these, Mount of Olives-Mount Scopus, immediately east of Jerusalem, forms a conspicuous border with the Judean Desert. The Judean Mountains are drained mainly by the Sorek River, one of the major watercourses of the Central Mountain Massif. The Sorek River discharges into the Mediterranean, and its markedly meandering valley proved sufficiently wide for the construction of the railway connecting Jerusalem with the Coastal Plains.

The Beth-El Mountains, covering an area similar in size to that of the Jerusalem Mountains—about 9 mi. (15 km.) in length—rise to summit heights exceeding 3,300 ft. (1,000 m.)— Baal-Hazor, 3,332 ft. (1,016 m.). One of their most important characteristics is that the watershed attains considerable width there. A road along one of the interfluves extending to the west (Beth-Horon Ridge) was formerly the main approach to Jerusalem from the Coastal Plains and consequently of particular strategic importance.

The Judean Desert. According to its appearance, the Judean Desert could be regarded as a northward extension of the arid Negev lands that border on it at the valley of the Ḥemar River. Genetically, however, it belongs to the orographic types of deserts, whose aridity—much less pronounced than in "true" deserts—is due mainly to the fact that the area is situated on the leeward side of the massive and high Judean Mountains, which intercept the rain-bearing winds. This effect is made more pronounced by the steepness of the eastern flank of the Judean anticlinoria toward the Dead Sea-Jordan Rift Valley, about 1,000–1,300 ft. (300–400 m.) below sea level. Actually, only the lower portions of this flank are arid. Even there, the larger part of the area receives more than 4 in. (100 mm.) of rain per annum—Jericho receives about 6 in. (150 mm.)—whereas on the upper portions the precipitation decreases gradually from about 16 in. (400 mm.) near the watershed region to the amounts mentioned above. The Judean Desert also comprises the eastern flank of the Samarian Mountains up to the wide valley of Wadi Fāriʿa and the spur of Qeren Sartaba protruding from the Samarian Mountains into the Jordan Rift Valley. It differs markedly from the Judean Mountains in lithology as well as in structure and is composed predominantly of chalky formations younger in origin than those forming the bulk of the Judean Mountains. In contrast to the latter, faulting—syngenetical with that which created the Dead Sea-Jordan Rift Valley—exerted a great influence upon the configuration of this desert, particularly by creating the step-like descent toward the Rift Valley. The relative imperviousness of the bedrock, the much lower resistance to erosion, and the steep overall declivity caused by a difference in elevation of about 4,000 ft. (1,200 m.) from the watershed zone to the Dead Sea, over a distance of only 19 mi. (30 km.), result in most of the precipitation turning into highly erosive runoff. Consequently the Judean Desert represents a "mountain wilderness," an apparently chaotic landscape of innumerable valleys of all kinds. Many of them are canyons cut in harder rock exposed along the flexures and fault lines (Ẓe'elim, Agurot, Mishmar), whereas the higher-lying portions form a maze of mostly flat-topped hills (some of which are famous as sites of ancient fortresses such as Herodium and Masada). In the Ḥatrurim area these hills impart to the landscape the appearance of badlands. It was mainly this type of relief, the absence of productive soils of the terra rossa type, and the very short duration and scantiness of the vegetation cover—almost excluding trees and actually confined to a few weeks during the rainy season—that throughout historical times rendered it a region of "desolation" and a refuge for fugitives from the law and prevented any permanent settlement or the establishment of communication networks.

Shephelah. Topographically, the Shephelah represents a transition zone between the Coastal Plains and the Hebron and Jerusalem Mountains. It is relatively narrow—about 8 mi. (13 km.)—in proportion to its south-north extension—about 35 mi. (60 km.). Though they form the foothills of the Judean Mountains, the Shephelah hills differ from the former in almost all respects. Structurally, they form a major synclinal part of the south Judean anticlinorium, composed mainly of chalky formations of Senonian-Eocene origin. Hypsographically, the Shephelah consists of two parts: a western one (the "Low Shephelah"), rising to a height of about 600 ft. (200 m.) above the Coastal Plains, and an eastern one (the "High Shephelah") about 600 ft. (200 m.) higher than the former. On the north the Shephelah borders on the tectonically conditioned Aijalon Valley, one of the main natural approaches to the Judean Mountains. The Shephelah is a region of gently sloped hills separated by the confluents of the major rivers descending into the area from the Judean Mountains. At their entrance into the Shephelah, these rivers, and several of their tributaries, form relatively wide-floored valleys that run for a considerable stretch along the border between the hill and the mountain region. Passage between these longitudinal valleys is relatively convenient, and this natural communication channel has been very important throughout history.

The Samarian Mountains. Morphotectonically, the Samarian Mountains (less frequently referred to as the Ephraim Mountains) form a transitional link between the massive Judean Mountains, which are influenced little by faulting, and those of the Galilees, where faulting has all but obliterated the other tectonic elements. No topographic features form any pronounced boundary between the two parts of the Central Mountain Massif, and it is only by convention that the upper reaches of the Shiloh River—a tributary of the Yarkon—are used for this demarcation. Structurally, the Samarian Mountains consist of two main parts: an eastern anticlinal one, built up of Cretaceous formations, and a synclinal western one, consisting mainly of rocks of Eocene origin. Characteristically, the highest elevations are found in the latter part. Here the twin mountains of Ebal and Gerizim attain heights of 3,083 ft. (940 m.) and 2,890 ft. (881 m.) respectively. Northward, approaching the valleys of Beth-Shean and Jezreel respectively, elevations become progressively smaller—about 1,300 ft. (400 m.) above sea level. The structure and its morphological expression are mainly influenced by faulting, which produced tectonic valleys and almost enclosed basins (the latter additionally affected and shaped by solution processes). Sequences of short ranges and mountain blocks thus rise steeply above their flat surroundings, which sometimes form relatively extensive intramontane plains. Thus, the wide tectonic valley of Shechem (Nablus) separates Ebal from Gerizim and continues eastward as Wadi Fāriʿa, which separates the southern, higher part of the Samarian Mountains from the spurs of a much lower northern part. The broad, tectonic valley of Dothan delimits the Samarian Mountains, in the narrow sense, in the direction of the Carmel, whereas in the interior parts, several wide alluvia-filled basins (Emek Shiloh, the Lubban Valley, Emek Hamikhmetat, and the largest of them, Marj Sānūr) endow the region with some features characteristic of Lower Galilee. The shorter distance between the Samarian Mountains and the sea, with no intervening foothill region, the many and wide valley openings, and the smaller amount of depression in the Rift Valley bordering it to the east resulted in a Mediterranean climate for almost all of Samaria, except for a narrow belt adjacent to the Jordan Rift, where semiarid conditions still prevail. Samaria receives larger amounts of precipitation than the Judean Mountains—28–36 in. (700–800 mm.) annual average rainfall—and the soil cover (terra rossa and rendzina) is also much more continuous. There is a great deal of evidence that considerable parts of Samaria were once covered by woods.

Mount Gilboa. According to its situation and structure, Mount Gilboa represents a direct continuation of the Samarian Mountains, although almost separated from the main body of these mountains by the Jenin Plain—an extension of the Jezreel Plain. It is bordered on the east and southeast by steep fault-scarps, which, together with some outcrops of volcanic rocks, indicate the complex tectonic processes that caused the separation of the Samarian from the Galilee Mountains, also resulting in the formation of the Harod-Jezreel Valley. Composed of Eocene strata, with outcrops of Senonian ones on the northeast side, the surface here is mostly barren, block-strewn, and covered by soil in patches only—probably as the result of intensive slopewash and consequent soil erosion, mainly caused by the differ-

The slopes of the Gilboa Mountain, looking north over the Jezreel Valley in the vicinity of Kefar Yeḥezkel and Merḥavyah. Courtesy J.N.F., Jerusalem.

ence in elevations of about 1,600 ft. (500 m.) over a distance of only about a mile between the mountain crest and the floor of the surrounding valleys. Precipitation amounts to about 18 in. (450 mm.) on the annual average. The barrenness of the Gilboa, in such strong contrast to the once forested landscapes of Samaria, may serve as the factual background to the explanation of the well-known biblical curse laid upon this mountain. Nowhere in Cisjordan is there such a concentration of springs, some very abundant in discharge, as is found at the bases of the fault escarpments of the Gilboa (Ein Moda, Ein Ḥumah, Ein Amal, En-Harod). These are now one of the most important sources of irrigation for the Harod and Beth-Shean Valleys.

Carmel Mountain. To the northwest a highland body branches off from the Samarian Mountains, differing from the latter in many respects, particularly in structure. In the regional literature of Cisjordan, this branch is usually referred to as the Carmel, although it consists of three very distinct parts of very different structure, lithology, topography, and consequent relief features. The Carmel, therefore, represents a triplet mountain body about 35 mi. (60 km.) long along its median axis and stretching southeast-northwest—a single major occurrence within Cisjordan, although recurring in some lesser ranges. Its general shape is that of an elongated triangle, the relatively short base of which is formed by the Dothan Valley, separating it from Samaria, with the two long sides facing the northern Sharon Plain on the west and the Plain of Haifa and the Jezreel Valley on the northeast. The apex of this triangle—the Carmel headland—abuts almost immediately on the Mediterranean; this is a feature that recurs only at Rosh ha-Nikrah. All the flanks of the mountain, as well as those of its parts, exhibit high and steep slopes, mainly created by faulting, rising abruptly above the adjacent plains. The three subunits of the Carmel (from southeast to northwest) are: the Umm al-Faḥm Block, separated from Samaria by the wide Dothan Valley; the Manasseh region, disjointed from the former by the tectonically conditioned Iron Valley; and the Carmel, in the narrow sense, its largest component, separated from the Manasseh region by the Jokneam-Tut Valley sequence, also of tectonic origin.

The Umm al-Faḥm Block (lately also called the Amir Range) forms a quadrangle-shaped plateau, whose undulating surface provides a gradual descent toward the southwest. Toward its northeast confines, the plateau becomes higher, with bolder relief, and ends in a scarp descent facing the Jezreel Valley. Structurally, it represents an upwarped and uplifted part of the Carmel and accordingly consists of resistant Cenomanian limestone and dolomite formations framed at the periphery of the block by formations of Turonian age. Relatively large areas are covered by basalts and volcanic tuff, a lithological feature recurring in the two other subunits of the Carmel. It receives a mean annual precipitation of about 20 in. (500 mm.) and the prevailing soils are of terra rossa type. There are very scanty remains of forests, and still larger areas covered by maquis, their degraded forms, indicate that in the past extensive areas here were wooded. With the exception of its southernmost part, the area is drained almost exclusively by tributaries of the Kishon River.

The region of Manasseh, similar in its quadrangular outline to that of Umm al-Faḥm, contrasts with it in almost all other respects. Composed predominantly of soft Eocene chalks, which also accounts for the scantiness of terra rossa and the wide distribution of rendzina soils in this area, its originally tabular surface became intensively dissected. The dominant relief features of the region are thus hills with moderate slopes rising to relatively small heights above the valley floors. The overall height of the region above sea level is about 600 ft. (200 m.) less than than Umm al-Faḥm Block and still less than that of the Carmel. Its slopes to the Jezreel Valley are also far lower and less steep and continuous than those of the two adjacent units. Due to the relative impermeability of the surface rock, and consequently the considerable percentage of runoff and particularly the erodibility of the bedrock, the drainage net is rather dense, flowing to the Kishon River in the north and to Ha-Tanninim ("Crocodile") and Daliyyah Rivers in the south, both of which discharge directly into the Mediterranean.

The singularity of the Carmel within Cisjordan—used in the Scriptures, together with Mount Tabor, as a paradigm of beautiful mountainous scenery—is based on the following factors: it appears as a very regularly shaped mountain block, well defined on all its sides, and conspicuously elevated above the surrounding plain; it is the only major mountain—about 22 mi. (35 km.) long along its central axis—in Cisjordan with an extended slope rising only a small distance from the Mediterranean; its apex forms a most conspicuous headland, and beyond its northern flank the coastline recedes, forming the only true bay of the country; fully exposed on both its flanks to the Mediterranean, it receives large amounts of rain—about 32 in. (800 mm.) per annum—and dew; arboreal vegetation persisted here, due to its great regenerative power, mainly as a result of favorable climatic conditions. Structurally the Carmel represents a sort of counterpart to the Umm al-Faḥm Block. It, too, was upwarped and uplifted and is mainly composed of Cenomanian-Turonian limestones and dolomites. Volcanic outcrops, in particular tuff, are relatively widespread, and the latter greatly influence the form of valleys. Whereas the valleys incised into the hard, intensively jointed calcareous rocks are deep, narrow, and have steep slopes—frequently actually minor canyons (Naḥal Me'arot, Daliyyah, Oren), those which developed in the tuffs are conspicuously wide and flat-floored, and exhibit relatively gentle valley slopes (Kerem Maharal, Shefeyah Valley). The calcareous parts are strongly affected by solutional weathering. Thoroughly corroded blocks cover large portions of the surfaces, and many of the almost perpendicular valley slopes contain caves, some of which are of considerable prehistoric importance. The Carmel is strongly affected by faulting, which not only gave rise to the almost uninterrupted slopes descending steeply to the Haifa Plain and to the

Jezreel Valley and less pronounced ones along the Jokneam trough, which separates it from the Manasseh region, but also strongly influenced the relief of its interior parts. Faulting here gave rise to several depressions and had a major influence upon the course of some of the valleys. The Carmel, like its adjacent mountain units, consists of two topographically differentiated parts: a higher one, its summit region, along its northeast flank—from Rosh ha-Carmel, 1,790 ft. (546 m.), to the somewhat lower Keren ha-Carmel—referred to in regional literature as the "High Carmel," and a far larger part sloping down to the Carmel Coast, the "Low Carmel." The latter consists mainly of broad interfluves, created by the many valleys descending to the Coastal Plain. The drainage net is characteristically varied in catchment area and pattern, in close accordance with the relief differentiation described above. The divide between the watercourses descending on the northeastern slopes and tributary to the Kishon runs a very small distance from the scarp rim. The valleys of these water-courses are short and relatively straight and are joined by very few tributaries. The watercourses running west and draining more than three-quarters of the total area of the Carmel are more numerous and intensely ramified, particularly the Oren and Daliyyah Rivers. Toward the south the Carmel juts out into the Plain of Sharon and up to the valley of the Ha-Tanninim River in a large spur separated from the main body by the valley of the Daliyyah River. Called the Zikhron Ya'akov Mountains, after the principal settlement, the spur encloses the Carmel Coastal Plain to the west and separates it from the Plain of Binyaminah, a northward extension of the Sharon.

The Valley Sequence. From the Jordan Rift Valley to the coast of the Mediterranean, Cisjordan is traversed by an east-west sequence of large, interconnected, elongated basins that are of preeminent physio- and anthropogeographical importance. These are: the Harod Valley, named after its main water artery, the Harod River; the Jezreel Plain, the largest component of the sequence; and the Plain of Haifa, which, genetically, forms the continental terminal part of this tectonic trough and continues westward as the Bay of Haifa. The three basins form relatively wide plains, enclosed on their southern and northern sides by abruptly rising, steep mountains, and constitute a marked discontinuity within the Cisjordan highlands north of the Beersheba Basin. The vale sequence subdivides the highlands very conspicuously into two main mountain complexes: a larger, southern one (Judean Mountains, Samarian Mountains, and Carmel) and a northern one, approximately one-third the size of the former, the Galilees.

THE HAROD VALLEY. This valley—the easternmost component of the sequence—represents, hypsographically, topographically, climatically, and lithologically, a westward salient of the Beth-Shean Valley. There is no major relief feature that could serve as demarcation between these two units; therefore the travertine terraces, more correctly their remnants near Beth-Shean, are used by convention for this purpose. Their correlative characteristics are as follows: the surface of the eastern part of the funnel-shaped vale gradually descends to below sea level and merges imperceptibly with the depression of the Beth-Shean and Jordan Valleys; temperatures and precipitation (in both amount and distribution) are very similar to those of the Beth-Shean Valley; a close likeness of soil cover in the two valleys, particularly in the types resulting from decomposition of basalts and travertine; the already-mentioned abundance of springs, particularly at the foot of the Gilboa scarps. In the past the Harod Valley was partly covered by swamps due to the relative impermeability of some of its soil cover, heavy flooding by the many watercourses reaching it from the nearby high, steep mountain enclosure, and the incapacity of the bed of the Harod, to contain the floodwaters. The many springs were an additional cause of swamp formation.

THE JEZREEL VALLEY. The largest intramontane basin in Cisjordan is the Valley of Jezreel, formerly also known as the Plain of Armageddon (after the fortress of Megiddo, which was renowned in the annals of the Fertile Crescent).

Roughly triangular in shape, it is bordered on the southwest by the Carmel, Manasseh Plateau, and the Umm al-Faḥm Block; on the north by the Lower Galilee Mountains; and on the east, discontinuously, by Mount Tabor, Givat ha-Moreh, and the Gilboa Mountains. The shape of this valley is straight only along the Carmel; at the other borders there are several embayment-like extensions of the plain into the surrounding mountains. The largest of these extensions is the Plain of Jenin, enclosed on the east by the Gilboa and joined on the southwest by the Dothan Valley. Eastward, the Jezreel Valley downgrades imperceptibly in the vicinity of Afulah into the Harod Valley and intrudes deeply into the Lower Galilee Mountains, separating their outliers, Mount Tabor and Givat ha-Moreh, by the wide Chesulloth Plain. The Jezreel Valley is connected at its apex with the Haifa Plain by a narrow passage 1,600 ft. (500 m.) wide created by the valley of the Kishon (at Kiryat Ḥaroshet) near the site of Bet She'arim, between the Carmel and the Lower Galilee Mountains. The winding course of the Kishon River begins near Afulah, less than 230 ft. (70 m.) above sea level and at a distance of about 25 mi. (40 km.) from the Mediterranean, into which it discharges. In the past it was inadequate to drain the valley, particularly in the rainy season. Its many affluents from the enclosing mountains, which receive about 8 in. (200 mm.) more precipitation than the Jezreel Valley, together with the many local topographic depressions and poorly permeable alluvial heavy soil cover, turned a large part of the valley into swamps. Consequently, it was sparsely populated and little utilized agriculturally. Only after the marshes were drained and malaria, once endemic in this area, eradicated, did the valley become the area of the most intensive and continuous cultivation within the mountain zone of Cisjordan. The physiognomy of the Jezreel Valley, and to some extent also of the Harod Valley, is largely determined by the two massive, high mountain blocks rising abruptly above the plain; Mount Tabor and Givat ha-Moreh.
 Pronouncedly isolated from each other and from the

highlands to the north and south, their summits attain heights of over 1,600 ft. (500 m.) above sea level and only slightly less above the surrounding plain. Because of the almost perfect dome shape of Mount Tabor, it was, together with the Carmel, often used to exemplify the beauty of mountainous scenery. Differing as they do in lithological structure (limestones and dolomites in Mount Tabor, outcrops of volcanic rocks in Givat ha-Moreh), these two mountains probably represent remnants of a highland zone connecting the Samarian Mountains with those of the Galilees that was shattered by the tectonic movements, which also formed the entire basin sequence.

HAIFA PLAIN. Despite its being a part of the Coastal Plains, according to its situation and surface configuration, the Haifa Plain (formerly referred to also as the Zebulun Plain) morphotectonically represents the westernmost unit of the vale sequence. The plain continues in its submerged part as the Bay of Haifa. Accordingly, the interior part of the plain, east of the dune belt, is covered by heavy alluvial soils with very little *ḥamra.* Drainage here was also greatly impeded, mainly by the dune belt (as evidenced by the deferred debouchures of its two main streams, Kishon and Na'aman), and marsh areas persisted up to the time of Jewish colonization.

The Galilee Mountains. Occupying a smaller area than the Judean or the Samarian Highlands, the Galilee Mountains are nevertheless far more complex in lithology, structure, and consequently morphology. Basalts (there is even a remnant of a true volcano—Karnei Ḥittin, the "Horns" of Ḥittin) cover large tracts in the eastern parts, a feature recurring only in Transjordan. This cover imparts to several of its landscapes a peculiar plateau-like relief of great uniformity, in vivid contrast to areas of much more variegated configuration in the west, where the surfaces consist of calcareous rocks. Faulting, however, has exerted a far more decisive influence. In the Negev and in the Central Highlands, fold structures are found almost everywhere and are visually recognizable as the most important tectonic element that determines the relief of the region even in its minor features. In the Galilees, however, the influence of fold structures upon the relief is largely upset, permuted, and even inverted by faulting. Tectonic activity seems to be continuing at present, as evidenced by the relatively frequent, and sometimes strong, earthquakes affecting the region. Generally characteristic of the landscape of the Galilees as a whole are closely spaced sequences of basins or valleys and mountain ranges that are uplifted unequally and thus tilted, so that one slope is much steeper than the opposite. Here mountain blocks, separated from their surroundings by faults and upthrusting, constitute some of the highest summit regions of Cisjordan. Since the prevailing direction of the major fault lines is west-east, the general trend of Galilean ranges follows this direction, in strong contrast to the Central Mountain Zone's prevailing meridional trend and particularly to the Judean Mountains, where a continuous watershed zone running south-north emphasizes the compactness of this body. Tectonic conditions, resulting in an increase of rock exposures, and the relatively large amounts of precipitation produced relatively abundant karst features in the Galilees. Among these there are simple and complex dolines (small solution basins), sinkholes, even a large polje, and caves several of which contain speleothems (stalactites, stalagmites, etc.) or have been found to be of prime importance as prehistoric sites. Thus, lithologically, and still more so morphologically, the Galilees form the most contrasted and variegated mountain province (excluding the Eilat Mountains) of Cisjordan. Although strongly disjointed by the numerous basins, tectonic valleys, and uplifted blocks, the Galilee may be clearly subdivided into two main regions: a southern one of moderate height, Lower Galilee, and a northern one, separated from the first by an extended tectonic valley (Valley of Beth-Cherem), and rising behind it to maximum summit heights in Cisjordan, Upper Galilee.

LOWER GALILEE. The Lower Galilee Highlands, which rise abruptly and steeply from the vale sequence in an in- and outcurving front, are markedly subdivided into an eastern part and a western one. The first is characterized by a widespread basalt cover of considerable thickness that buried a former, probably intensively sculptured relief, turning the area into groups of plateau-topped mountain bodies. This landscape, which is geologically recent, is now subject to vigorous dissection by rivers (many of them perennial) that discharge into Lake Kinneret or into the Jordan (Ammud, Ẓalmon, Ha-Yonim and Tabor Rivers). They flow through deeply incised gorges created by their great erosive power, resulting from very considerable height differences between their respective source regions and their places of debouchure, which are respectively about 700 ft. (200 m.) above and 800 ft. (250 m.) below sea level and are only 12 mi. (20 km.) apart. The rivers also subdivide eastern Lower Galilee into many units, several of which form small plateaus, rising steplike, one above the other (Kokhav—the site of the crusader fortress of Belvoir—and the Jabneel-Kefar Tabor plateau are the largest of them). In the other two-thirds of Lower Galilee, the surface rock consists of limestone (subject to strong solutional processes and to the formation of karstic features, such as dolines, sinkholes, caverns), chalk and marl, generally intensively interbedded. In this part of Lower Galilee almost all of the landforms bear visible evidence of the decisive role played by faulting in determining the relief of the present landscape.

Central Galilee consists of a series of basins, separated by generally narrower ranges, usually representing remnants, partially uplifted portions, of the former highland surface. The series begins with the Plain of Jezreel, which, from the general morphotectonic point of view, represents the foreland of Lower Galilee. It is separated from the Tiran Basin by the abruptly rising, steeply sloping Nazareth Mountains. Beyond the Tiran Basin lies that of Bet Netofah (the largest one), separated from the Tiran Basin by the Tiran Range. The Tiran Basin now contains a large storage lake, part of the National Water Carrier System. It is bordered on the north by the Yodefat Range, which, in turn, separates it from the Sakhnīn Basin. The Shezor (Sājūr) Ridge extends north of the Sakhnīn Basin, near the boundary valley of Beth-Cherem, beyond which the first group of the Upper Galilee Mountains rises, wall-like to heights exceeding 3,280 ft. (1,000 m.). The interbasin ranges are not compact, but rather form series of rounded hills separated by wide saddles, being the short fluviatile valleys of tributaries of the major rivers that drain the basins (Ẓippori and Ḥillazon Rivers). The rivers draining the basins, however, were inadequate to collect and carry off the waters flowing down to them from the enclosing ridges. Large areas of them were flooded during the rainy season and the thick cover of heavy soils, mainly a product of slope erosion, greatly impeded infiltration. In addition to the flatness of the basin floors, the sluggishness of the flow of waters in their main channels, due to the very small gradient, strongly enhanced marshy conditions.

UPPER GALILEE. Most of the essential differences between the Lower and the Upper Galilee are conspicuous at their boundary, Valley of Beth-Cherem, one of the most distinct morphotectonic border zones of Cisjordan. Here, without any transition, the slopes of several mountain blocks rise abruptly to the highest summit heights in Cisjordan—Mount ha-Ari, 3,434 ft. (1,047 m.), Mount Kefir, 3, 221 ft. (982 m.)—culminating slightly to the north in the three summits of the Meron Block with heights of 3,621, 3,745, and 3,962ft. (1,104, 1,151, and 1,208 m.). Structurally these mountains, as well as the majority of the mountains throughout Upper Galilee, are horsts, i.e., blocks separated from their surroundings by faults and partially uplifted to very considerable heights. The relative abundance of the horsts, which predominate over other tectonic structures, seems to be a result of the variety of fault directions. Whereas in the Lower Galilee the major fault lines generally trend east-west, conditioning the pattern of basins and intervening ranges that follow the same directions, in Upper Galilee faults running in these directions are intersected obliquely or even at right angles by other faults. This is one of the prime causes of the isolation of the individual blocks and their apparently random pattern. The difference in height between the blocks is primarily the result of the amount of uplift rather than of different rates of denudation. The Upper Galilee Highlands, as a whole, slope down to the northwest, and their lowest parts, already within the boundaries of Lebanon (Lebanese Galilee), are adjacent to the Qasimiye Valley. Faults also strongly influence the pattern and the individual courses of the valleys, which form almost parallel gorges only several kilometers apart (Ga'aton, Chezib, Beẓet Rivers within Israel; Shamaʿ and ʿAzziyya in the Lebanese Galilee). In contrast to Lower Galilee, Upper Galilee is predominantly built up of Cenomanian and Turonian limestone formations, framed in the west by a belt of less resistant Senonian ones, which also form the surface rock of the region's intramontane basins. Eocene formations, generally consisting of hard rock sequences, are more extensive in the eastern part of the region. Another important difference between the Lower and Upper Galilee is the much smaller surface covered by basalts in the latter, where they are virtually restricted to some small plateaus (Dalton, Ram Plateaus).

Upper Galilee, being northernmost of all the mountain regions of Cisjordan, with only a narrow coastal plain interposed between it and the Mediterranean to "intercept" the early rains, in particular, and affect their amounts, as in the case of the Judean Mountains, is the region with comparatively the highest precipitation within Cisjordan. Very few parts of the region receive less than 24 in. (600 mm.) while the amount of precipitation on its summit areas exceeds 40 in. (1,000 mm.) annually. Snowfall occurs almost yearly. The large amounts of precipitation combined with the hard, intensively jointed limestone bedrock and the abundance of exposed surfaces (the result of tectonic shattering and fracturing and of the erosive activity of the watercourses) have made Upper Galilee the region most strongly affected by solution processes. Accordingly, it contains almost a full

Karstic landscape in Upper Galilee (Naḥal Avivim). The pillars are formed by solutional weathering, with numerous caverns formed by corrosion. Photo I. Schattner, Jerusalem.

The polje of Kadesh Naphtali looking toward the Arab village of Qadis, 1939. Courtesy J.N.F., Jerusalem.

inventory of subaerial and subsurface karstic features. This is the only area where a sort of "holokarst" has developed, i.e., landscapes whose surfaces are primarily affected by solution and that display almost the whole gamut of specific features. Large surfaces are rilled and corroded into a maze of small, sharp-crested ridgelets separated by even narrower minute channels (lapies). Dolines are widespread (particularly in the vicinity of Sa'sa and Alma) as are sinkholes, many of which are tens of meters deep. This is also the site of the only large "true" polje within Cisjordan, i.e., a basin of considerable size (Kadesh Naphtali), mainly a product of solution. Upper Galilee is, in addition, the site of the most abundant and intricate caves in Ereẓ Israel (some of which include a full inventory of speleothems—stalactites, stalagmites, stalagnates, dripstone-draperies, etc.).

The same basic conditions—the large amounts of precipitation and the prevalence of limestone-dolomite surface rock—produced a relatively continuous cover of terra rossa on most moderately sloping areas. These conditions also apply to the relatively large areas of forest, which have great regenerative ability, so that even in the past, when forests were utterly depleted through man's agency, considerable parts of Upper Galilee remained covered by high-grade maquis.

Upper Galilee is an analogue of Lower Galilee in its physiographic subdivision, on the basis of lithological and morphotectonic conditions. The eastern part of Upper Galilee was apparently affected by faulting to a smaller extent, imparting to the landscape a more uniform aspect than in the adjacent parts. Several areas form small plateaus, mainly due to their basalt cover. Basins of considerable size, as well as relatively long mountain ranges, running almost unbroken and not partitioned into isolated blocks, are found here. One of these, the Naphtali Range, with summits over 2,900 ft. (900 m.) high, extends almost due north up to the Qasimiye River. Its eastward slope is precipitous—1,600 ft. (500 m.) difference in height over a distance of only about a mile—a marked fault-scarp facing the upper Jordan Valley, the Ḥuleh Basin and the Marj ʿAyyūn Basin farther north. Plateau-like on its top surfaces, and strongly affected by karstification, the Naphtali Range forms a wall-like enclosure around the Ḥuleh Basin, uninterrupted by major valleys, and a pronounced watershed zone between this basin and the rivers draining to the Mediterranean. South of this range lies the Safed region, flanked on its east by Mount Canaan and on the west by the dominant Meron Block. Here the surface is divided into individual mountain groups, due largely to the numerous steeply incised valleys of the tributaries of the Ammud River. The central Upper Galilee Highlands are separated from the eastern Highlands by the gorge of the Ammud River, running almost due north-south. Here, as in the portion extending southward to the Beth-Cherem Valley, typical Mediterranean mountain scenery reaches its climax within Cisjordan. Slopes, mostly terraced, rise from deep valley gorges to heights surpassing 3,000 ft. (1,000 m.) above sea level. Covered by patches of trees or scrub growth, they culminate in the gently domed summits of large mountain bodies such as Mount ha-Ari, Mount Hillel, and Mount Addir, which are overshadowed by the summit region of the massive Mount Meron. The western part of Upper Galilee, much lower in absolute and relative heights, is characterized primarily by a large number of valleys (originating in the Central Highlands). As noted earlier, the valleys are very closely spaced, and form deep gorges in their upper and middle reaches (Chezib and Beẓet in the Israel part of the area and Samara, Shamaʿ, and ʿAzziyya in the Lebanese). These intensively dissected highlands mainly form extended interfluve ranges, the widest of which, the Ḥanitah-Rosh ha-Nikrah Range, ends with a headland into the Mediterranean (Rosh ha-Nikrah).

Rift Valley. The Rift Valley, within Ereẓ Israel, is part of the approximately 3,700 miles (6,000 km.) Rift Valley system that begins in Africa near the Zambezi Valley and peters out north of the Amanus Mountains. The Red Sea and its two gulfs, Eilat and Suez, are submerged parts of the system, whereas in Ereẓ Israel, as mentioned earlier, the Rift Valley is the prime determining factor of a complex of morphotectonic features unique in the world. Some of the tectonic movements that generated the Rift Valley seem to be still active here, as proved by the frequent earthquakes affecting the valley and the adjacent regions. Other evidence is provided by the many hot springs along the boundaries of the Rift Valley, indicating the presence of near-surface magmatic bodies. Geologically recent volcanic activity also played a major role in forming the basic surface configuration of the valley and its adjacent regions. Streams of lava, extruding mainly in the Bashan (particularly in the Hauran and Golan), formed an almost continuous basalt cover extending as far as to the south of the Yarmuk Valley. The lava moved down into the northern part of the present Jordan Valley, consolidated, and dammed up the valley, thus differentiating it into the Ḥuleh Valley—the head part of the Jordan River system—and a section lying about 800 ft. (250 m.) lower, at present occupied by Lake Kinneret. A vast inland sea covered the Rift Valley floor in the Middle Pleistocene, extending from the present Lake Kinneret to far beyond the southern shores of the Dead Sea. It is termed the Lashon (Lisān) Lake after the wide peninsula, or "tongue" (Heb. *lashon;* Ar. *lisān*), that protrudes into the present Dead Sea and divides it into two basins connected by a narrow strait. The level of the Lashon Lake was once about 700 ft. (200 m.) higher than that of the Dead Sea. Sediments deposited on the floor of the Lashon Lake (accordingly called the Lashon formation)—overlying very thick sediment accumulations of former lake formations, which appeared and disappeared in accordance with climatic variations during the Pliocene and Lower Pleistocene eras, and other fill-in material—are of very specific character. They consist of thinly layered clastic material, particularly clays, and evaporites, i.e., sediments produced by chemical precipitation caused mainly by evaporation. With the gradual regression of the Lashon Lake (evidenced by the many terraces along the Dead Sea slope enclosures marking the former coastlines), the Lashon formation sediments were bared. These sediments, covering the floor and the slope bases of the Rift Valley from Lake Kinneret in the north to Ein Ḥaẓevah about 20 mi. (30 km.) south of the Dead Sea, are easily eroded and thus condition microreliefing processes of the highest intensity. These processes create mazes of badlands containing almost the entire gamut of configuration features in miniature, due mainly to the innumerable gullies that dissect this former floor of the Lashon Lake. Another extremely important lithological characteristic of the Rift Valley is the abundance of rock salt and gypsum forming the bedrock of prominent features (for example, Mount Sodom).

The Rift Valley, sunk in, troughlike, in some places to considerable depths below the sea level, forms a unique climatic region with very distinct characteristics and exerting great influence upon its adjacent zones. Climatic conditions in the Rift Valley have a decisive influence on the surface relief of its southern and central parts, i.e., from the Gulf of Eilat to Lake Kinneret. The Rift Valley receives very small amounts of precipitation, as it is leeward of the moisture-bearing winds coming from the Mediterranean, due to the interposition of the highlands of Cisjordan. Precipitation averages 1 in. (25 mm.) annually at Eilat, 2 in. (50 mm.) at the southern end, and less than 4 in. (100 mm.) at the northern end of the Dead Sea and gradually increases to approximately 12 in. (300 mm.) annually at Lake Kinneret, the terminal area of the depression below sea level. North of Lake Kinneret, where the Rift Valley floor is well above the level of the Mediterranean, precipitation is 16 in. (400 mm.) annually, imparting to this section subhumid characteristics. The topographical conditions that influence the amounts of precipitation are also the major reason for the generally extreme temperatures and their variations in the Rift Valley. Geomorphologically more important than the temperatures themselves, which frequently reach the highest values within Ereẓ Israel, is the

Arabah landscape in the vicinity of Ein Ḥaẓevah. The rift floor is covered mainly by gravel supporting scanty xerophytic bush vegetation. In the foreground is one of the numerous canyon exits into the Rift Valley.

extreme evaporation potential they cause, which greatly influences the bedrock and the processes affecting it, particularly weathering. The above-mentioned climatic conditions, together with particular lithological conditions (the high proportion of evaporites), have resulted in large parts of the Rift Valley being devoid of proper soil and vegetational cover, and these develop here only under specific hydrographic or hydrological conditions. The Jordan, for instance, from its exit from Lake Kinneret almost up to its debouchure, is accompanied by a dense gallery forest covering its floodplain. In the vicinity of springs and in areas where topographical conditions cause the formation of salt marshes a type of tree oasis is common.

Hydrographically, the Rift Valley is a vast endoreic basin (i.e., without a discharge outlet to the sea), presently in a state of equilibrium between the amount of inflow from its catchment area—about 15,500 sq. mi. (40,000 sq. km.) in area—and the amount of loss caused by evaporation and infiltration. The level of the Dead Sea, its discharge terminal, does not change in height appreciably from year to year. From the physiographical, and particularly morphotectonic, points of view, the portion of the Rift Valley within Ereẓ Israel may be subdivided into the following major units (dealt with here according to their south-north sequence, which to some degree also follows their genetical order of succession): Arabah, Dead Sea Region, Ḥuleh Basin, and the Jordan Sources Region.

ARABAH. North of the Red Sea and the Gulf of Eilat, the Great Rift Valley again becomes a continental feature. Its first portion here extends for about 100 mi. (160 km.) up to the Dead Sea, constituting the longest and largest Rift unit within Ereẓ Israel. It is relatively narrow, as its maximum width is only about 12 mi. (20 km.), and, according to its topography (especially its hydrographic conditions), it consists of two parts. The southern part, about 43 mi. (70 km.) long, ascends gradually from the Eilat coast to a divide between the latter and the Dead Sea about 600 ft.

(200 m.) above sea level. From here the valley floor slopes down to below sea level in its last third and merges with the large salt marsh at the southern shore of the Dead Sea. This northern area is drained by the Arabah River and its many tributaries, whereas the southern area lacks any organized drainage, particularly any distinct river channel discharging into the Gulf of Eilat. Another significant characteristic of the southern portion of the Arabah is several major topographical depressions that function as discharge terminals for various very short, sporadic watercourses flowing in shallow, indistinct, rill-like beds and for the sheet floods occurring after each heavy rain.

Southern Arabah. The southern section of the Arabah is bordered by the coast of Eilat-Akaba, which is less than 6 mi. (10 km.) long and runs southwest-northeast. This coast differs in several respects from that bordering the Mediterranean. It is covered by coarse sands and shingle, created by the disintegration of magmatic rocks and Nubian Sandstone, which compose the mountains framing the Gulf of Eilat and the Arabah, and by fragments of corals and associated organisms that populate the Gulf. The widely distributed beachrock consists mainly of pebbly material deposited on the coast by the rivers descending from the crystalline Eilat Mountains and their Transjordanian counterpart, the Edom Mountains, in addition to the above-mentioned organogenic material. After somewhat protracted or concentrated rainfall, the coastal part of the Arabah is frequently flooded. In the absence of discharge channels it becomes a kind of playa (i.e., salty marsh) that, after its ensuing desiccation, exhibits wide areas of polygonal clay shards encrusted by salt crystals. Farther north the floor of the Arabah is covered by detritus of various sizes reaching a depth of more than 3,300 ft. (1,000 m.). This layer has been deposited by numerous streambeds that carry only floodwaters (from Roded, Sheḥoret, Amram, Reḥam, and Timna on the western enclosure and Yitm, Mulghān, and Muhtadī on the eastern one). Another very important depositional factor is slope wash and gravitational movements (rockfall, sliding, slumping, particle creep) that continuously take place on the mountain slopes flanking the Arabah, which lack stabilization by soil and vegetational cover. These slopes, as mentioned earlier, are lithologically heterogeneous. In the southern part of the Cisjordan Arabah, they are composed mainly of magmatic-metamorphic rocks and Nubian Sandstone (Eilat and Timna Massifs); farther north limestones and dolomites prevail. The Transjordanian side of the mountainous enclosure consists predominantly of crystalline rocks and Nubian Sandstone.

The floor of the southern part of the Arabah is not flat. It is differentiated by many rises and wide shallow depressions. The former originate in alluvial fans spreading out widely into the Arabah at the exits of all the valleys. The fans on the east side are generally more numerous, larger, and longer as a result of the larger supply of detritus. The abundance of this supply is conditioned by several factors. The mountains bordering the Arabah to the east are much higher than the Negev Highlands and receive far larger amounts of precipitation because of their westerly exposure. These two factors endow the watercourses descending from the eastern side with considerably greater erosive power. In addition, the bedrock there, which consists of crystalline rock and sandstones almost along the entire extension of this flank, is subject to intensive disintegration under the prevailing arid conditions and supplies the watercourses with the bulk of the coarse material that is borne down and deposited at their exit into the Arabah. Thus, on the east side an almost continuous detritus apron of coalesced fans envelops the bases and the lower slopes. Where the fans extend farther into the Arabah or meet fans formed by watercourses from the west side (generally smaller in size), rises or topographical swells originate. The floor between the rises is basin-like; runoff is deflected into these basins with consequent flooding and salt marshes of short duration are formed. In several of these basins (Avronah, Yotvatah, and Saʿīdiyīn are the largest), halophytic vegetation has developed and even trees are able to subsist on brackish subsurface water. Another characteristic of both the southern and northern Arabah is the relatively wide areas of dunes, particularly between the basins of Yotvatah and Saʿīdiyīn.

Northern Arabah. The northern, larger part of the Arabah, which begins with a wide protrusion of the Paran Plateau into the trough valley, differs in several respects from the southern part. The latter is relatively narrow, limited on the east by the relatively straight and continuous fault scarps of the Edom Highlands and on the west by the irregular outline of the southern Negev Highlands with their many mountain outliers and riverhead cirques. The influence of faulting is less pronounced there. Conversely, the northern Arabah often widens into the mountains bordering it, which are in turn frequently interrupted by wide valleys intruding deeply into the confining mountain flanks. The most significant difference between the southern and the northern parts of the Arabah, however, is the presence of a river course almost throughout the length of the latter. It is very indistinct and erratic, functioning mainly as a collecting artery of the many tributaries joining it from the east and west. The existence of this relatively dense drainage net, although it carries flash-flood waters almost exclusively, precludes the existence of any major basins turning into a salt marsh or extensive dune areas. The bed of the Arabah River, several hundred meters wide, is not contained by any permanent or continuous banks and is defined mainly by the accumulation of pebbles and associated fluviatile material. It does not run along the median axis of this part of the Rift Valley, but consistently deviates westward due to the fans growing and spreading out from the eastern side of the valley. These fans receive more alluvial material than those spreading out from the Negev, due to the greater height, larger amounts of precipitation, and consequently greater erosive and tractive capacities of the Transjordanian affluents.

 The northernmost part of the Arabah was covered in the

Middle Pleistocene by the Lashon Lake. Its surface accordingly consists mostly of laminated, highly erodible marls. The Arabah River and several others (in particular the Amaẓyahu River, almost parallel in course to the former) have cut spectacular canyons into these sediments, accompanied by labyrinthal badlands. The Arabah River does not reach the Dead Sea through a clearly defined bed channel, but disappears in the Sodom playa—the salt marshes south of the Dead Sea—which is flooded periodically by any considerable rise of the Dead Sea and/or by the rivers that discharge into the Dead Sea. Only one river in this area, however, the Zered (Ḥasāʾ)—delimiting Edom from Moab—has a direct debouchure into the Dead Sea. It drains an area in Transjordan that reaches heights of over 3,280 ft. (1,000 m.), receives over 10 in. (250 mm.) precipitation on the annual average, and is fed by numerous springs. Due to these factors, the Zered exhibits perennial flow up to its entrance into the Rift Valley, and after rains it discharges very large quantities of floodwater. A large spring is also located in that section of the valley through which the Zered flows, and this northeast corner of the Arabah (the region of Zoar) forms a sort of an enclave, characterized by plentiful, almost tropical vegetation.

DEAD SEA. The deepest part of the Rift Valley is covered by an inland sea about 50 mi. (80 km.) long, 10 mi. (17 km.) wide, and generally similar in shape to the rift lakes in East Africa. With no outlet to the sea and an inflow of river water balanced by evaporation from its surface area of over 380 sq. mi. (1,000 sq. km.), the salt contents of the sea (mainly magnesium, sodium, and calcium chlorides), carried as solutions by the rivers and the other sources of discharge into it (such as springs with a high mineral content), became progressively concentrated. This salt content now amounts to about 28–33%, depending on the depth of the water layer. The Dead Sea consists of two widely differing parts: a southern, small, and very shallow basin—20 ft. (6 m.) deep—with a higher percentage of salinity; and a northern basin, over three times the size of the southern one, and considerably deeper than it—about 1,300 ft. (400 m.). The two basins are connected by a strait about 2 mi. (3 km.) wide, formed by the westward protrusion of the Lashon Peninsula into the sea. According to topographical and historical indications, the strait was formerly more shallow and probably narrower, and it is assumed that in the geologically recent past the two basins were virtually separated. The Lashon Peninsula rises about 200 ft. (60 m.) above the Dead Sea and was probably formed by diapiric movements of underlying deep-seated salt masses (i.e., an upward thrust of salt deposits rendered plastic and mobile by the pressure exerted on them). Its tabloid surface consists of Lashon Marls, as do the steep sides of the peninsula, which are subject to strong wave abrasion. Except for its northern and southern coast and small stretches along its sides, the Dead Sea does not have any shore flats. It is almost immediately bordered along its entire length by steep slopes that sometimes protrude into the sea and form bold capes (Rās Fashkha, south of the site

The cape of Rās Fashkha, at the northwestern end of the Dead Sea. Courtesy J.N.F., Jerusalem. Photo David Dafnai, Jerusalem.

of Qumran, is the most pronounced). Conversely, many rivers, particularly those coming from the Judean Desert, create rather extensive deltas quite close to the exits of their canyons (Kidron, Daraja, the combined deltas of Mishmar, Ẓe'elim and Masada). These deltas impart to the western coast its sinuous outline, in contrast to the relatively straight coastline on the eastern side, where the deltas built out into the sea are fewer in number and generally far smaller in size. Thus, for example, the delta of the Arnon River, second only to the Jordan in the amount of water it supplies to the Dead Sea, is small; when the sea is at its high-water stage, its waters even extend up to the river's canyon exit. Even less pronounced is the subaerial delta of the Zarqā Māʿīn River, the third most important contributor to the Dead Sea. This variance in delta size seems primarily to be the result of the greater depth of the sea floor near its eastern coast, probably a consequence of the major fault line running close to it.

Mount Sodom, bordering the southeastern shore of the Dead Sea. Photo Prior, Tel Aviv.

A singular relief feature found on the southeastern side of the sea is Mount Sodom. It rises over 600 ft. (200 m.) above the sea, with jagged, almost perpendicular slopes close to the water line, and gradually slopes down on its western flank. About 6 mi. (10 km.) long, it is composed mainly of salt and gypsum layers capped by Lashon Marls. The mountain is of diapiric origin, i.e., salt and other evaporites have been squeezed upward along an elongated fault, thus uplifting the overlying sediments and then spreading them out sideways. The great solubility and erodibility of the evaporites, augmented by their strong tendency to form cracks as a result of the enormous stresses exerted on the rock masses when they are thrust up and intensively contorted, resulted in the formation of this almost unique mountain ridge. Closely spaced fissures (continually widened and deepened by solution), washout, and corrasion by gully waters created a multitude of pillar-like features ("Lot's Wife"). Their surfaces are pitted by innumerable hollows, crisscrossed by rills ("salt-lapies"); in their flank facing the Dead Sea caverns developed, one of them an actual cave, connected with the upper mountain surface by a chimney-like conduit. The interior of this cave exhibits a rich inventory of speleothems (stalactites, etc.), somewhat more elaborate than those found in limestone caves.

THE LOWER JORDAN VALLEY. The Lower Jordan Valley morphogenetically represents the floor of the Lashon Lake laid bare after its recession. The valley of the Jordan progressively developed on this floor, as did the lowermost courses of its tributaries, which formerly discharged into the Lashon Lake. Hypsographical, lithological, and climatic conditions resulted in the formation of a unique riverscape, connected with and focused on the course of the Jordan River from its exit from Lake Kinneret to its debouchure into the Dead Sea. The Jordan and its tributaries are deeply entrenched in the layers of the Lashon formations, which thicken progressively southward. They did not succeed, although greatly aided by the innumerable

The delta of the Jordan and its distributaries. The evaporation pans in the middle portion of this aerial photograph, taken in the 1940s, no longer exist. Courtesy Keren Hayesod, United Israel Appeal, Jerusalem.

gullies that developed on the former Lashon Lake floor, in dissecting and reducing it considerably, so that two distinct surface levels exist along the Lower Jordan Valley. The higher one, generally flat, featureless, and only moderately affected by river dissection, is the remnant of the Lashon Lake floor and is referred to as the Ghor (Kikkar ha-Yarden in Hebrew). On both sides it borders high and steep mountainous slopes, formed mainly by scarps and composed predominantly of hard limestones and dolomites. Near the Jordan course, however, the Ghor becomes intensively dissected by innumerable gullies that turn it into intensive and characteristic badlands. Tens of meters below the Ghor extends the alluvial valley of the Jordan formed by its vertical and lateral erosion and much narrower than the Ghor. The Jordan valley, in the narrow sense, consists of the riverbed, about 80–100 ft. (25–30 m.) wide when not in bankful or overflooding stage, and a discontinuous floodplain covered by a dense gallery forest. Walled in by the steep, intensively gullied badland slopes, it contacts the bases of the mountain slopes enclosing the Rift Valley in only a few places.

The length of the Rift Valley between Lake Kinneret and the Dead Sea is about 65 mi. (105 km.); the course of the Jordan along this part of the Rift Valley, however, is approximately 125 mi. (205 km.). The near doubling in length is the result of the river's intricate meandering, despite the great drop in height between its exit from Lake Kinneret and its entrance into the Dead Sea. Despite its tortuous course, the river's gradient and the velocity of its current are still quite considerable, endowing it with great erosive power—factors which are generally adverse to the full development of a meandering course. The intensive meandering of the Jordan—often cited as an example of the phenomenon—seems causally to be connected with the tributaries joining it, which built out progressively growing fans into its valley and thus deviate its course. The rivers contributing the greatest amounts of discharge to the Lower Jordan are its affluents from the Transjordanian side: the

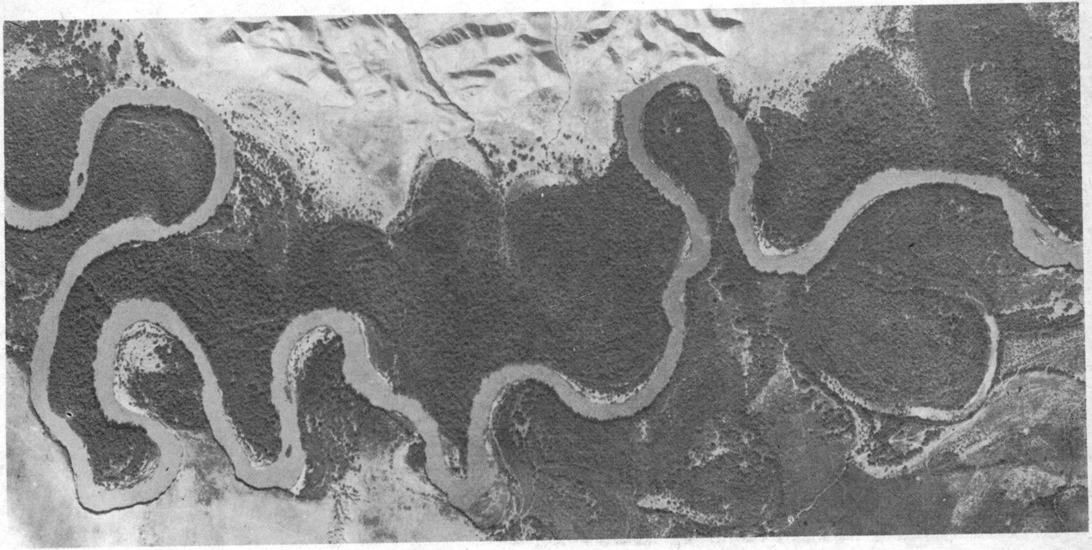

The meandering course of the Jordan, south of the embouchure of the Jabbok. The floodplain is covered by the dense gallery forest, "the pride of the Jordan." Parts of the abandoned channel, characteristically crescent-shaped, stand out clearly. The alluvial valley is bordered by badlands formed in the highly erodible Lashon marls.

Yarmuk contributes about 17 billion cu. ft. (480 million cu. m.) annual discharge, compared with about almost 18 billion cu. ft. (500 million cu. m.) of the Jordan flowing at their confluence; the Jabbok provides approximately 2 billion cu. ft. (about 60 million cu. m.); the Arabah River, over 1 billion cu. ft. (30 million cu. m.); and the other major tributaries contribute only 210–350 million cu. ft. (6–10 million cu. m.) Because the tributaries coming in from the western side of the valley discharge far less, the Jordan is permanently deflected westward. Another factor in determining the river's course is the larger amounts of riverborne material supplied by the eastern affluents (particularly at the flood stages), due to the greater height at which these rivers originate, the larger amounts of precipitation their catchment areas receive, and consequently their far greater erosive and tractive capacities. In addition, exceedingly large amounts of material are delivered to the river from the Rift floor, particularly from the badland zone. Since this material is deposited within the riverbed, where the current is extremely unequal, irregular, and frequently deviated in its course by the outbuilt fans, the large discharge injections are an additional major factor behind the meandering tendency. Finally, waste movements, activated by undermining the river erosion banks, or even—although far more rarely—by earthquakes, bring vast amounts of debris down into the riverbed. According to both historical and contemporary eyewitnesses, this activity has even caused temporary cessation of the river's flow for some time.

The Lower Jordan Valley is fringed on its eastern side by the high scarp-slopes of the Transjordanian plateaus, which are only insignificantly punctuated by the canyon exits of the rivers descending into the Rift Valley. Less linear in outline is the western enclosure, in which the Jordan tributaries created wide valleys, extending far into the eastern flank of the Judean and particularly the Samarian Mountains (ʿAwjā and Fāriʿa Rivers). Some 18 mi. (30 km.) south of Lake Kinneret, the western mountain enclosure is

The Yarmuk Valley, cut into basaltic cover rocks. Courtesy Government Press Office, Tel Aviv.

broken by the tectonic valley of Beth-Shean, which begins the valley sequence traversing the width of Cisjordan. Hypsographically and climatically it represents a transition zone. The valley's level rises progressively from about 800 ft. (250 m.) below sea level at its eastern limit—the Jordan River—to about 300 ft. (100 m.) above sea level at its conjunction with the Harod Valley. Two surface levels exist within this embayment of the Rift Valley: a higher one adjacent to Mount Gilboa and predominantly composed of travertine, precipitated mainly from the many fault-conditioned springs at the base of this mountain; and an eastern, lower one, separated from the former by a step slope (now indistinct because of cultivation), merging imperceptibly with the Ghor. The Beth-Shean and Jordan valleys exhibit semiarid characteristics, mainly as a result of the amounts of precipitation (exceeding 12 in. (300 mm.) on the annual average). Conversely, the prevailing temperatures are still very similar to those in the southern part of the Lower Jordan Valley.

KINNERET REGION. This region comprises Lake Kinneret (also called the Sea of Galilee or Lake Tiberias) and the narrow plains situated between it and the high, steep mountain slopes enclosing it to the west and east. To the south the plain into which the Jordan exits from the lake and in which the embouchure of the Yarmuk into the Kinneret is situated merges imperceptibly with the Beth-Shean Valley. The lake, however, covers a larger area—about 70 sq. mi. (170 sq. km.)—than all its surrounding plains combined. Lake Kinneret itself, whose maximum depth is only about 200 ft. (60 m.), was created by complex and protracted tectonic movements involving faulting and volcanic activities (the mountains enclosing the lake are to a large extent covered by basalts). These movements, which seem to continue to this day, as may be inferred from the earthquakes of considerable strength that affect the region from time to time (the town of Tiberias was heavily damaged and about 700 people were killed in the earthquake of 1837) and from the presence of hot springs (Tiberias, al-Ḥamma, the

Lake Kinneret, near Tiberias.

ancient Ḥammath-Gader, in the Yarmuk Valley). Another indirect source of evidence is the many mineral springs issuing from the lake bottom and contributing considerably to the relatively high salinity of the waters—300 mg./liter. Fault lines are the main factor behind the pronounced asymmetry of the shoreline. Whereas the eastern shore, conditioned by a fairly meridional fault sequence, runs relatively straight, the western one curves out sharply due to crescent-shaped fault lines. Asymmetry is also characteristic of most of the other features of the lakescape. Steep, high slopes rising almost immediately from the eastern and western sides of the lake face littoral plains on the opposite shores. The northern and southern shores of the lake are also very different in configuration. At its northern tip the Jordan River enters the lake in a complex braided course; several branches of it split up and join alternatively, uniting into a single bed only a small distance from the embouchure. The small river plain thus formed is the head of the al-Buṭayḥa (Bet Ẓayyada) Plain, which extends farther southeast and is composed mainly of the alluvial deposits of six small streams descending from the Golan Heights into the lake. South of this plain, and separated from it by a steep mountain spur, extends the shore plain of Ein Gev, dominated by Mount Susita and progressively widening and finally merging with the Yarmuk Plain.

In bold contrast to the northern and eastern sides of the lake, where alluvial plains are prograded into the lake, the southern shore is subject to incessant, strong abrasion and thus to regrading by the wave activity caused by the prevailing north winds. The recession of the shore is strongly aided by the high erodibility of the Lashon formation materials framing the lake. Into this bedrock, which also contains many basalt outcrops, the Jordan has cut its bed in a course that meanders almost from its exit from the lake. The west side of Lake Kinneret is fringed from the exit of the Jordan up to the debouchure of the Arbel River by a steep slope rising in several steps to about 600–800 ft. (200–250 m.) above the level of the lake —700 ft. (212 m.) below sea level. A large littoral plain—the Plain of Ginnosar—developed only at its northwest corner. This plain was created by the coalescence of deposits brought down from Eastern Galilee by several rivers (Arbel, Zalmon, Ammud).

Ḥuleh Basin and Jordan Source Region. At least two subsequent lava flows, descending from the Golan Heights into the Rift Valley north of the present Kinneret Lake and consolidating there, formed a basalt sill that dammed up the flow of the Jordan southward. A result of this stoppage was the formation of a lake whose waters quickly reached a level higher than the sill and finally began to overflow it. This process resulted in the formation of a riverbed incised progressively deeper into the basalt block, and the lake eventually became greatly reduced in surface area and depth. This reduction was probably accomplished in a relatively short time because of the considerable difference in height between the floor of the basin and the surface of Lake Kinneret that must have existed before the up-damming. At present the difference in height amounts to about 900 ft. (270 m.) over a distance of only 10 mi. (17 km.)—the steepest gradient in the Jordan's course, giving it great erosive power, despite the hardness of the basaltic bedrock (as evidenced also by the steepness of the banks along the bed cut into it). The Ḥuleh Lake, which was small—about 5 sq. mi. (14 sq. km.)—and only about 20 ft. (6 m.) deep, and the adjacent Ḥulatah swamps, which occupied an area of about 12 sq. mi. (30 sq. km.) covered by papyrus and kindred hydrophilic plants and populated by waterfowl, buffalo, etc., represented the natural remnants of the former lakescape. Drained off by the lowering, widening, and straightening of the Jordan bed and by artificial channels dug through the marshy areas in the 1930s—uncovering soils extremely rich in organic matter and thick layers of peat—the region underwent one of the most pronounced anthropogenous landscape transformations within Ereẓ Israel. At present it is one of the most intensively cultivated areas in the country (with the exception of a small reservation where the former conditions are preserved); however, it faces the problem of surface subsidence due to the progressive shrinkage of its underground, caused by the draining off of its interstitial water contents into the channels.

North of the former swamp area and lake, which occupied the lowest part of the basin, the land surface gradually rises to the Hills of Metullah, interposed between the Naphtali Range in the west and the Golan Heights in the east. This region is characterized mainly by its many watercourses—the headrivers of the Jordan: namely, from west to east: the Senir (al-Ḥaṣbānī), Dan, and Hermon (Banias) Rivers. All these rivers, as well as several brooks that discharged independently into the Ḥulatah swamps—like the Ijon (ʿAyyūn), which drains the basin bearing the same name farther north—are fed mainly by spring waters.

The Senir (al-Ḥaṣbānī) Valley. Courtesy J.N.F., Jerusalem.

The springs are partly supplied by rainfall and snow melting on the Hermon and fed by subterranean conduits, created by solution. The three above-mentioned headrivers, of which the Senir has the longest course, beginning at the northwest base of the Hermon, flow in deeply incised, precipitously sloped valleys in beds with very irregular gradients, which at times become highly steep and form waterfalls. There are several waterfalls along the course of the Hermon River and some smaller ones along that of the Dan. The most impressive waterfall within Cisjordan, however, is the *Tannur* ("Chimney") of the Ijon River near Metullah.

The Hermon River first joins the Dan, and only some distance from their confluence with the Senir does the Jordan River begin its course in a single bed. Before the swamps were drained, this united flow continued for only a small distance, after which the flatness of the basin bottom and the marshes covering it caused a division of the Jordan's course into several indistinct branches that discharged into the swamps and contributed to their existence. Thus the Jordan proper, in terms of the continuity of the river, and the singleness of its bed, began only at its exit from the Ḥuleh Basin. All these conditions were essentially changed by the draining of the Ḥulatah swamps and the regulation of the river courses discharging into it. The numerous watercourses perennially flowing down from the Hermon foothills, the Golan Heights, and the Naphtali Range—totalling an average annual inflow of over 26 billion cu. ft. (about 740 million cu. m.)—and the abundant springs (among them the largest in Ereẓ Israel) impart to the source region of the Jordan hydrographic characteristics infrequently encountered in the Levant.

Ijon Region. The 8.5 sq. mi. (22 sq. km.) basin of Ijon (Marj ʿAyyūn), which is situated within Lebanon, is separated from the Ḥuleh Basin by the Metullah Hills. It represents the northernmost portion of the Rift Valley drained by the Jordan, and also of the endoreic part of the Great Rift Valley System. The basin is over 1,600 ft. (500 m.) above sea level and it also is a tectonically conditioned depression. It is much smaller than the Ḥuleh Basin, with which it shares some properties, particularly its considerable marsh areas and associated vegetation. On its north the Rift Valley continues in the Beqa, which divides the Lebano-Syrian region into two main physiographical parts: a western one (Lebanon, Ansariye, Amanus Mountains) and an eastern one (Antilebanon, Syrian Plateau). In this area as well, both structure and hydrography are largely conditioned by the Rift, but drainage is essentially different from that of the Rift Valley within Ereẓ Israel: the two collecting trunk rivers (Leontes and Orontes) flow in opposite directions and discharge into the Mediterranean.

4 CLIMATE

Ereẓ Israel is situated between the subtropical arid (Egypt) and subtropical wet (Lebanon) zones. This location helps to explain the great climatic contrast between the light rainfall in the south and the heavy rainfall in the north in all four orographic belts: Coastal Plain, Western Mountain Ridge, Jordan Valley, and Transjordan. In the rainy season the centers of the barometric depressions crossing the eastern Mediterranean from the west normally pass over Cyprus. Most of Egypt and southern Ereẓ Israel lie in and partly outside this area of cloudiness and precipitation, whereas northern Ereẓ Israel is nearer to the center of the vortex. The cyclonic depressions of the eastern Mediterranean are usually smaller, both in area and in axis length, than the Atlantic depressions. The difference in pressure between the center and the periphery does not exceed 10–13 millibars, with differences between highs and lows not exceeding 17–20 mb. Pressure gradients in winter storms in Ereẓ Israel, however, are just as steep as those in Europe or America.

In the winter, depressions arrive in Ereẓ Israel from the west along two trajectories. The first, of decisive influence on the climate of the country, comes from northern Italy along the Adriatic Sea to Greece and the Aegean Sea. There it divides into two sections, one leading to the Black Sea and the other to Syria. The second leads from southern Italy and Sicily to the central Mediterranean and thence to the southeastern corner of the Mediterranean and Ereẓ Israel. A rare path extends along the North African coast through Egypt to Ereẓ Israel. Depressions sometimes pass along a narrow belt from the Red Sea northward and cause sudden cloudbursts accompanied by torrential floods in the normally dry Sinai Desert, Negev, Jordan Valley, and Syrian Desert. Mediterranean depressions are prevalent in the eight months from October till early June, when cold air penetrates from Eastern Europe through the Balkans to the Mediterranean, influencing the activity of the depressions. Rainfall in the eastern Mediterranean, including Ereẓ Israel, is directly related to the intensity of cold airstreams over Eastern Europe in the winter. The lower the temperatures fall in Eastern Europe, the stronger the influence of the cold airstreams on the depressions moving into the eastern Mediterranean. A narrow belt of high pressure descends from the Balkans and pushes depressions lying to the east. If, simultaneously, a second area of high pressure zones, connected to the great Siberian winter high-pressure system, extends over northern Iraq and Turkey, the activity of the eastern Mediterranean depression increases. Depressions are followed by high pressures, normally centered over northern Syria and Turkey, which are usually connected to the winter anticyclones of central Asia. In such cases, cold air descends from the high mountains of Armenia, which, though warming in descent—sometimes through tens of degrees—is often cold enough upon reaching Israel to cause freezing and frost. Visibility is exceptional. Snowcapped Mt. Hermon and the mountains of Lebanon are then visible from Mt. Carmel—a distance of 60 mi. (100 km.)—and even from Tel Aviv and high points west of Jerusalem—over 100 mi. (nearly 180 km.) away. Barometric pressures are higher in winter than in summer, being low only on stormy days. The difference between winter and summer pressures is smaller in Ereẓ Israel than in Turkey or Iraq.

Lower summer pressures result from Ereẓ Israel's location on the western periphery of the extensive low-pressure system of southern Asia, which causes the Indian monsoon. There is a summer monsoon in Ereẓ Israel too, though it is not accompanied by the heavy precipitation typical of Indian monsoons. The latter, however, affect summer conditions in Ereẓ Israel. Normal monsoons in India result in normal summers in Ereẓ Israel; insufficient pressure gradients and abnormal Indian monsoons cause "abnormal summers" in Ereẓ Israel and the entire eastern Mediterranean. In a normal summer, strong, humid, westerly and northwesterly sea breezes prevail continuously for weeks or months, resulting in extensive dew formation. These are the "etesian winds" known to the ancient Greeks. Other airstreams arise only in the transition months of spring and fall, arriving chiefly from the hot and dry deserts in the east. These are the *ḥamsin* (or *sharav*) winds (see below). *Sharav* winds from July to October are abnormal in summer, indicating undeveloped Indian monsoons.

CLOUDINESS. The frequency of depressions between October and May and their scarcity or total absence between June and September result in marked differences in cloud forms. Between October and May, or sometimes even June, all forms of high, medium, and low clouds occur. In summer only low clouds form through condensation of marine air currents ascending the mountain slopes. Toward the end of September, high ice clouds, then medium, and

Table 1. Monthly Mean Barometric Pressure in Jerusalem

	Millimeters
January	690.1
February	690.1
March	689.7
April	689.8
May	689.6
June	688.5
July	687.1
August	687.6
September	689.7
October	691.4
November	691.5
December	691.5

finally waterladen low cumulus clouds form. Summer clouds are also of the cumulus type, but they are higher than winter clouds. In summer low clouds also approach from the west, carrying more humidity than in winter, but they do not cause rain, lacking ice crystals and the necessary conditions for rainfall. Over high mountains, such as Mt. Hermon and the Lebanon range to the north, penetration of the sun's rays is reduced by these summer clouds. The western, seaward slopes and valleys are mostly covered by an afternoon mist that rises from the sea. Clouds over the mountains of Ereẓ Israel at night are very low, while during the day they occur at altitudes of 6,500–10,000 ft. (2–3 km.). Mist clouds are found in mountain valleys on summer mornings and disappear after sunrise. In Upper Galilee summer cloudiness exceeds that in the south, and morning mists are more prevalent. In the winter, cloudiness in the mountains exceeds that in the coastal region; the opposite is true in summer. The Jordan Valley differs from the rest of the country in this respect as few clouds occur even in winter.

There are no completely overcast days in summer: a quarter of the summer days are partly cloudy; the rest are completely clear. Mist occurs in the Coastal Plain in winter and the transition months. In the inland valleys, such as the Jezreel Valley, mists occur mostly in summer. Heavy morning fogs cover the coast on *sharav* days, while morning mists in inland valleys are the result of temperature inversion. Low places in the Jezreel Valley have mist on clear winter mornings and on summer mornings with no easterly wind. Unique fogs rise in the winter from the Ḥuleh Basin and the Dead Sea. The former is covered by heavy mists on cold nights; over the latter, fogs form after sunrise in the wake of depressions, when cold air flows in pushing the local air up the slopes of the Judean Mountains in the west and the Moab Mountains in the east. After sunrise, these fogs ascend to the mountain tops, over altitude differences of 4,000–5,000 ft. (1,200–1,500 m.). They reach Jerusalem late in the morning, thicken toward noon, and scatter in the late afternoon, though they sometimes remain till evening or even throughout the night. Fogs do not cross the mountain crests to the west, but remain stationary in the strong westerly wind as a westward-pointed wedge hundreds of meters thick.

RADIATION. Ereẓ Israel is a sunny country because of its location in the subtropical zone, its low degree of cloudiness, and its extensive desert areas. In the long summer days the sun ascends to over 80° above the horizon, and radiation reaches the ground in 98% of all potential hours of sunshine; in the winter the sky is cloudy, on the average, through half the day. The annual mean daily radiation is 5 million calories on each square meter. On a summer day it is about 7.5 million, on a clear winter day 3 million, and on a cloudy winter day 1 million. Few countries can compete with Ereẓ Israel in abundance of sunshine. Horizontal surfaces receive illumination of some 90 kilo-lux-hours at noon in summer, and an area perpendicular to the sun's rays receives over 130 k.l.h., nearly the absolute maximum the sun can provide. These quantities are reduced by one-third in the winter. Southern slopes as well as southern-oriented walls and rooms receive the greatest amount of sunshine in the winter. In other directions, no marked differences exist between the various seasons.

RAIN. Rainfall normally begins in Ereẓ Israel in November, increases in intensity to about January-February, and decreases again to May, which is sometimes completely dry. First rains sometimes fall earlier and sometimes later. Likewise, the rainy season may end before Purim (March), though small quantities of rain may fall till Shavuot (around the end of May). Most of the rainfall, some 72% of the seasonal total, occurs in December, January, and February. Five types of yearly rainfall can be discerned: 1) normal, with even distribution; 2) rainy in early winter and dry in its second half; 3) dry in early winter and rainy later; 4) heavy rains in the middle of winter with relatively dry early and late seasons; 5) twin- (or even

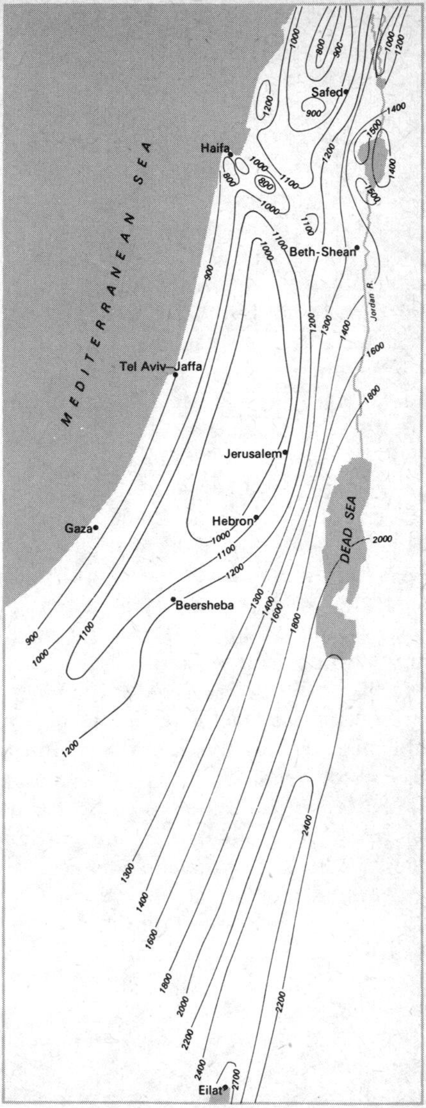

Annual potential evaporation in Ereẓ Israel in millimeters.

multiple-) peaked season, with dry intervals between peaks. The first type occurs in Jerusalem in about 33% and in Haifa in some 42% of the winters. The second type is found in Jerusalem and the Judean Mountains in about 20% of the winters and only in 6% in northern Israel. The third type is more frequent in the north (31% in Haifa) than in the south (13% in Jerusalem). The fourth type is rare, occurring in 2–3% of all years. The fifth type is most frequent in the Judean Mountains (35%), with some 24% in Haifa. Regional differences in rainfall are much larger in Ereẓ Israel than in other countries of comparable size. In Israel there is an absolute desert with under 1.2 in. (30 mm.) rain per annum—the Arabah; semi-desert areas with 2–3 in. (50–75 mm.) to 6–8 in. (150–200 mm.)—the Negev and Dead Sea Valley; agricultural regions with 12–18 in. (300–600 mm.); and mountain areas with 20–32 in. (500–800 mm.) in Judea and Samaria and up to 44 in. (1,100 mm.) in Upper Galilee. Mountains receive more rain than the Coastal Plain or the Jezreel Valley. Amounts of rainfall increase from south to north in all regions: the Coastal Plain, the western and eastern mountain ridges, and the Jordan Valley. Similarly, the number of rainy days in northern Ereẓ Israel exceeds that in the south. In dry years both the amount of rain and the number of rainy days are reduced; in very wet years both may be doubled. Most cultivated areas are those with over 12 in. (300 mm.) rainfall per annum. Contrary to common belief, the amount of rainfall in agricultural areas in Ereẓ Israel is no less than that in agricultural countries in the temperate zones. The difference lies not in the annual amount of rain, but in the number of rainy days and in the intensity of rain per hour or per day. In Ereẓ Israel the entire annual amount falls in 40 to 60 days in a season of seven to eight months. In temperate climates precipitation occurs on 180 days spread over 12 months.

DEW. The formation and amount of dew are dependent both on meteorological conditions—relative humidity and nocturnal cooling—and on the properties of the cooling

Flash flood in the Negev, Naḥal Boker. Courtesy J.N.F., Jerusalem. Photo Zilla Lidor.

surfaces—soil and vegetation. The regional distribution of the number of dew nights and the amount of dew is greatly diverse. Richest in dew are the northwestern Negev and the western and central Jezreel Valley, followed by the Coastal Plain from Gaza to Binyaminah. The central Ḥuleh Basin and parts of the lower Beth-Shean Valley also have large amounts of dew. They are surrounded by the Golan and the Naphtali mountain slopes, which are dry on most nights of the year. Hilly coast regions (Mt. Carmel), regions near the mountains (Western Galilee), and the Jezreel Valley have smaller amounts of dew and fewer dew nights per month and per year. Still smaller is the amount of dew in the mountains of Jerusalem and Galilee. The eastern slopes of the mountain ridge descending into the Jordan Valley, as well as the western foothills, receive smaller and sometimes negligible amounts of dew. The Carmel foothills and those of Western Galilee, Ephraim, and Judea have almost no dew at all. The mean annual number of dew nights exceeds 200 in the entire Coastal Plain and the Jezreel Valley and 250 in

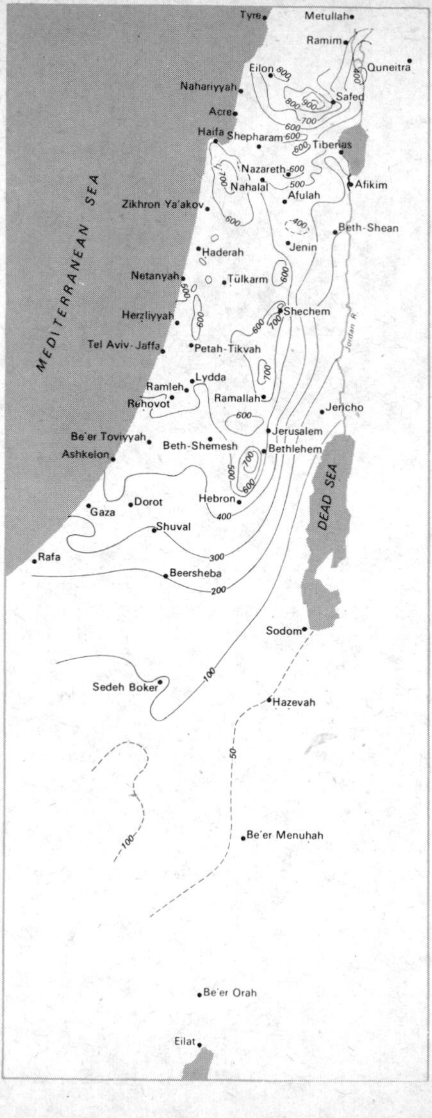

Mean annual rainfall in Ereẓ Israel, 1921–60, in millimeters; broken lines indicate insufficient data.

the northwestern Negev. The mountains have only 150–180 dew (and fog) nights per year; the western foothills have 100, and the Jordan Valley (excluding lower Beth-Shean Valley and central Ḥuleh Basin) has under 50. An

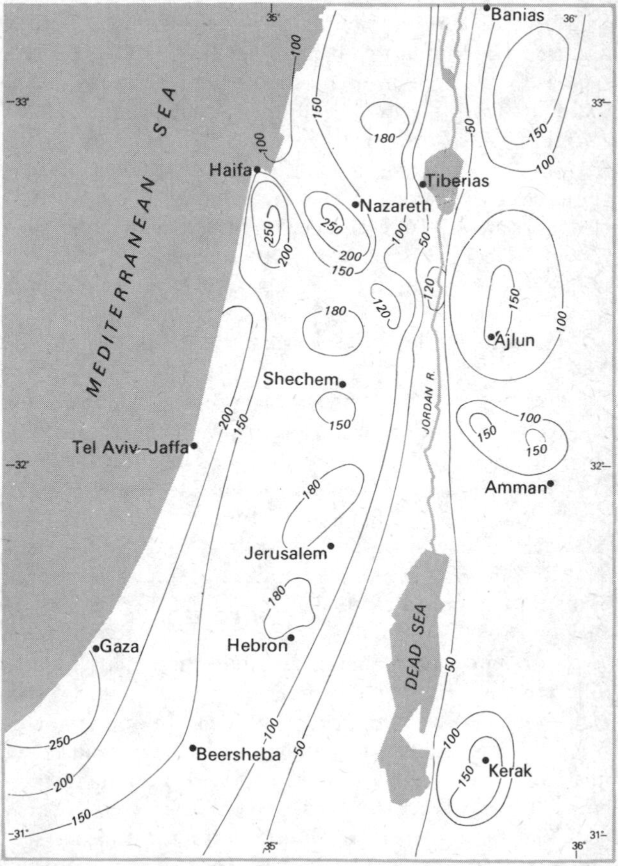

Annual number of dew nights in Ereẓ Israel.

abundance of dew is important for agriculture and settlement. For example: as a result of the dew formation on most summer nights, the vicinity of Khan Yunis in the western Negev which receives only scanty winter rainfall, is a center for growing watermelons, a typical summer crop. Unirrigated summer field crops (sorghum, corn, sesame) can be grown only in areas with sufficient dew.

SNOW. In certain mountain areas snow is a normal occurrence. Mountains of 2,500–4,000 ft. (800–1,000 m.), such as those of Hebron and the Upper Galilee, as well as those of Transjordan—elevation 4,000–5,500 ft. (1,300–1,700 m.)—have snow nearly every year. Mt. Hermon and the Lebanon range, rising to some 10,000 ft. (3,000 m.) above sea level, receive most of their precipitation as snow, which feeds a relatively large number of perennial streams. Most snow falls in Ereẓ Israel in January or February, but it has been known to occur in November and December and even in March and April. The heaviest snowfall recorded in Jerusalem in the last half century was 38 in. (97 cm.) in February 1920.

TEMPERATURE. Air temperature depends on elevation and distance from the sea. Valleys have higher, mountains lower mean temperatures; the higher the location, the lower the air temperature. The highest temperatures are recorded in the Rift Valley, a few hundred meters below sea level, with peak temperatures in the Arabah, south of the Dead Sea. The lowest mean temperature is found in Upper Galilee. The mean annual temperature in the coastal regions is 68°–70° F (20°–21° C) with differences between coastal plains that are near mountains and coastal plains that are not. Haifa has lower temperatures than Acre, Netanyah, Tel Aviv, and even El-Arish. Coastal temperatures vary only slightly in summer, and even in winter their fluctuations are smaller than elsewhere. Maximum temperatures in summer are not high, and winter minima not very low. Fluctuations increase with the distance from the sea; the maximum rises and the minimum decreases markedly. The annual mean temperature is 3° C lower in Jerusalem than in Tel Aviv—difference in elevation 2,624 ft. (800 m.)—but in the winter the difference is larger.

The annual means in the Jezreel Valley and the Coastal Plain are similar, but monthly fluctuations inland, as well as differences between maxima and minima, are larger than on the coast. Temperatures are lower in the Ḥuleh Basin than around Lake Kinneret or the Dead Sea. The mean annual temperature at the southern end of the Dead Sea is 78.3°F (25.7°C); at the northern end, 74.3°F (23.4°C); at Tirat Ẓevi 71.6°F (22.0°C); and at Kinneret, 72.1°F (22.3°C). The annual mean in the Ḥuleh Basin is similar to that on the coast—67.8°F (19.9°C)—though the extremes differ widely. Great climatic differences are hidden by a similarity of mean annual temperatures; evaluation of climatic conditions must also take into account the extremes of diurnal cycles and of hourly differences.

DIURNAL CYCLE. Regional differences are most outstanding in the daily temperature cycle. On the coast temperatures reach their maximum values long before noon. The sea breeze prevents any further increase and the temperature remains almost constant till late afternoon. The temperature peak is thus replaced by a "flat ridge." The same is true of the minimum at night, which lasts for several hours after midnight. But, with increasing distance from the sea, both maximal and minimal temperatures decrease in duration. In the Jordan Valley the diurnal cycle is different. Near the northern Dead Sea in the summer there are two

Mean Temperatures, Tel Aviv and Jerusalem

	Tel Aviv	Jerusalem
January	13.9°	8.6°
March	16.3°	12.0°
May	21.9°	20.4°
July	26.7°	23.2°
September	25.9°	21.6°
November	18.5°	15.3°

peaks. There is an early morning and a late afternoon maximum near the Dead Sea. At Ein Gev on Lake Kinneret the two daily peaks are less developed but still quite prominent. Along the entire Jordan Valley the afternoon peak in temperature results from the adiabatic warming of the westerly wind that descends from the western mountain ridge into the deep Jordan depression. On the southern shore of the Dead Sea the cycle is similar to that near the Mediterranean coast, but the basis temperature values are entirely different. The mountains to the west of this area are not as high and adiabatic heating of the descending air does not increase the temperature above that prevailing locally. The shallow water at the southern end of the Dead Sea has an equalizing effect on daytime temperatures and also maintains high values at night.

Heat Waves. A *ḥamsin,* or heat wave, occurs when a depression approaches Israel from the west, with easterly winds backing first to south and later to west. It is broken when cool and humid maritime air replaces the hot air; when this occurs temperatures may fall by 45°F (20°C) or more. During a *ḥamsin* the temperature always rises and the humidity decreases. In midwinter, clear days with temperatures rising by 10°C or more in a day are a pleasant phenomenon. Such a temperature rise in spring or fall, however, is far from pleasant, since air temperature may reach body temperature. Mountains are hit first by a heat wave and, although temperature rises are relatively small, it is felt strongly because it lasts longer than in the valleys near sea level. When a *ḥamsin* reaches the valleys temperatures are always higher than in the mountains and reach the absolute maxima recorded in Ereẓ Israel. In May and June and in October and November there are often such severe days with high temperatures. But they may occur in the rainy season, with its centers of low and high pressure arriving from the west.

Another type of *ḥamsin* develops with rising barometric pressure under anticyclonic conditions. A northeasterly wind, turning easterly, blows toward the area from a center of high pressure over Iraq, Syria, and sometimes also Turkey. Such a strong east wind in winter is referred to in the Bible as *kadim* (e.g., Ex. 10:13; Ps. 48:8; Jonah 4:8). Owing to the very low humidity, the air is very clear. At first the temperature is low, but it rises daily while the air becomes both dry and hazy. When pressure begins to fall, the conditions are similar to those occurring in a depression *ḥamsin*, but an anticyclonic *ḥamsin* is not only as hard to bear, but it is often stationary and of longer duration. The action of the sun's rays is weakened during such days, and there is only a slight wind. Humans and other warm-blooded creatures feel unwell because the normal functioning of the body's cooling processes are impaired. Delicate winter plants wither in a spring *ḥamsin* because high evaporation causes excessive loss of moisture, and the winter green vanishes as if by magic. The *ḥamsin* is harder to bear near the coast than in the mountains, chiefly because of the high relative humidity of the hot air, which prevents the evaporation of perspiration.

COLD WAVES. Every barometric depression is followed by a high pressure system generally centered over Syria or Turkey. Air flowing in from the northeast usually comes from Siberia in winter, reaching Ereẓ Israel after some warming over the mountains of Armenia, Iran, and Turkey, or, if coming from the north, northwest, or west, over the Black and Mediterranean seas. Such cold waves bring air at temperatures of 14°–19°F (–7° – 10°C) to the Euphrates Valley and 23°F (-5°C) in the Transjordanian Mountains. Each cold wave from the east penetrates first into the Jordan Valley before reaching the Western Mountain Ridge. In such cases, temperatures near the Dead Sea start to fall some 12 hours earlier than in Jerusalem. The danger of frost in winter is thus greater in the northern Jordan Valley than in the western valleys or the Coastal Plain.

TEMPERATURE EXTREMES. The highest temperature ever recorded in Israel was 131°F (54°C, Tirat Ẓevi, Beth-Shean Valley, June 1942). On the same day the temperature was 122°F (51.5°C) at the Dead Sea, 113°F (45°C) on the

Coastal Plain, and 118°F (48°C) in the Jezreel Valley. In the mountains, temperatures exceeding 111°F (44°C) have not been recorded for the past 100 years. In most heat waves, temperatures rise to 110°–113°F (43°–45°C) in the Jordan Valley and 97°–100°F (36°–38°C) on the Coastal Plain; 100°F (38°C) is considered very hot for the mountains. The lowest temperature recorded in Jerusalem in the past 100 years was 19.4°F (-7°C). Even in the Jordan Valley 28°–32°F (-2° to 0°C) was repeatedly recorded. The Coastal Plain, however, seems to be immune to frosts; only twice on record did temperatures fall below freezing. In early 1950, all of northern and central Ereẓ Israel down to the Mediterranean was covered by snow.

HUMIDITY. The relative humidity of the air is highest near the coast and higher at night in summer than in winter. Humidity reaches its daily minimum around noon. Mountain areas are drier, and the humidity there in winter exceeds that in summer, in spite of the dry easterly winds. Conditions in the Jezreel Valley are similar to those near the coast, with high nocturnal humidity in summer. Humidity is lowest in the Rift Valley, especially in the Arabah, and around the Dead Sea. The Dead Sea has higher humidity at the northern end than at the southern end; but the diurnal cycle is different at each end. In all areas the daily cycle is simple, with a minimum at noon and a maximum late at night or throughout the night. At the northern end, however, the relative humidity rises to its maximum at noon in summer when the Dead Sea breeze lowers the temperature. In the afternoon and near sunset, when temperatures reach a maximum, the humidity is minimal due to the western breeze that warms up while descending into the valley.

Absolute humidity in the valleys is higher than in the mountains. The Coastal Plain not only has a high relative but also a high absolute humidity, which causes physical discomfort in summer. Absolute humidity near the Mediterranean is similar to that near the Dead Sea, or even exceeding the latter in summer, although temperatures near the coast are lower. In the Beth-Shean Basin the absolute humidity is also high because of the very high summer temperatures. Since a low humidity facilitates evaporation of perspiration, conditions in the mountains are more pleasant.

WINDS. Simple wind conditions prevail on the Coastal Plain. In summer, a sea breeze blows all day and a land breeze blows at night. Wind conditions on clear winter days are similar to those in the summer, but when a barometric depression covers the sea, easterly winds blow at first, slowly backing to the south and southwest. These winds bring clouds and sometimes rain from the sea, until northerly winds disperse the clouds and the sky clears. In summer northwesterly winds blow over the mountains for weeks and even months on end. The strength of the wind rises from near calm in the morning to a maximum in the late afternoon. Local winds are rare in the mountains, where mainly regional winds blow. These winds are dependent upon pressure distribution around centers of high or low pressure. Local winds occur in summer around the lakes of the Jordan Valley as well as near the Mediterranean. The latter receives the sea breeze throughout the day, while the inland lakes generate land breezes only at certain hours. This is a result of the Mediterranean breeze neutralizing all local activity on reaching the Jordan Valley, so that even the lakes become involved in the general climatic conditions. The landward breeze from the lakes is of biological importance in the hot season. The Mediterranean sea breeze generally has a cooling effect; but upon descending into the valleys lying hundreds of meters below the surrounding mountains and even below sea level, the breeze undergoes such a rise in temperature that, instead of cooling, it heats the area. In summer the westerly winds in the entire Jordan Valley are thus hot and dry. The biological cooling effect of the westerly winds in the Jordan seems to vary. A moist and perspiring body is cooled by it; but upon drying, only the effect of moving air remains, imparting a false sensation of cooling.

Weak winds prevail in the Coastal Plain, the Jezreel Valley, and the Negev. The mountains and the Rift Valley, especially the southern Arabah, experience strong winds. Average wind force is higher in summer than in winter throughout the country; but in a winter storm, velocities in January and February equal or surpass those in the summer. Isolated cases of high winds in winter often lead to a general impression of high winter averages. Wind speeds may reach 50 mph. (80 kph.) and even more in winter, but between storms near calm may prevail. In summer, on the other hand, strong winds blow regularly at certain hours. While these are not as strong as the winter storms, summer averages are generally higher than winter ones. In the Manarah Mountains in Upper Galilee, for example, winds of "winter force" blow on summer days, especially at dusk. The diurnal cycle of wind strength in the mountains reaches its maximum in the afternoon, and on the coast and in the Jezreel Valley at noon. Mornings are usually calm in most areas of the country, as are nights, except in the mountains and the southern Arabah.

HISTORY OF CLIMATE RESEARCH IN ISRAEL. Scientific climate research in Palestine started in the mid-19th century. The first instruments for weather observation were used at the English Hospital in Jerusalem in 1845, where regular observations were taken until World War I. The records of the first 14 years have been lost, but those for 1860–1913 have been preserved intact. The Scottish Mission also took observations at various places, which were supervised from 1860 by the Palestine Exploration Fund and its meteorologist, G. Glaisher (until 1903). M. Blanckenhorn took meteorological observations for the Deutscher Palaestina-Verein from the mid-1890s.

The first results of these observations are assembled in F. M. Exner's work *Zum Klima von Palaestina* (1910), including the first rainfall map of Ereẓ Israel and the adjacent areas. French and American convents, schools, and scientific institutions also set up meteorological stations in Palestine, Syria, and Lebanon. Jews entered the field of climatic research in Ereẓ Israel only in the 20th century. In 1910 the Palestine Office of the World Zionist Organization set up rainfall stations in several towns and villages. Soon after World War I Dov Ashbel set up a network of meteorological stations in Jewish villages from Metullah to the Negev, and a number of stations were installed by the British Mandatory administration. Meteorological research after 1937 was conducted at two centers. One was at the meteorological station maintained by the government Department of Civil Aviation at Lydda Airport, where upper-air conditions were studied with advanced technical equipment. The other was run by the department of meteorology of the Hebrew University of Jerusalem, which controlled the network of meteorological stations in Jewish settlements. The government set up stations in parts of the country populated by Arabs, formerly inaccessible to Jewish research. The Transjordan government also organized a network of observation stations between Akaba and the Yarmuk River. During World War I, the opposing air forces studied upper winds and upper-air meteorology in Palestine. In World War II, the Allied air forces in the whole Middle East theater systematically collected a mass of meteorological data resulting in a revision of concepts of the conditions in the area. The network of Jewish stations was extended in the latter years of the Mandate.

After the establishment of the State of Israel, meteorological operations were developed by both the civil authorities and the Israel Air Force, being carried out on a national scale for both civilian and military needs. These operations include extensive upper-air observations with radio-sondes as well as meteorological satellite research in collaboration with other countries.

5 GEOLOGY

Outline of Stratigraphic Evolution. THE PRECAMBRIAN BASEMENT. Upper Tertiary to Recent faulting and uplift led to many exposures of the basement rocks along the flanks of the Arabah graben, the southeastern corner of the Dead Sea, the Eilat area, and eastern Sinai. The morphology of the Precambrian basement rocks is characterized in Sinai and in the Ḥejaz, situated opposite Sinai, by a conspicuously barren and rugged relief (e.g., Mount Sinai, Wadi Yitm), contrasting remarkably with the tabular landscape of the Paleozoic-Mesozoic sedimentary cover. Varieties of granite and granite-porphyry, syenite, diorite, and gabbro, interchanging with gneiss and mica schists, constitute the principal plutonic and metamorphic basement rocks. Volcanic tuffs and lava sheets also occur, as well as abundant acid and basic dikes. Swarms of dikes invade the whole of the crystalline complex, as well as the unmetamorphosed sediments of the Saramūj series.

The Saramūj series consists principally of multicolored conglomerates analogous in rock character and deposition to the Molasse and Verucano of the Alps. Like these Alpine formations the Saramūj series are of simple fold structure, giving reason to assume strong mountain building during the late Precambrian. The Precambrian "Alps" were then leveled on a regional scale, only a few monadnocks remaining on the enormous erosion and abrasion surface of the Lipalian peneplain. Ore deposits of economic importance have not yet been discovered in the basement complex. The feldspar-, barite-, and mica-bearing pegmatites are of very limited economic value.

Typical erosion form in the Paleozoic Nubian Sandstone of *Amudei Amram* ("Amram's Pillars"), north of Eilat. Courtesy Israel Ministry of Tourism, Jerusalem. Photo A. Strajmayster.

Paleozoics. Above the Lipalian peneplain (principal unconformity) there is an extensive cover of continental and marine sediments of Paleozoic to Recent age. The sedimentary material is derived either from a landmass in the east,

The Jordan Valley near Naḥal Argaman halfway between Jericho and the outlet of Wadi Fāriʿa, with the Mesozoic formation of Gilead in the background. The center of the valley is covered by the horizontally bedded formation of soft Lashon marl. Courtesy J.N.F., Jerusalem.

the "Arabo-Nubian" shield, or from the transgressive "Tethys" sea in the west. The few marine Lower Paleozoic outcrops known from Timna, Eilat, and Petra or from Wadi al-Ḥasā' and Zarqā Mā'īn at the Dead Sea all appear as thin beds of shallow epicontinental limestone-dolomite, shales, and littoral sands; these are intercalated between sandstones hundreds of meters thick. This continental, as well as littoral, sandy complex is included in the Nubian Sandstone. Reminiscent of the "Old Red" of Europe or the "continental intercalaire" of Africa, the Nubian Sandstone has built the impressive colorful rock escarpments of Petra and the eastern cliffs of the Dead Sea. Erosion and corrosion have sculptured these sandstones to fantastic rock forms, especially well developed in the Ḥismā plains and in the Wadi al-Rūm of the Ḥejaz province. It is also in this region that the complete atmospheric disintegration of the Nubian Sandstone has supplied the sandy fillings of the present extensive valleys of the Ḥismā; in the region outside our map it has provided the material for the large belts of dunes of the Ḍahna and Nafūd of inner Arabia. Copper of an average 1.5% is found as a cementing carbonate in the Paleozoic Nubian Sandstone and is mined at Timna. In the same area, manganese deposits have been mapped (mostly psilomelane) but their economic value is still under discussion.

Mesozoics. Dating the Nubian Sandstone is a persistent difficulty, particularly where there are no marine intercalations. This is the case in the Arabah and Dead Sea graben. Thus in the north-south canyons and steep western slopes of Moab, Sodom, and Midian and in the area opposite, between Eilat and Timna, Triassic and Jurassic marine interbeds are remarkably absent. There the massive sandstone rests directly on the Precambrian or the marine Lower Paleozoic Cambro-Silurian beds and is overlaid by marine Cenomanian strata. In this part of the country the Nubian Sandstone may therefore be of any age from Paleozoic to Mesozoic. Fossil plants found in the uppermost layers of sandstone (here somewhat clayey and shaly) are of continental Lower Cretaceous or Wealden character. Genuine marine Triassic in the Transjordanian part of our map is known from the surroundings of the northeastern corner of the Dead Sea and from the deeper wadi-cuts of the Jabbok River. In the high Negev of Sinai and Israel, Triassic is exposed in the erosion windows of Mt. Arif and Ramon. The predominantly calcareous, occasionally marly beds display lithological affinities with the "Germanic" epicontinental Trias—the Muschelkalk—though their fauna also contain many "Mediterranean" elements. Quasi-continental conditions during the Upper Triassic led to the deposition of gypsum evaporites and to faunistically sterile dolomite varves and Keuper-like variegated marls. The lowermost outcropping strata of the marine Triassic again appear in the "Nubian" facies.

Marine Jurassic is recorded from the neighborhood of the Triassic outcrops of Transjordan and on the Cisjordanian side from the anticlinal cores in Makhtesh Ramon, Ha-Makhtesh ha-Gadol and Ha-Makhtesh ha-Katan; yet none of the calcareous and marly epicontinental formations of the Jurassic or Triassic in Transjordan and in the Negev are completely devoid of sandy intercalations, demonstrating shallow sea conditions in the vicinity of a dune-framed continent. At Ramon, terrestrial influence is also marked by residual deposits of bog-iron and flint clays (up to 55% Al_2O_3) at the Jurassic-Triassic boundary, as well as by a few hundred meters of continental Nubian Sandstone containing some thin intercalations of marine Jurassic. Striking gravel formations recorded from the Jurassic-Cretaceous passage beds of the Ramon in the Negev, as well as of the Lebanon, indicate uplift and widespread erosion at the end of the Jurassic.

The Ramon outcrops are finally distinguished by numerous trachytic dikes and sills of possibly Upper Jurassic age, since they penetrate both Jurassic and Triassic sediments. The syenite-essexite plutonics of the anticlinal core have also been assigned to the Jurassic. The "intermediary" magmatics differ somewhat in rock type from the

The southeastern slope of Mt. Hermon, with Jurassic in the center and Cretaceous cuestas at the foot. The Druze village of Ma'sada is built on basaltic ground. Courtesy J.N.F., Jerusalem.

more basic volcanics, which are extensively represented in the Hermon-Lebanon mountains. In contrast to the continental and epicontinental Jurassic of the Negev and Transjordan, the Middle and Upper Jurassic of Lebanon and Hermon are developed as a 1,000–1,500-meter-thick marine complex prevalently of dolomite and limestone, suggesting deposition in an oceanic basin fairly remote from shore and land.

The recent material obtained from oil-exploration drilling in Israel leads to the conclusion that the Mid-Upper-Jurassic marine sedimentary troughs of Lebanon-Hermon extended south and southwest to Galilee, Carmel, Judea, the Coastal Plain, and the western Negev lowlands. The continental sphere of influence during this period is restricted to the Negev proper and to Transjordan. This paleogeographic zoning of sedimentary conditions persists to a greater extent in the following epoch, during the Lower Cretaceous. Thus in Transjordan and in the Negev-Arabah, the principal representative of the Lower Cretaceous is a uniform sandstone of continental habitus assigned in the map to the "Nubian" complex. Mostly regarded as the time-equivalent of the Wealden, this Lower Cretaceous Nubian Sandstone (kaolinic at the base) is again well exposed in the erosion windows of Ramon, the Makhtesh ha-Gadol, and the Makhtesh ha-Katan. There are, howev-ever, a few thin marine intercalations.

In the western regions, in the Coastal Plain as well as on Mount Carmel and in Galilee, evidence of the hegemony of the Tethys sea during the Lower Cretaceous is found in the cuttings and core samples from the recent wells at Ḥeleẓ, Tel Ẓafit, Moẓa, Zikhron Ya'akov, Caesarea, Haifa, Ein Na'aman (Kurdāna), Mount Tabor, and Tiberias, as well as in the outcrops of central and northern Galilee (Sartaba-Tabor, Bet Netophah, Har Ḥazon, Har ha-Ari, Manarah) and of eastern Samaria (Wadi Māliḥ-Fāriʿa). The lithology of the Lower Cretaceous is predominantly marly and occasionally sandy. Limestones are less frequent and like the other formations are of shelf and littoral character. The presence of lignite in the sandy beds also indicates the proximity of the continent. The abundance of hydroxides and oxides of iron gives the Lower Cretaceous rocks of Galilee their dominant and characteristic brown colors. Enrichment in a shallow sea led to the deposition of oolitic iron ores. The best ore (28% Fe) was found in the "minette" of the Aptian of Manarah in northernmost Israel (30,000,000 tons of minable ore have been evaluated).

Cenomanian-Turonian. Whereas the Triassic, Jurassic, and Lower Cretaceous appear in restricted outcrops in the anticlinal erosion cirques, Makhtesh Ramon, Ha-Makhtesh ha-Gadol, and Ha-Makhtesh ha-Katan, in the wadi-cuts at Ramallah and Wadi Māliḥ-Fāriʿa, and in the uplifted fault blocks of Galilee, more than half of the exposed mountain formations of Israel belong to the marine Cenomanian-Turonian. Thus the prominent mountain bodies of the northern Negev, Judea-Samaria, Carmel, and Galilee are built of Cenomanian-Turonian rocks up to 2,500 ft. (800

The downfaulted intermontane basin of Levona (Lubban) near the watershed of the Judean-Samarian mountains. A typical Cenomanian landscape on the Ramallah–Nablus road. Courtesy J.N.F., Jerusalem. Photo E. Orni, Jerusalem.

m.) thick. The principal strata, hard limestone and dolomite, weather to a rough and rocky karstic landscape characteristic of Mediterranean calcareous terrains. Subdivided by very thin marly (e.g., Moẓa Marl) or by thicker flint-bearing chalk beds (e.g., the Carmel promontory of Haifa), these dolomites and limestones have become the main groundwater aquifer exploited during the last few decades in Israel.

In the central Transjordan section, in the Arabah-Dead Sea Rift Valley, and in the southernmost Negev (Timna), the Cenomanian limestone protrudes as a hard, vertical cliff overlying the rim of Nubian Sandstone escarpments. In southern Transjordan, the lower stage of the Cenomanian is still in the Nubian Sandstone facies. The main Cretaceous transgression starts there only with the Upper Cenomanian, or even, in places, with the Turonian. In northern Transjordan, however, in the upwarped region of the

Cenomanian chalk cliffs of Rosh ha-Nikrah, on the Israel-Lebanon border. Courtesy J.N.F., Jerusalem.

Typical terrace landscape in the Cenomanian rocks and terra-rossa soil of the Judean Hills. Courtesy J.N.F., Jerusalem. Photo A. Strajmayster, Jerusalem.

Typical smooth morphology of the Senonian chalk formation near Safed in Galilee. Courtesy Keren Hayesod, United Israel Appeal, Jerusalem.

Jabbok-ʿAjlūn, the marine development of the Cenomanian is again complete, of considerable thickness and surface distribution. The landscape here is very reminiscent of the Judean-Samarian uplands. In the Carmel and Umm al-Faḥm mountains, submarine lavas and tuffs are interspersed in the Cenomanian-Turonian.

Senonian (Including Paleocene). The Cenomanian upwarps and anticlines of the Israel mountain bodies are everywhere framed on their flanks by narrow strips of Senonian, which continue in larger extension in the synclinal areas. Flint-bearing hogbacks and flat-irons are characteristic morphologic features of the asymmetrical slopes of the Negev and Judean anticlines. The greatest surface extension, however, is that of the synclinorial downwarps of the Judean Desert, the Desert of Zin, and the Paran (Jirāfī) and Ẓenifim deserts in the southern Negev. The dominating Senonian of these regions is also distinguished in the landscape by a white to light gray color and badland dissection of its principal rock type, the chalk. Where unexposed to the atmosphere, the Senonian chalk is usually bituminous. Intercalated flints and the now exploited phosphatic limestones are other representative rock-types of the Senonian. In the Negev section of Sinai and of Edom, opposite, the harder flints are the principal components of the pebble pavement of the large ḥamada plains and plateaus.

Eocene. The surface occurrence of the Eocene is similarly associated with the downwarped regions. The anticlinal ridges of the Cenomanian-Turonian, including their asymmetrical flanks, are practically devoid of Eocene. Eocene is of great extension west of the Ramon and Dimonah ranges in the structural depressions which start from the Avedat plateau down to Niẓẓanah, Revivim, and Beersheba. From Beersheba to the north it extends along the western foothills as far as Ḥuldah. Eocene is likewise extensively represented in the downwarped fold region of Paran and ʿAqof (ʿIqfī) in the southern Negev.

The folds of these synclinorial regions (and this applies also to those of the north) are usually smaller, shallower, more symmetric, and frequently of the brachy-anticline type. Undulations of this kind are developed in the uplifted high plateaus of Transjordan. In Samaria the exposed Eocene is distributed between Ebal-Gerizim and the Umm al-Faḥm range and in Ephraim proper between Umm al-Faḥm and Mount Carmel. A large area of Eocene is analogously situated (though disturbed by faults of the Kishon Valley) between Carmel and southwestern Galilee (Shepharam to Nazareth). In spite of the strong block-faulting which dissected the Galilee in the Pleistocene and the extensive basalt and Neogene cover, it is nevertheless possible to trace the Eocene on the southeastern flanks of the Galilean upwarp. On the western flank of this upwarp,

The Arabah Valley, with arid Senonian and Eocene chalk formations of its eastern border in the foreground and the blockfaulted escarpments and heights of Edom in the background. Courtesy Government Press Office, Tel Aviv.

parallel to the Senonian-Paleocene sedimentary girdle, Eocene appears in sporadic outcrops, intimating that its major portion lies hidden below the Coastal Plain and the sea. The Eocene in the foothill region of the Negev and Judea, western Galilee, and Ephraim consists primarily of chalk interspersed with flint and chalky marl. Lithologically it frequently resembles the Senonian and is accordingly marked by a common egg-shaped smooth hill-morphology. Harder limestones in the higher Negev (Avedat plateau) and in Sinai produce an esplanade landscape with enormous regional plateaus and cuestas. In the Lower Eocene table landscape of Edom-Moab, there is much interstratification of phosphatic limestone. Harder limestone and marble limestone of uppermost Lower to Middle Eocene age are widely distributed in central and eastern Galilee, evolving a pronounced karstic rough-hewn landscape which differs sharply from the smoother relief forms found in the foothill regions of Israel. There, rare occurrences of Upper Eocene are still developed in the chalky marly facies of the Middle to Lower Eocene foothills. Some of Galilee's largest springs derive from the Eocene karst, e.g., Gilboa, Migdal, Naḥal Ammud, Kinnerot (al-Ṭabigha), Kefar Giladi.

Oligocene. The Oligocene Tethys sea never reached far inland. The few limited outcrops in the foothills of Bet Guvrin, Ramleh, and Ephraim, as well as the drilling samples of the Coastal Plain, all point to shore deposits of chalky and detritic character. Marine Oligocene, therefore, plays no significant role in Israel's surface formations; continental Oligocene has not, so far, been discovered. Israel's emergence from the sea may have commenced in the Late Eocene from submarine ridges which already existed here and there in the Senonian; but the major elevation and hence the final anticlinal-synclinal fold pattern came about at the end of the Oligocene or earliest Miocene.

Marine Neogene. The beginning of the Neogene coincides with the most widespread rising of the region above the sea since the end of the Precambrian, i.e., since before the first appearance of the Paleozoic Tethys

(Lipalian interval). Emergences had taken place before, such as at the end of the Triassic and Jurassic and the end of the Lower Cenomanian, but the whole of the country was not affected then, as shown by the results of recent deep borings in the Coastal Plain.

With the approach of the Miocene, the Tethys ceased to exist, its waters merging with and filling the Atlantic and Indian Oceans. At a later time, this region became connected with these two oceans only by means of small sea branches. Europe and Africa-Arabia were then united by isthmuses or divided by inland seas and the Mediterranean originated. In place of the widespread Mesozoic and Eocene transgressions of the Tethys, marine ingressions are henceforth limited to local embayments of the Mediterranean. These occurred primarily during the two Neogene stages, the Miocene Vindobonian and the Pliocene Astian-Plaisancian. Surface outcrops of the marine Neogene are very small in Israel and restricted to the foothill area or to the Beersheba and Kishon plains. Marine Neogene thus plays a very minor role in the morphology of the country.

The littoral Miocene is found today from Haifa Bay and the Ephraim Hills (Ein ha-Shofet) in the north to Beersheba and Dimonah in the Negev, up to a height of 1,600 ft. (500 m.) above sea level. In all the known exposures, it appears with sharp erosional unconformity on folded Eocene and Cretaceous rocks. The marine Miocene strata consist of lagoonal, sandy marls, beach sands, coarse-grained sands, and coral limestone. Both the facies and the fauna point to a connection with the Red Sea and the Indian Ocean. After the retreat of the Miocene sea, due to uplift in the Pontian of some 700–1,000 ft. (200–300 m.), there followed a new subsidence, accompanied by the Pliocene ingression.

The Pliocene sea in the north again occupied the Kishon Valley, the Jezreel Valley, and eastern Galilee as far as Tiberias. In the south it reached Nevatim, east of Beersheba, and again washed the foothills bounding the present Coastal Plain. The character of the Pliocene

(Astian) littoral sediments is similar to the Miocene, except for the absence of coral reef limestone, indicating disconnection from the Red Sea and Indian Ocean. Uplift movements at the end of the Pliocene and during the Pleistocene brought the Pliocene littoral beds to their present height of 700–1,000 ft. (200–300 m.) and the Miocene to 1,600 ft. (500 m.). Where subaerial erosion has removed the Neogene sediments, the ancient abrasion planes often appear as tilted "peneplains."

The marine Miocene-Pliocene lying below the Quaternary of the Coastal Plain has been studied in hundreds of water wells and in many petroleum-exploration drillings. As so-called Sāqiyya beds, it consists of several hundred meters of plastic clays, silty marls, and marly sands; there are some local lumachelle layers and even basalt flows. In the deeper horizons it becomes markedly lagoonal, with several gypsum horizons, but this part of the section may be assigned to the Miocene-Oligocene.

Continental Neogene. The varying relief of Israel and neighboring Levant countries demonstrated by the Neogene irregular gulf and headland coastal configuration is also expressed by the development of large intermontane depressions, with their fill of predominantly continental deposits. Limnic freshwater and brackish sediments, evaporites (Menaḥemiyyah gypsum, Sodom salt), fluviatile gravel, red beds, and desert sands attaining hundreds of meters of thickness have been described under various formation names: Herod, Sodom, Ḥaẓevah (Ḥoṣeb), etc. They occur in the Jezreel Valley, the Jordan Valley, the Negev, and near the Dead Sea. Although of lesser thickness and geographical extension, these inland sediments may be compared in facies and age with the Bakhtiyārī and Fars series of Iran, Iraq, and Syria.

The continental Neogene, like its contemporaneous marine Mio-Pliocene, rests discordantly upon all pre-Miocene formations, frequently starting with a basal conglomerate, e.g., Kefar Giladi, Har Hordos, al-Dhrāʿ, Dimonah, etc. In the folded mountain of the Negev it is associated

Columnar basalt, representative of large parts of the Golan Heights, seen at the Hameshushim pool.

with synclinal basins (as in the Palmyra chains of Syria), e.g., Naḥal Malḥata (Wadi Milḥ) east of Beersheba, synclinal valleys between Yeroḥam and the Ha-Makhtesh ha-Gadol (Ḥatirah) anticlines, the Ḥaẓevah-Sodom-al-Dhrāʿ basin, and the Upper Paran downwarp. In the Jezreel Valley and eastern Galilee the continental Neogene occurs as filling masses within the huge fault depressions that extend from the Kishon to the Tiberias area. This is the same region of tectonic tension in which Upper Miocene and, more visibly, Upper Pliocene continental basalt eruptions took place and even continued during the Pleistocene. Pleistocene and Pliocene sheet lavas have built up the extensive volcanic plateaus of Hauran and eastern Galilee. They cover Neogene and pre-Neogene sediments, which, due to Pleistocene block and rift faulting, are exposed along the slopes of the Jordan graben and in the transversal fault valleys of Naḥal Tabor (Wadi Bīra), Harod, and eastern Dayshūn.

Quaternary. Uplift and desiccation of the inland lakes not only brought the marine and continental Pliocene into a higher topographic position, but was also accompanied by the complete retreat of the sea far to the west of the present Levant shores. Contemporary with this uplift, fault-dissection on a regional scale produced the graben-trough of Eilat-Arabah, the Dead Sea, and the Jordan Valley and accompanying step-fault blocks. The branching off of diagonal faults both in Cis- and Transjordan gave origin to transversal fault valleys and fault-block mountains, which are especially well developed in Samaria and the Galilee. The Negev, south Judea, Shephelah, and Sharon were far less affected by fault tectonics, and thus the mid-Tertiary fold pattern of anticlinal ridges and synclinal valleys, upwarps and downwarps, remained well preserved. In the synclinal valleys and on the ḥamada-plateaus of the Paran hinterland, continental deposition may have continued from Upper Tertiary to Recent.

Along the western border of the Judean Mountains, gravel fans and terraces plunge below the Coastal Plain (as

Badlands of loess soil in the Beersheba area. Courtesy J.N.F., Jerusalem.

far west as the Mediterranean) and are found in groundwater exploration wells at depths of 330 ft. (100 m.) overlying the Neogene strata. These clastics are assigned to the Lower Pleistocene or Villafranchian, indicating the extremely high precipitation of this Pluvial stage, synchronized with the Guenz-Mindel glacial time of Europe. Younger gravels of Mid-Upper Pleistocene age interfinger the fossil indurated dunes of the Coastal Plain, known as *kurkar* sandstone. The *kurkar*, which constitutes another important aquifer, is frequently subdivided by a terra-rossa-like, sandy, loamy soil, the *ḥamra* (Ar. *ḥamrāʾ*) or "red sands" of our citrus belt. The unconsolidated dunes are of Recent age. They run along the Coastal Plain and extend into the northern Negev, as far inland as the neighborhood of Beersheba. The undifferentiated Quaternary signifies the loamy, loess, and swampy soils, as well as Recent gravels and silts blanketing the coastal and interior alluvial plains. Pleistocene marine sediments are found as foraminiferal limestone in the Haifa-Acre plain (e.g., Kurdaneh) and as marine *kurkar* around the western Carmel border. The water boreholes in the Coastal Plain encountered marine Pleistocene only as far inland as Rishon le-Zion, but this is missing in the Jezreel Valley and the Shephelah foothills. The lower Pleistocene is thus the most insignificant of the ingressions of the Cenozoic Mediterranean Sea. During the Upper Pleistocene, Mousterian man already lived near the present shores.

In the newly formed Quaternary Dead Sea-Jordan graben, the Lower to Middle Pleistocene is distinguished by gravel and freshwater lake and swamp deposits. At the southern end of Lake Tiberias (ʿUbaydiyya), many extinct mammals, skeleton remains of primitive man, and implements both of pebble culture and of Abbevillian were discovered. Slightly younger, but not older than Middle Pleistocene, were the proto-Acheulean tools and extinct fauna found at the Jordan, south of Lake Ḥuleh. During this period volcanic activity was renewed and many basalt layers accumulated, derived in part from the Hauran district. They were partly responsible for separating the

Ḥuleh graben section from the Tiberias and southern Jordan graben and for the accumulation of thick peat deposits in the Ḥuleh Valley. The Tiberias region, the middle and southern Jordan Valley, the Dead Sea, and the northernmost Arabah Valley were occupied during the Upper Pleistocene (some 60,000 years ago) by a large brackish inland lake in which were deposited fine-bedded clays, gypsum, and chalk, called the Lashon (Lisān) formation. This formation is interfingered with large fluviatile deposits of gravel and silt. At the end of the Pleistocene (some 20,000 to 15,000 years ago), the ancient Lisān lake receded from its highest stand at the -720 ft. (-220 m.) level to about -1,300 ft. (-400 m.), the present level of the Dead Sea. Young rivers spread their gravels upon the dried-up Lisān lake and cut out the present floodplain of the Jordan River. The raising of the Sodom salt mountain also started in the Lower Pleistocene.

STRUCTURAL PATTERN. The tectonic structures formed by the folding movements that modelled their final features during the Mid-Tertiary are best preserved in the dry climate of the Negev. However, south of the Yotvatah area, the influence of the Plio-Pleistocene graben faulting with its step faults, parallel and transversal to the Arabah graben depression, markedly disturbs the fold pattern that is still well observable at Ẓenifim. From Naḥal Paran as far as Makhtesh Ramon the direction of the folds is close to east-west and this trend persists into Sinai. The folds then turn in a northeast-southwest direction and dominate the central and northern Negev. Their anticlines are mostly asymmetrical on the eastern flanks and frequently limited by reverse strike-faults. These folds are grouped into one unit forming the main anticlinorial uplift, with culminations in the Makhtesh Ramon and Ha-Makhtesh ha-Gadol. In the structurally low areas, such as the central Arabah Valley and the synclinorium of Ḥaluẓah, the folds are smaller and more symmetrical, representing small domes and brachy-anticlines.

 The mountainous region of Judea and Samaria is a broad

The Pleistocene fill of the Lisān deposits around the Dead Sea Rift Valley adjoining the fault escarpment of the Upper Cretaceous limestone mountains near Masada. Courtesy Government Press Office, Tel Aviv.

arch, rising to a considerable height, that is subdivided into folds by the anticlines of Maon, Yatta, Ẓāhiriyya, Modi'im, etc. and the synclines of Netiv ha-Lamed-He and Ẓorah. The arch and its folds, again with a northeast-southwest trend, are distinctly asymmetrical, descending unequally to the Coastal Plain in the west and to the Jordan-Dead Sea graben in the east. Thus the pronounced northwest asymmetry observed on the western slopes of the Judean arch contrasts with the southeast asymmetry of the dominant folds of the Judean Desert and the northern Negev. These asymmetrical anticlinal folds are difficult to relate to pressure exerted by the Arabo-Nubian massif, but are apparently connected with the mechanism of epeirogenic and taphrogenic uplifts.

As in most rift valleys of regional extent, it is not always possible to define the exact location of the main border faults. In the case of the Pleistocene Jordan-Dead Sea graben, a throw of a thousand meters or more has been determined at a number of places. The western cliffs of the Dead Sea graben and the graben slopes between Beth-Shean and Lake Kinneret are, moreover, divided by numerous step faults that run parallel to the main border fault. They are also hidden to some extent by *en échelon* faults that have their origin in the main graben. A number of transversal faults, such as those between Wadi Fāriʿa and Jericho, as well as in the foothill region near Tulkarm, cut the anticlinorium of the Judean Mountains.

On the Coastal Plain, just as in the northern Negev and the southern part of the Judean Mountains, the structural lines are directed northeast-southwest. It is not yet clear whether this direction applies only to the folds or, as in the Ḥeleẓ area, to deep-seated faults as well. Petroleum wells of the Ḥeleẓ-Beror Ḥayil ridge indicate the presence of a wide and deep depression filled with Tertiary sediments, constituting the regional (Ashkelon) fault-conditioned trough.

In the Sharon a number of small transversal faults have been observed. It is possible that these constitute the continuation of faults exposed in the foothill area. There are no surface indications of a main, larger border fault, as found along the Jordan graben. Nevertheless one may assume that the great thickness of Tertiary sediments in the Sharon Plain is the outcome of a downfaulted coastal depression that began during or at the end of the Mid-Tertiary, as presumed also for the Ashkelon trough. If the existence of main faults below the young fill on the Coastal Plain and the continental slope area of the Mediterranean should be proved, then a general tectonic picture would evolve presenting Judea as a major horst limited on both sides by major grabens or by downfaulted depressions.

Mount Carmel forms a structural unit by itself. It is an extensive faulted uplift. The direction of some of the smaller anticlines (ʿUsifiyyā, Oren) is northwest-southeast. That is to say, they are not in harmony with the strike of other fold structures in the country. The view has been expressed that the major faults that limit Mount Carmel to the north have been responsible for producing the small anticlinal bends of this exceptional direction. Although the folds in Upper Galilee are more or less obliterated by the predominance of faulting, a certain east-southeast asymmetry of the rudimentary folds, and especially of the central upwarp, is still noticeable. Whereas in eastern Galilee faults are primarily directed northwest-southeast and their fault escarpments face north, in western Galilee, i.e., west of the main watershed, the faults run principally east-west, and their tilted block escarpments usually face south. The region of the watershed thus serves as a structural backbone where both the western and eastern fault systems meet. It is here, at Mount Tabor, Ḥazon, Ha-Ari, Meron, and Addir, that the faults frame the horst blocks on all sides.

In geological maps of Transjordan, many faults are indicated. Among the principal ones, there is the north-east-southwest Wadi Shu'eib fault, which turns into a north-south fault in the Dead Sea, thus becoming the eastern boundary fault of the graben. Between Wadi Ḥasā' and Petra, sets of faults in various directions build an extensive series of blocks in which the influence of the graben tectonics is heavily felt. The most outstanding of these faults extend southward from Petra, forming the eastern boundary fault of the southern Arabah graben and the western boundary of the Midian horst.

6 FLORA AND FAUNA

Flora. The range of flora to be found in Ereẓ Israel is among the richest and most varied of any country in the world. On both sides of the Jordan River there are close to 2,300 species belonging to about 700 genera, which in turn belong to 115 families of flora. To these should be added scores of species found in Golan and in Sinai. No other place in the world has such floral wealth concentrated within such a comparatively small area. This density of species is due to several factors, among them being the varied history, beginning from the earliest geological periods, of the region's landscape, the diversity of its topography and climate, the lengthy period of its agriculture, and especially the fact that it is the meeting place of three phytogeographic areas: the Mediterranean, the Irano-Turanic, and the Saharo-Sindic, with enclaves here and there of the Sudano-Deccanic.

THE FLORA OF THE MEDITERRANEAN AREA. Of the three phytogeographic areas, the most important is the Mediterranean, which includes agricultural land in the mountains and valleys. In it the amount of water precipitation varies from 14–40 in. (350–1,000 mm.). This precipitation, the result of winter rains (with a small additional amount of melted snow from the high mountains), makes the nonirrigated cultivation of plantations and of winter and summer crops possible. The area is subdivided into mountain and coastal subareas.

The Mountain Subarea. This was once agriculturally the most developed area (having since been superseded in importance by farming lands in the valleys and the Coastal Plain). The intensive agricultural cultivation of mountain

Natural grove of Aleppo pine *(Pinus halepensis)* near Bet Me'ir in the Judean Hills. Photo A. Eris.

lands has curtailed or prevented the development of forests in this, their natural habitat, so that only remnants of forests and groves are left. In this subarea several types of forests are to be found, such as that of the Jerusalem pine—the Aleppo pine *(Pinus halepensis)*, the tallest forest tree in Israel. Flourishing in gray, chalky soil, which is particularly suitable for mountain agriculture, the Aleppo pine has been extensively felled and is now to be found only

Terebinth *(Pistacia atlantica)* in autumn in Wadi Napleh in the Negev Plateau, an area of Irano-Turanic vegetation. Photo Yosaif Cohain.

in Gilead. Associated with the pine are the common oak, the Palestine terebinth, the mastic terebinth, the carob, the arbutus, and the rhamnus, as well as many shrubs and wild grasses. Most of the woods in Israel consist of the group of the common oak *(Quercus calliprinos)*, and the Palestine terebinth *(Pistacia palaestina)*, which can reach a considerable height but are usually shrubby as a result of having been cut or gnawed by sheep and particularly goats. This bush grows extensively on mountains of an altitude between 1,000–4,000 ft. (300–1,200 m.) above sea level. There is also the gall oak *(Quercus infectoria (boissieri))*, a deciduous tree with a tall trunk, alongside which grows the hawthorn *(Crataegus azarolus)*. Under favorable humid conditions there also grow in this subarea the sweet bay

(Laurus nobilis) and the Judas tree *(Cercis siliquastrum)*, which in spring adorns the mountains with its lilac flowers. On the western ridges of the Carmel and Western Galilee and on the western slopes of the Judean Mountains, there is maquis, where grow the group of the carob *(ceratonia siliqua)* and the mastic terebinth *(Pistacia tentiscus)*, along with many species of shrubs, climbers, annuals, and perennials. A third genus of oak—the Tabor oak *(Quercus ithaburensis)*—predominates on the western ranges of the Lower Galilean mountains, accompanied by the storax tree *(Styrax officinalis)*. In the northern Ḥuleh Valley it grows alongside the Atlantic terebinth *(Pistacia atlantica)*. These two species of trees are the largest in Israel, some in the neighborhood of Dan having trunks 20 ft. (6 m.) in circumference and reaching a height of c. 65 ft. (20 m.).

All these are types of forest trees. Another genus of Mediterranean plant comprises flora groups called garigue

Common oak *(Quercus calliprinos)* and Palestine terebinth *(Pistacia palaestina)* in an area known as "Little Switzerland" near Bet Oren. Courtesy J.N.F., Jerusalem. Photo E. Orni, Jerusalem.

The branching palm *(Hyphaene thebaica)*, found in the vicinity of Eilat. Photo Pri-Or, Tel Aviv.

which in Israel consist predominantly of shrubs and dwarf shrubs no taller than a man. The characteristic plants of the garigue are the calycotome thorn bush *(Calycotome villosa)*, the rock rose *(Cistus villosus)*, and the salvia *(Salvia tribola)*. At times the garigue flora groups are the developing stage of a forest, at others an indication of the former presence there of a forest since destroyed. Characteristic of the unforested Mediterranean landscape are dwarf shrubs, of which the most widespread is the poterium thorn *(Poterium spinosum)*. Reaching a height of less than half a meter, it grows densely and is one of the principal factors in preventing the erosion of mountain soil. Where these plants have been destroyed by being used either for firewood or for burning lime, the ground has been denuded by the eroding effects of wind and rain.

The Coastal Subarea. The soil here is sandy or a mixture of sandy chalk and sandy clay, which, being poor in organic substances and in its capacity to retain rainwater, is unsuitable for the growth of plants (unless irrigated). In this subarea grows flora that strikes deep roots, and desert and Arabah plants that can exist on small amounts of water, as well as annuals which sprout and ripen during the rainy winter months. Here can be found flora of Israel's three phytogeographic areas, as well as that of the Sudano-Deccanic, such as the sycamore *(Ficus sycomorus)* and the wild jujube *(Zizyphus spina-Christi).* Sand flora is in constant danger of being covered by moving sands and of having the sand under its roots blown away by the wind. Yet many sand plants are able to survive under such conditions, either by striking deep roots or by developing new shoots above the branches covered by sand. Near the sea, where the winds carry sea spray onto the flora, plants grow which are insensitive to sea water, such as the Russian thistle *(Salsola kali)* and species of fig marigold *(Mesembryanthemum).* Most of the sandy-clav soil is planted wіth citrus groves. The flora group of the love grass *(Eragrostis bipinnata)* and of the thistle *(Centaurea procurrens)* grow extensively here, as do the group of the cistus and of the calycotome on the brittle sandy-chalk hills in the Coastal Plain area, and the group of the carob and of the mastic in the hard sandy-chalk soil.

FLORA OF THE IRANO-TURANIC AREA. This is concentrated in the loess (arid soil) of the northern Negev, the Judean Desert, and the Transjordanian highlands. Here the climate is dry, with a rainfall varying from 8–14 in. (200–300 mm.), these being the limits for nonirrigated plants which thrive in rainy years (cf. Gen. 26:12). In this area there are almost no forests, but only sparse trees, such as the plant association of the Atlantic terebinth and the lotus jujube *(Zizyphus lotus).* Characteristic of the slopes bordering on the Jordan and Beth-Shean Valleys is the *Retama duriaei* association. Here the most important plant association is of a species of wormwood *(Artemisia herba-alba)* which grows extensively in the Negev, the Judean Desert, and Transjordan.

FLORA OF THE SAHARO-SINDIC AREA. This area, which extends over most of Israel but has the poorest flora, includes the southern Negev, the Arabah, the desert regions of Edom, Moab, and the Sinai Peninsula. Its rainfall, which is limited to a shorter period in winter, does not exceed c. 8

Hammada Scorpio, a desert shrub found in stream beds of the Sinai Peninsula. Courtesy J. Feliks, Jerusalem. Photo Ehud Enoch.

in. (200 mm.) and is usually much less, and there are even parts which in some years are almost completely rainless. The soil here is infertile and includes hammada, desert, gravel, and rocks. Trees grow only in wadi fissures. There are saline tracts bare of all flora, which is in any event very sparse here. The most typical plant in the hammada is the small shrub *Zygophyllum dumosum*, which is capable of surviving in areas with a rainfall of less than 2 in. (50 mm.). Since desert plants have to contend with a severe shortage of water, only those with special properties are able to survive here. Most of them spring up and flower quickly after a shower of rain; some, only a few weeks after germinating, scatter their seeds, which are capable of preserving their power of germination for many years. Other species here are bulbous plants which hibernate in dry periods. Generally, desert flora has long roots so as to utilize the sparse amount of water over a wide area, and hence the infrequency of these plants. Many species of desert flora have a great ability to absorb groundwater; one species, the *Reaumaria palaestina,* developing an osmotic capacity of more than 200 atmospheres. Other desert plants shed their leaves in a dry season, thereby curtailing the area of evaporation. Still other species are succulents, which are equipped with cells that in the rainy season store water for the dry period.

In sandy desert regions the flora is usually more abundant, the predominant species here being the haloxylon and the broom *(Retama roetam).* In the Arabah and in the lower Jordan Valley, where there is widespread salinity, saline flora, including species of atriplex and salicornia, grows densely.

In desert regions near sources of water there are oases, where tropical Sudano-Deccanic flora grows, the characteristic plants here being species of acacia, wild jujube, etc. These also grow in wadi fissures in desert regions. In places where the ground becomes sodden from winter floods, crops can be grown and plantations established.

Hydrophylic flora grows near expanses of water in all the areas of Israel. Large numbers of the poplar *(Populus euphratica),* as well as species of the willow *(Salix)* and of the tamarisk *(Tamarix),* grow on river banks, as do the plane *(Platanus orientalis)* and the Syrian ash *(Fraxinus syriaca)* on the banks of streams in the north. Alongside these trees there usually grows the oleander *(Nerium oleander),* together with numerous species of annuals and

Water buffalo *(Bubalis bubalis)* at al-Butayhah, near the entry point of the Jordan into the Sea of Galilee. Photo Werner Braun, Jerusalem.

perennials. The reed and the cattail are found near almost every expanse of water. The papyrus once flourished extensively in the Ḥuleh swamps, but since they were drained it grows in extremely limited areas. Due to the draining of swamps in Israel and the piping of river water, hydrophytic flora has progressively decreased. On the other hand, some species of riparian plants flourish near fish ponds, the area of which has greatly increased.

CULTIVATED PLANTS. Ereẓ Israel has a long and varied history of agriculture. In addition to the older plants cultivated in the country for centuries, many have been introduced from various parts of the world, especially from America, among these being numerous ornamental plants. Together with these plants, their companion wild grasses have also come into Israel and have flourished alongside the older wild grasses, in particular the prickly species which are a characteristic feature of Israel's landscape, especially in the burning hot days of summer.

Fauna. HISTORY. The history of Ereẓ Israel's fauna a long one, going back to the earliest geological periods. Of these the Pleistocene epoch was the most dynamic and decisive in this respect by reason of the considerable changes which took place in its zoological character, mainly as a result of the influx of animals from various regions. In this period, fauna at present characteristic of East African savannas predominated in the country, To this period belong the bones, uncovered in the country, of animals no longer extant in Israel, such as warthog, hippopotamus, rhinoceros, and striped hyena, as well as various species of gazelle. The bones of elephants and of mastodons, brought to light in the Jordan Valley, belong to the Lower Pleistocene Age. In later periods animals penetrated to the country from Western and Central Asia, among them the wild horse, the wild ass, gazelles, wolves, and badgers. From the north there was a limited influx of animals as a result of the Ice Age in Europe.

During the Upper Pleistocene Age a tropical climate, warm and humid, predominated in Ereẓ Israel. This was followed by a dry period which led to the destruction of the tropical fauna. And indeed an examination of the bones of animals found in the caves of prehistoric man in the Carmel shows that the principal game hunted by him consisted of mammals still extant in Israel, this being true also of the bones of birds brought to light in Early Stone Age caves, although several mammals and birds are of species extinct in the country in historical times. As early as the end of the Stone Age (4,000 B.C.E.) there was to be found in the country the fauna characteristic of it since biblical days.

 With the enlargement of the settled area in the biblical

Kingfisher *(Alcedo atthis)* near the Sea of Galilee. Photo Werner Braun, Jerusalem.

and later in the mishnaic and talmudic periods, changes took place in the distribution of animals, now forced into the uninhabited areas. The invention of rifles led to the extinction of the large carnivores as well as of the large ruminant game.

The present-day Jewish agricultural settlements have

altered the distribution of the various animals. Some of them have disappeared, while others, finding favorable conditions in developed farming areas, have begun to multiply. Thus the increase in waterfowl is due directly to the increase of fish ponds, in which aquatic mammals (such as the marsh lynx) have also begun to establish themselves. New species of birds have started to nest in plantations and citrus groves. The State of Israel's fauna preservation laws have saved several mammals from threatened extinction and some have begun to multiply greatly, such as the gazelle, at present to be found in various parts of the country. The ibex, too, has increased in number and herds of it may be seen in the mountains of En-Gedi and Eilat. On the other hand, toxic substances used to exterminate agricultural pests and jackals have led to the extinction of birds, particularly carrion-feeding ones. In this way the

Jackal *(Canis aureus)*, found near areas of settlement throughout Israel. Photo Werner Braun, Jerusalem.

Serpent eagle *(Circaetus gallicus)*, one of the "birds of prey" of the Bible. Photo Werner Braun, Jerusalem.

griffon vultures, found in large numbers in the country up to the 1930s, have become almost extinct, only a few surviving at present.

THE ZOOGEOGRAPHY OF EREẒ ISRAEL. The fauna in the country is extremely varied, the reason for this being, as in the case of the flora, that Israel is the meeting place of three climatic and floral regions. The regional distribution of the fauna corresponds almost exactly to that of the flora.

To the Mediterranean fauna belong the hare, chukar partridge, swallow, agama, and others: to the Saharo-Sindic, the desert mice, desert lark, sandgrouse, gecko, cobra, and many other species; to the Irano-Turanic, animals that inhabit the northern Negev and the Judean Desert, such as the tiger weasel (*Vormela*), bustard, isolepis, and agama.

The Sudano-Deccanic animals inhabit the Jordan Valley as far as the Arabah. Here are to be found representatives also of tropical fauna, such as the cheetah, honey badger, tropical cuckoo, and carpet viper. In contrast to these animals that love the warmth, there are also representatives of the Holarctic fauna, such as the shrew and meadow pipit.

Unlike its flora, which has been thoroughly studied and surveyed, the fauna of Ereẓ Israel is not properly known. The catalogue of the names of animals thus far studied testifies to a wealth of fauna. At present approximately 88 species of mammals are known, 359 of birds, 76 of reptiles, 434 of sweet and salt water fish, and seven of Amphibia. Much larger is the number of invertebrates. These are extensively represented among the insects, of which some 8,000 species are known in the country, their aggregate number being 22,000 according to Bodenheimer, who maintains that there are about 900 species of other *Arthropoda*. Probably more than a thousand additional species have not yet been studied. Of the invertebrates, other than the *Arthropoda*, some 300 species are known, their total number being estimated at about 2,750.

7 COMMUNICATIONS

The Road System. The country's topographical scheme, in general, does not favor traffic. The hill ridges, running mostly from north to south, bar the way inland from the coast, especially in Judea. The Coastal Plain and Transjordan Plateau thoroughfares, relatively the easiest, became two of the main highways of antiquity, the Via Maris (Sea Road) and the King's Way from the Eilat shore through Edom, Kir-Moab (Kerak), Dibbon, Heshbon, Rabbat Ammon and Ashtaroth to Damascus. An important side branch of the King's Way descended from Petra to the copper site of Punnon in the Aravah Valley, and crossed the Negev and the Sinai Peninsula into Egypt.

Of the local thoroughfares, the longest was the Hill Road. Least continuous was the road through the Rift Valley, the existence of which can be verified only from the Second Temple period. Most of the west-east roads were of local importance connecting major centers of habitation with the principal north-south roads.

Principal road junctions in the Coastal Plain were Gaza in the south and Acre in the north; at a later stage, Jaffa and Caesarea also became traffic centers. In Judea, Jerusalem became a major crossroads only under King David. During the Second Temple period, roads radiated out in all directions, despite topographical difficulties. In Samaria, Shechem and Shomron rivaled for supremacy as traffic centers. In the Jezreel Valley, the strategic site of Megiddo constituted the most important crossroads until its decline under Roman rule. Among the outstanding Roman-built highways in the country are the routes Caesarea-Antipatris-Jerusalem, Gaza-Jerusalem Jerusalem-Jericho-Philadelphia

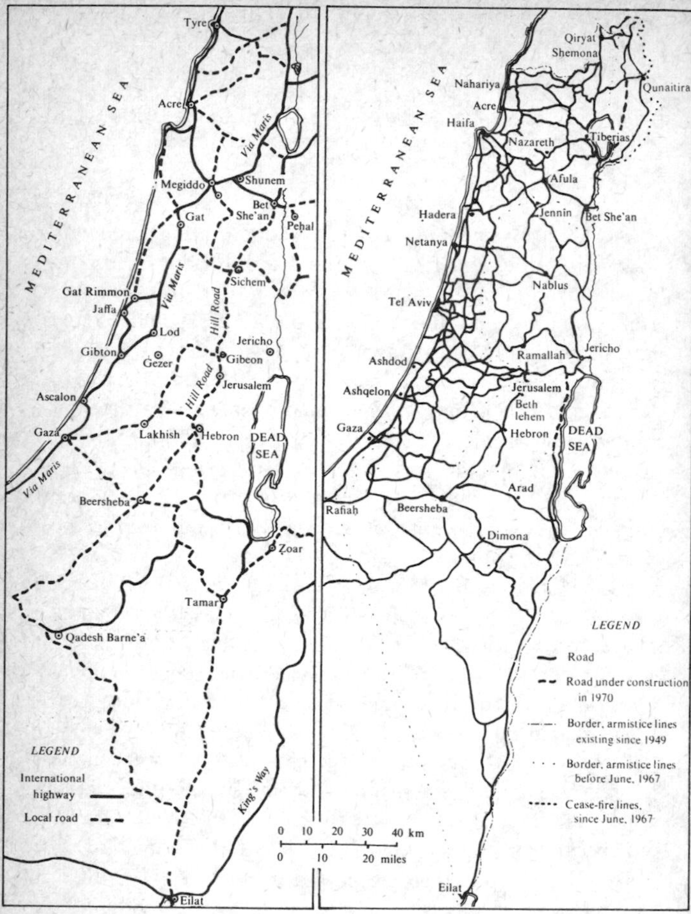

The ancient (left) and modern (right) road system (from E. Orni, *Geography of Israel*, Jerusalem, 1971). The ancient system was more confined by topographical considerations; the modern system shows the limiting influence of armistice lines.

(Rabbat Ammon)-Gerasa, Jerusalem-Legio (Megiddo), and Acre-Tiberias.

With the end of Roman rule, roads fell into disrepair. The Crusaders tried to improve some of the highways but never attained the standards of Roman times. Until the end of the 19th century, there were no paved roads, goods were transported on camels or donkeys, and travel was either by foot or on horse and camels.

The development of seafaring in the Mediterranean Sea and the growing stream of pilgrims to the Holy Land at the end of the 19th century made a thorough improvement of the road system inevitable. The existing tracks were partly adapted to the passage of caravans and coaches ("diligences"). Prime attention was given to the roads leading to sacred sites, e.g., the links between Jaffa and Jerusalem, Haifa and Nazareth, or the lengthwise route of Hebron-Bethlehem-Jerusalem-Nablus-Nazareth. These tracks were paved and provided with bridges and culverts, so that they became all-weather roads. Before World War I, they totaled 450 km. (280 mi.) in length.

The first years of the British Mandate saw much repair, improvement, widening and asphalting of roads to fit them for motorized traffic. In 1932, the road network reached a length of 950 km. (590 mi.). The increase in immigration and citrus exports of the 1930s necessitated a further expansion of the road network, and the mounting prosperity in the country provided the means to finance it. In 1936, the first highway running the whole length of the Sharon was finally built between Tel Aviv and Haifa: a road link was also established between the port-city of Haifa and the flourishing farming region of the Jezreel Valley.

Efforts to complete the road system were redoubled during World War II. In the south, and even more in the north, new roads were laid out. Among these was the Megiddo-Afula road in the Jezreel Valley, which created a direct link between the Coastal Plain and the Sea of Galilee. The country's road system was connected with Transjordan and Syria to the east and north as well as with

Egypt, through the Sinai Peninsula. On the eve of Israel's statehood, Palestine had 2,660 km. (1,650 mi.) of motor roads.

The road network still mirrors, to some extent, the country's morphological structure although today's technical means enable builders to overcome topographical difficulties. The borders existent between Israel and her neighbors between 1949 and 1967 put many roads out of use completely or in part, lent increased importance to other roads, and necessitated the construction of new highways to replace those cut by the frontiers, e.g., the section of the Jerusalem-Tel Aviv highway built by Israel immediately after the cessation of hostilities in 1948, between Sha'ar ha-Gai and Ramleh ("the Road of Courage") to circumvent Latrun, then in Jordanian territory. Furthernore, new economic requirements, expansion of old and contruction of new urban centers, as well as regional settlement projects necessitate investment of large means and efforts in roadbuilding. To cope with the ever-increasing traffic, all major interurban highwasy continually have to be widened.

Israel's principal traffic arteries connect the three main cities of Tel Aviv, Jerusalem, and Haifa; lead from Tel Aviv and Jerusalem south to the Negev and Eilat; and from Tel Aviv and Haifa north and east, to Galilee and to the Central and Upper Jordan Valley. The Tel Aviv-Haifa highway bears by far the heaviest traffic.

Extremely important is the connection between Haderah in the Coastal Plain through the Iron Valley to Afula in the Jezreel Valley and thence to Tiberias; this follows the track of the ancient Via Maris. Another heavy-duty road links Tel Aviv with Lydda Airport.

In the Southern Coastal Plain, three highways today run parallel to each other; nearest to the shore is the road which passes from Tel Aviv through Yavneh and Ashdod to Ashkelon up to the northern end of the Gaza Strip near Yad Mordekhai and thence southeast where it joins the parallel eastern road near the new urban center of Sederot.

 A second highway runs from the Bet Dagan junction and

splits near the development town of Kiryat Malakhi; its western fork links up with the Gaza-Beersheba road near the kibbutz Sa'ad, while the eastern one passes Kiryat Gat and reaches the Beersheba highway near Eshel ha-Nasi. The third road branches off the Tel-Aviv-Jerusalem highway at the Naḥshon Junction, runs west to join the former road for a short stretch between the Re'im and Aḥim junctions, and then turns south and southeast to lead directly to Beersheba.

Great strides in roadbuilding have been made in the Negev, and further highways are under construction or projected for the near future. A highway built in 1957 links Beersheba through Dimona and Miẓpeh Ramon with Eilat, and another, 127 km. (79 mi.) long, descends from Dimona to Sedom. The new Arad development region is crossed by a road from Beersheba to Arad and the Dead Sea shore north of Sedom. The En Gedi-Sedom-Eilat highway runs a straight course along the Dead Sea and the Aravah Valley, and is paralleled in the northwest by a link connecting the Arad-Sedom and Beersheba-Dimona-Sedom highways.

The main highways of the central and northern valleys and of Galilee are the following: Haifa-Acre-northern border; Acre-Safed; Haifa-Nazareth-Tiberias; Haifa-Afula-Bet Shean; and Bet Shean-Tiberias-Rosh Pinnah-Kiryat Shemonah-Metullah.

Railroads. In 1892 a railroad line running from Jaffa to Jerusalem was constructed by a French concessionary company. In 1914 the Turks built the special-gauge Hejaz Railroad connecting Damascus with Medina through Amman, with a branch via Ẓemaḥ and Afulah to Haifa and a spur to Acre, and during World War I extended the line southward from Afula to Tulkarm. A further extension via Beersheba reached Quseima in 1916. Also during the war the British built the standard-gauge Sinai military Railroad from Qantara to Haifa. In 1941 it was extended from Haifa to Beirut and at the end of the Mandate there were 290 mi. (470 km.) of railroad in Palestine. Only 75 mi. (121 km.) could be brought into operation in the State of Israel after the War of Independence. New standard-gauge lines were laid from Haderah to Tel Aviv in 1953 and from Na'an to Beersheba in 1956. The latter was extended to Dimonah in 1965 and later extended to reach the Oron phosphate works. The Israel railroad system has about 425 mi. (over 760 km.) of standard-gauge line.

Harbors. Israel's three modern deep-water harbors—Haifa and Ashdod on the Mediterranean and Eilat on the Red Sea—are managed, maintained, and developed by the Ports Authority. The lighter harbor at Jaffa which had served the country since the second millennium B.C.E. and was the only port of entry for the early Jewish immigrants, and the one at Tel Aviv, which was built during the Arab riots of 1936–39, were closed in 1966 when Ashdod came into use. The decision to build this new deep water harbor, with an annual capacity of 2.5 million tons, was taken in 1961, as the deep water port of Haifa, built by the British in 1934, was rapidly becoming saturated with the expansion of commerce in both directions. The Red Sea deep-water port of Eilat, opened in 1965, has an annual capacity of half a million tons.

Air Transport. Civil aviation has made a significant contribution to tourism, exports, rapid internal communications and economic development. Israel's location at the junction of Europe, Africa, and Asia makes it a convenient focus for air transport. Regular air services enable Israel to maintain close contact with world Jewry, and the Israel national air carrier is widely used by Jews everywhere.

Lydda (Lod) airport, the international airport for passengers and freight, began to operate in 1936 and was taken over by Israel in 1948. Considerable investments were also made in Eilat airport. Jerusalem's airfield at Atarot (Kalandia) served internal traffic after the Six-Day War. The airfield at Rosh Pinnah serves Upper Galilee, and Sedeh Dov, near Tel Aviv, serves as a transit point for passengers bound for Eilat and Rosh Pinnah. The Arkia company began to operate internal airlines on the establishment of the state. There are regular services to Eilat, Jerusalem, Rosh Pinnah, Masada, Sharm el-Sheikh, and Nicosia.

8 NATIONAL PARKS

The National Parks Authority was established by law in 1963 to take over the functions carried out from 1956 by the Department for Landscaping and the Preservation of Historic Sites in the prime minister's office. These functions are: the preparation, laying out, and maintenance of park areas for the general public; the restoration, landscaping, and preservation of historical and archaeological sites; the construction of access roads and amenities for recreation and leisure; and, in the case of ancient sites, the provision of explanatory notice boards and pamphlets. The Authority has also established museums at several historic sites.

Israel is rich in biblical sites and the remains of post-biblical Jewish, Roman, Byzantine, Muslim, and Crusader settlements, often in surroundings of beauty, and most of the national parks have been linked with these sites. Many had suffered from centuries of neglect, since they were of little interest to the successive occupying authorities. The Authority had to clear overgrowth and thick layers of debris, undertake restoration programs where possible, and provide amenities and access for visitors, both local and from overseas. Some parks were laid out without any connection with a historic site, in order to preserve rural areas from the encroachment of urban development. Occasionally, archaeological sites were taken over for preservation and maintenance by the Authority, where the excavations had been particularly dramatic, as at Masada; or where scholars had made spectacular finds of wide public interest, as at Hazor, the Bet She'arim necropolis, the ancient synagogues at Bet Alfa, Baram, and Hammath (Tiberias), the Roman theater at Caesarea, and the excavations at Bet Yeraḥ and Ramat Raḥel. At some sites the National Parks Authority was responsible for the excavations, undertaken by specially commissioned archaeologists, as well as for their restoration and current maintenance. Examples are: the Crusader city of Caesarea, complete with moat, walls, gates, and towers; the crypt, tunnels, and some of the walls of Crusader Acre; the castles of Yeḥi'am and Belvoir; the Roman theater at Beth-Shean; the Nabatean-Byzantine city of Avedat, with its citadel, acropolis, and two churches; and the Nabatean cities of Shivta and Kurnub. At Masada, much of the restoration work was carried out at the same time as the excavations.

The Authority is responsible for 50 sites designated as national parks. Those already open to the public, in addition to the ones already mentioned, are; Ḥurshat Tal in Upper Galilee, with its streams, pond, lawns, and woods; the spring, bathing pool, and woodland slopes of Ma'ayan Ḥarod in the Valley of Jezreel; the three natural pools and

The national park on the Ashkelon seashore, which includes a camping site and an antiquities area. Photo A. Strajmayster.

Gan ha-Sheloshah, the national park in the eastern Jezreel Valley formed from three natural pools.

landscaped banks of Gan ha-Sheloshah, also in Jezreel; the seashore park and antiquities of Ashkelon; the natural pools of Ein Avedat in the northern Negev; the 25,000-acre parkland and forest of Carmel; and the Crusader remains at Aqua Bella (Ein Ḥemed) near Jerusalem. The Authority has also renovated some of the medieval synagogues of Safed, and improved the amenities at the tomb of Maimonides in Tiberias. It has carried out site-improvement work at Mount Zion in Jerusalem and at the tomb of R. Simeon b. Yoḥai at Meron. The Authority was one of the initiators in setting up the park at Yad Mordekhai, which contains a reconstruction of the Egyptian attack on the kibbutz in 1948 and a small museum devoted to the defense of the southern kibbutzim during the War of Independence. Among the new parks for which plans have already been completed by the Authority is the Jerusalem national park—a green belt circling the Old City walls and covering 500 acres. The number of visitors to the national parks in 1968 exceeded 2,000,000.

9 NATURE RESERVES

Israel has an extraordinarily varied landscape and a rich array of flora and fauna. There are some 2,500 different species of indigenous wild plants—an extremely high number in relation to the area—in its three geobotanical regions: Mediterranean, Saharo-Sindi, and Irano-Turani, as well as enclaves of tropical and European flora, the most northern and southern known. About 250 of the plants are endemic. The fauna is also varied, though it is only a remnant of the wild life of biblical times; at least 15 large mammalian species have become extinct. There are more than 20 varieties of freshwater fish, several species of amphibians and eight of reptiles, 400 varieties of birds (150 of which nest in Israel, the remainder being migratory or winter visitors), and about 70 species of mammals, mostly small rodents and bats. Gazelle, wild boar, ibex, hyena, wolf, jackal, hyrax, caracal, and lynx are still to be found.

The dynamic development of modern Israel has inevitably affected plant and animal ecology. Some 500 new villages and a score of new towns, as well as the rapid expansion of existing ones, have encroached on areas of hitherto undisturbed wild life and natural vegetation. The quadrupling of the population, the rise in the standard of living, and the vast expansion of tourism, have brought large numbers of hikers and trippers to the countryside.

To protect the flora and fauna, a Nature Reserves Authority was established by the government in 1963. Some 120 areas have been selected as nature reserves in which landscape, flora, and fauna are protected in their natural condition. Some are large reserves, in which the flora and fauna maintain an equilibrium, for instance on Mt. Meron

Spring at the En-Gedi nature reserve in the Judean Desert. Photo Werner Braun, Jerusalem.

(about 70,000 dunams; 17,500 acres). There are also the smaller areas maintained for specific scientific reasons, e.g., winter pools to preserve lower crustacea and amphibians, a ridge of sandstone with its typical flora, islands on which common tern nest, and sites such as Ḥurshat Tal and Circassia as reminders of the landscape that once existed. While most of the reserves are open to the public, some are closed to preserve their scientific value. Facilities for visitors have been provided at Tel Dan, the "Tannur" near Metullah, the cave of "Pa'ar," the "Masrek" near Jerusalem, En-Gedi, etc., and the work is being extended to other places throughout the country. The Nature Reserves Authority has also undertaken to reintroduce species that have become extinct. At the *Ḥai-Bar* (wildlife) Biblical Game Reserve at Yotvata (34,500 dunams; 8,650 acres), attempts were begun in 1966 to breed some of these extinct species, with the approval of the World Wildlife Fund.

10 MAPS OF EREẒ ISRAEL

Graphic descriptions from factual data, of the topography and history of Ereẓ Israel, are valuable sources for the reconstruction of the physiographic and anthropogenic conditions prevailing at the time they were drawn. They are also nearly always far more important as documents which give evidence on contemporary developments of cartography in general. In this respect the cartographic representation of Ereẓ Israel differs fundamentally from that of any other country. The main reason for that was its unique status and special significance for believers in the three monotheistic religions which had such a decisive influence upon the culture and history of the Occident. Consequently Ereẓ Israel became a main—at times almost a sole—object of cartography for several countries. There are innumerable maps depicting the "Holy Land," and they date back to the very dawn of cartography. Another important aspect is that there is no major break in the cartographic representation of Ereẓ Israel over more than a millennium and a half; thus the subsequent depictions of the country reflect the general developments of cartography and at times are even the principal reason for it. This resulted from the fact that the "Holy Land" was treated as a very special, even unique, geographical-historical and even cosmological object, involving specific problems as to adequate cartographic expression and therefore necessitating techniques and means that were not applied at all, or applied only partially and usually much later in maps dealing with other countries.

Ereẓ Israel in Ancient Cartography. Only four map-like documents dating back to classical times are known at

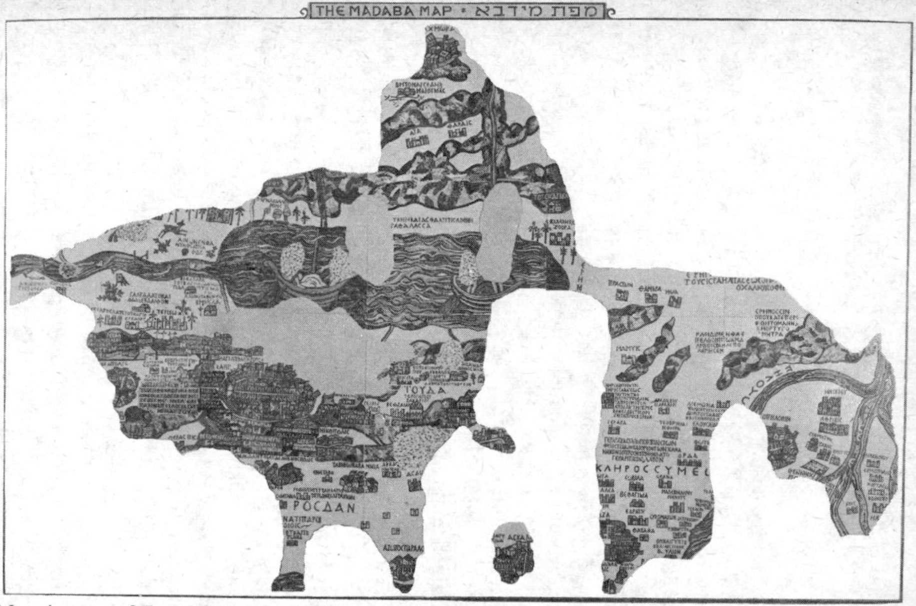

Mosaic map of Ereẓ Israel from a sixth-century church at Madaba, Jordan. From *Atlas of Israel,*

present. Of these only one has been preserved in the original (Madaba Map mosaic), while the three others exist in medieval copies only.

MADABA MOSAIC. This mosaic, partly destroyed when a church floor in Madaba was unearthed, is a typical pictorial map whose subject is the biblical countries, i.e., besides the Land of Israel—to which it is mainly devoted—it depicts parts of Lower Egypt, Sinai, and southern Syria. It became one of the most important and reliable sources for the reconstruction in particular of the anthropogenic landscape of Ereẓ Israel in the Byzantine period.

THE PTOLEMAEUS MAPS. In the maps which are ascribed to Claudius Ptolemaeus, a second-century Alexandrian cartographer, and which are drawn presumably to illustrate his treatise Γεωγραφικὴ ὑφήγησισς (preserved only in medieval copies), Ereẓ Israel is represented in the map entitled "The fourth part of Asia." Its scale is very small; nevertheless, it is of great value since it contains much information pertinent to Ereẓ Israel in the period of the Antonine dynasty. From the cartographic point of view its greatest importance lies in the fact that (as will be detailed below) it changed thoroughly all the fundamental long-held clichés concerning the representation of the Holy Land, and introduced northern orientation and an exact scale by the use of the longitude and latitude grid.

THE PEUTINGER TABLE (TABULA PEUTINGERIANA). The Peutinger Table seems to have been one of the very common road maps in use in the Roman Empire. The original table seems to have been drawn in the third century, and the extant copy probably dates from the 13th century. It is exceedingly long in proportion to its width (682 ×33 cm.), and its main subject, to which all other details are subordinated, is a communications network of the contemporary Roman Empire, specifically emphasizing its stations and the distances between them. Originally drawn in one piece, it was apparently cut into a series of sections of equal size later on. Ereẓ Israel is depicted on it in the lower portions of the sections IX and X. It is assumed that the copy does not differ appreciably from the original; the most pronounced variances are, significantly, several "Christian" additions localizing, illustrating, and explaining sites and events of Christian-biblical interest and thus mainly found in the portion depicting Ereẓ Israel and the adjacent regions. It has been assumed, therefore, that this preserved map was copied in order to serve as a guide to pilgrims traveling to Ereẓ Israel and Rome. The map is not drawn to any scale, and the location of the provinces represented on it is dictated merely by the space provided by the elongated shape of the map which led to extreme distortions in their outlines and situation.

THE "SAINT JEROME MAPS." There are two maps known as the Saint Jerome Maps, both of these copies drawn in the third century. They are included in a manuscript in St. Jerome's *De hebraicis quaestionibus et interpretationibus nominum Veteris et Novi Testamenti,* and their contents provide evidence that the originals were produced at the time of the Church Fathers, but not necessarily by Jerome himself. Both are rather crude black-ink sketches very generalized in style and content, and were thus important as precursors of a great number of maps drawn by monks in the medieval period. One of the drawings depicts the Roman Empire according to its division into provinces, emphasizing the places of special interest to Christians. As a portion of this map is missing, only the northern part of Ereẓ Israel appears on it: the Mt. Hermon area and the sources of the Jordan (designated here as "Jor" and "Dan"—a toponymic deduction from the name of the river that prevailed throughout the Middle Ages). The second sketch contains both the whole of Ereẓ Israel and the adjacent countries, Egypt, Syria, and Mesopotamia. Some of the most characteristic features of almost all the "scholastic" medieval maps are also present here: Ereẓ Israel occupies the central part of the drawing and is represented out of all proportion to the surrounding countries, which appear as small unimportant appendages. Similarly, only places and topographical features of biblical interest appear on this map sketch.

In the Middle Ages. Although in general, cartography in the Middle Ages was of a low standard, cartography of Ereẓ Israel reached a peak in this period, both in quantity and quality. For several centuries, Ereẓ Israel was the sole, or at least the most important and prominent, subject of map making. Two kinds of maps existed in the Middle Ages:

a. World maps *(mappae mundi),* almost all of which were of an abstract nature, and were largely the work of monks. Their purpose was to explain and illustrate contemporary ecclesiastical views of cosmography and geography, which, rather than being based on a knowledge of reality, were based on the Scriptures, as interpreted by the Church Fathers and the scholastics, as well as on the writings of ancient polyhistors such as Pliny, Pomponius Hella, and Solinus. Not only was the content of these world maps decisively influenced by the Bible; even their shape (a circle or rectangle) was a result of dogmatic interpretations of certain biblical passages. The world maps are "oriented," i.e., their top denoted the East, the presumed site of Paradise (which is shown on many of these maps as a geographical actuality). In all the maps, Ereẓ Israel occupies a prominent place, in many instances as much as a sixth of the entire space (as for example in the famous "Anglo-Saxon" map). In some of the maps, which are so abstract in conception and drawing as to represent mere cartograms, Ereẓ Israel takes up so much space that the other countries tend to appear as insignificant background only. The description of Ereẓ Israel on these maps consists entirely of biblical topography, with an addition of explanations and traditional identifications of places. Furthermore, from the beginning of the Crusades up to the 16th century, Jerusalem, believed to be the "navel of the world," was placed at the very center of all world maps. This, of course, dictated the whole framework, structure, and composition of the map, fulfilling the role played in present maps by the reference location of the poles and the equator. The proportionally great detail of the historio-geographical and physiogeographic facts in which traditional particulars of Ereẓ Israel were depicted or verbally denoted on the maps (such as Mt. Gilboa, Mt. Tabor, various springs, caves, trees, holy places, etc.), however, made it necessary to invent new forms for expressing such details, and this seems to have had a lasting effect upon the development of symbols and signs used in maps in the following centuries. Among medieval maps there were many sketchlike maps of Jerusalem, that were generalized and geometrical and served as guides to pilgrims and Crusaders.

b. The portolano maps, which appeared in the late Middle Ages, were used mostly for purposes of navigation and were probably derived from charts developed as early as the Byzantine period. Many Jewish cartographers were involved in the production of this kind of map, in particular those of the Catalan school, centered in Majorca. The most renowned representatives of this school were Abraham and Judah (Jaime) Cresques; the latter drew the Catalan Atlas, the most beautiful and advanced project of the portolano cartography. Although on these maps Ereẓ Israel no longer occupies a disproportionate amount of space, it continues to exhibit many specific aspects, both as to content and cartographic execution. Since these maps were sea charts aimed at serving navigation, they concentrated primarily on the delineation of coastlines and the location of ports, and show hardly any details of the interior, except perhaps for a flag (banner?) signifying the political control of the country. An exception is made in the case of Ereẓ Israel, for which the relevant portion of the map shows great inland detail, such as the Jordan and its lakes, holy places, and important churches and monasteries. The Red Sea is shown in red or crimson (whereas other bodies of water are shown in blue or light green); a white strip marks the site where the Israelites are presumed to have crossed the Red Sea. It has become increasingly certain that the portolano maps served as the basis of the few regional maps made in the Middle Ages (at least the few that have been preserved). All of these maps (with one exception, which also contains Britain; see the Matthew Paris map, below) have Ereẓ Israel as their subject. Considering the period in which they were made, these are exceptional maps: a) They are the outcome of either direct observation or factual and critically adapted information. b) Their contents are of a topical nature, describing Ereẓ Israel during and after the time of the Crusader Kingdom of Jerusalem, though they also contain many details based on biblical tradition—so important for every Christian pilgrim in the Middle Ages but not corresponding to the reality of the country and in contrast to the factual content of the map. c) They generally serve a practical purpose, i.e., as guides for armies or pilgrims. d) Some of the maps and techniques exhibit specific features that denote marked progress in cartography and were used in the maps of other countries only much later.

The outstanding medieval maps of Ereẓ Israel that have been preserved are the following: 1. A large map (2,080 sq. cm.), preserved at Florence, that is extraordinary not only with regard to its delineation of the coast, which corresponds closely to reality as is the rule with portolano maps, but also as to its wealth of detail. The details, however, are of a much lower standard; for example, the markings of locations—which is a major subject of all medieval maps—are out of proportion to the areal extension of the map. The map is oriented to the East, in contrast to the portolanos, thus reflecting the prevailing influence of the *mappae mundi* and their affinities. 2. A sketch map of Ereẓ Israel at Oxford, whose portolano origin is evidenced by its orientation to the North. It contains a great number of topical details, including some based on observation, such as a unique description of the road leading from the coast to Jerusalem.

 3. Another map kept at Florence, outstanding in the quality of its

illustrations and colors, but inferior in content to the two maps mentioned above. Because of its highly heraldic and ornamental designs and its wonderful coloring, it represents one of the most pronounced examples of the artistry employed in the late Middle Ages. 4. A map drawn by Matthew Paris of England (1250 C.E.), outstanding for its unique description of the road system and its allusions to caravan traffic between Ereẓ Israel and Syria. Some places, especially Acre, the most important Crusader fortress, are depicted in great detail in a separate small vignette. Paris was also the author of an illustrated road guide (England to the Holy Land) which is unique in cartography. The map has the form of a long strip and signifies with miniature designs the stops along the route between the two countries; the stops were usually churches or monasteries that pilgrims customarily visited, and even the roads leading from one stop to the next are indicated by two parallel lines. 5. Medieval cartographic presentation of the Holy Land reached its climax in a series of maps and sketches attached to a memoir by the Venetian Marino Sanuto, appealing for a renewal of crusading *(liber secretorum fidelium crucis).* The map appendage consists of a map of Ereẓ Israel, a rather stereotyped *mappa mundi,* a map of the Near Eastern countries, and a detailed, extremely accurate sketch of Acre, and a far more conventional one of Jerusalem. It is now established that at least the maps of Israel and of the Near East were drawn by Pietro Vesconte, a noted portolano cartographer. The map of Ereẓ Israel is an astounding piece of work, anticipating various future cartographical developments by several centuries. It is not only relatively exact in scale—a characteristic common to most portolanos as far as the coasts are concerned—but also exhibits a grid of longitudinal and latitudinal lines equally spaced throughout at a distance of 1 "leuca" (approx. 2,500 meters). The location of the towns and villages, at least those existing at the time, is rather exact, as are the sites of most topographic features represented in the map. Another extraordinary feature is the wealth of information (besides the usual indication of biblical sites, the areas assumedly occupied by the tribes of Israel, and pertinent remarks and explanations derived from the Bible) on the contemporary situation, based, as were the above-mentioned features of the map, on the author's personal observation and/or intensive study of the memoir. Because of its relative accuracy and abundance of detail, the map served as a pattern for other maps during the Renaissance period; however, its grid was generally replaced by the Ptolemaic latitude and longitude grid. 6. A map drawn by William Wey in the 15th century. It is a typical medieval depiction of Ereẓ Israel, in which all the elements of medieval presentation of this country are incorporated and superbly executed; in particular the pictorial embellishments and the coloring (illumination).

Ereẓ Israel in Arab Cartography of the Middle Ages. In general, medieval Arab maps were more exact, more detailed, and more comprehensive than European maps, but in technique they were far more uniform and stereotyped, employing outlines and symbols of a strictly geometric nature. In Arab maps, Ereẓ Israel did not occupy the most prominent place. The best and most comprehensive Arab map of Ereẓ Israel was made by Idrissi, whose cartographic works represent a mixture of Moslem and Western European style and content.

In Modern Times. The cartographical representation of Ereẓ Israel underwent some fundamental changes in modern times: 1. As a result of constantly growing geographical knowledge (gained from the works and maps of Ptolemaeus) and the extensive discoveries of whole continents, accompanied by the development of the sciences, in particular those dealing with the earth—its astronomical position, movements, and surface nature, Jerusalem could no longer be regarded as the "navel of the world" and ceased to be used as the center of world maps. 2. The mathematical and astronomical fixing of locations—by means of lines of longitude and latitude—based upon the method used by Ptolemaeus and arrived at by exact measurements, made it possible to establish the proper outlines of the countries and their relative size. Each map was now based on a distance scale and it was no longer possible to exaggerate the size of Ereẓ Israel in comparison with the other countries of the world. 3. However, whereas the maps of other countries usually contained only details of a contemporary nature, maps of Ereẓ Israel retained their historical character. The main purpose of these maps was to describe the topographical and geographical background of the events described in the Bible and the Gospels, and they ignored the actual landscape of the country, and in particular, the anthropogenic features (villages, roads, etc.). For this reason, a contemporary map of Ereẓ Israel *(tabula moderna)* was usually attached to the Ptolemaeus maps, made to a much larger scale, orientated to the East, and containing many traditional topographical designations. Most of these maps were based on that of Sanuto. Nevertheless, for a variety of reasons, maps of Ereẓ Israel retained their special importance in the early modern period: 1) For various historical and religious reasons (the Reformation, Bible translations), the invention of printing made maps of Ereẓ Israel the most popular and most widely distributed maps; they were also the first to be produced in print. 2) The competition resulting from the wide demand for maps of Ereẓ Israel that provided the location of sites mentioned in the Bible, caused these maps to become generally the most splendid and beautiful ones produced in this period; this applies particularly to the signs and symbols used on the maps, the decoration of the margins, and the cartouche, i.e., the part of the map separated by an ornamental enclosure containing the title of the map, its author, the scales, sources, and so on. The historical content, that seemed to illustrate the background of the Bible and Gospels with the little contemporary geographical detailing that was available during the Renaissance period, made it possible to experiment with the maps and even led to innovations as regards scales, symbols, shading, coloring (illumination), etc. Thus the first indication of magnetic variation was made on a map of Ereẓ Israel.

Ereẓ Israel in the Era of Atlases. The magnificent atlases produced during and after the Renaissance, in Western and Central Europe, usually contained at least two maps of Ereẓ Israel, which were the works of different cartographers and were scarcely compatible with each other. One of the maps forms an integral part of each atlas and is usually based on Ptolemaeus; it is oriented to the North, contains some slight changes in the delineation of the coast and some additional relief features and hydrographic details, and a wealth of place-names mentioned in

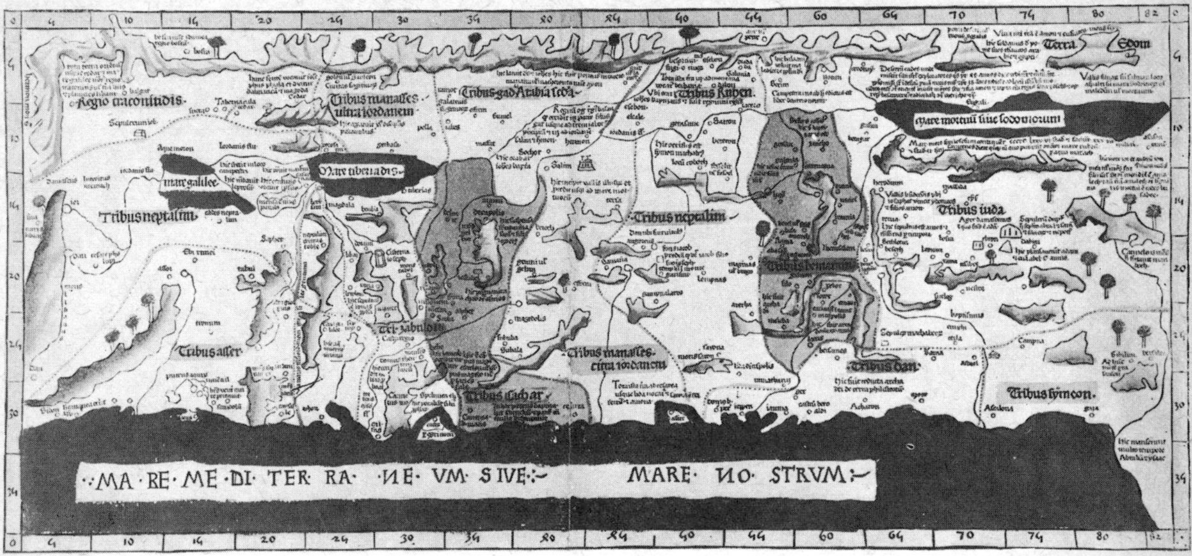

Map of non-Ptolemaic design, Pietro Vesconte, 14th century. Jerusalem, J.N.U.L.

the Scriptures, in the works of Josephus and so on. Thus, in essence, the map depicts Ereẓ Israel as it is shown in "The fourth part of Asia" by Ptolemaeus. There are numerous instances, however, in which the Ereẓ Israel map in the atlas is oriented to the East and is much closer in content and nature to the Sanuto map, with the important addition of the use of the astronomic longitude and latitude grid derived from Ptolemaeus. The second map of Ereẓ Israel (and sometimes even a third, produced by yet another cartographer) is found among the numerous addenda *(additamentum)* that were attached to the atlases in this period. Important Ereẓ Israel maps in this period were produced by Ortelius, Mercator, Tilemanus Sigenensis, Laicstein, Blaeu, Janszon, Homann, Sanson, Seutter, de Lille, Bonne, and d'Anville. The maps made by the last three cartographers mentioned (who represent the French school) were superior to others in the precision of their content and may be regarded as the most advanced maps prior to those of the 19th century. There were also maps of Ereẓ Israel that were attached to the numerous cosmographies published in this period (of which that by Sebastian Muenster was the most widely distributed). Even more important, as a source for the maps appearing in the atlases, were the various works on Ereẓ Israel, which contained maps made to a large scale. Among these, mention should be made of the works of Jacob Ziegler, Adrian Adrichomius (1590), and last and most important, Hadrianus Relandus' *Palaestina ex monumentis veteribus illustrata,* which contains a number of detailed and relatively precise maps, especially one showing the relief and the consequent physiographic division of the country into coastal plain, the mountains, the Valley of the Jordan and the Transjordan plateaus. Only a single map of Israel, made in 1483 by Bernard Breitenbach, is based entirely on the author's personal observation and describes the country as he saw it. Combining both the medieval and modern cartographic style, the map enjoyed great popularity.

The 18th, 19th, and 20th Centuries. The first mapping of Ereẓ

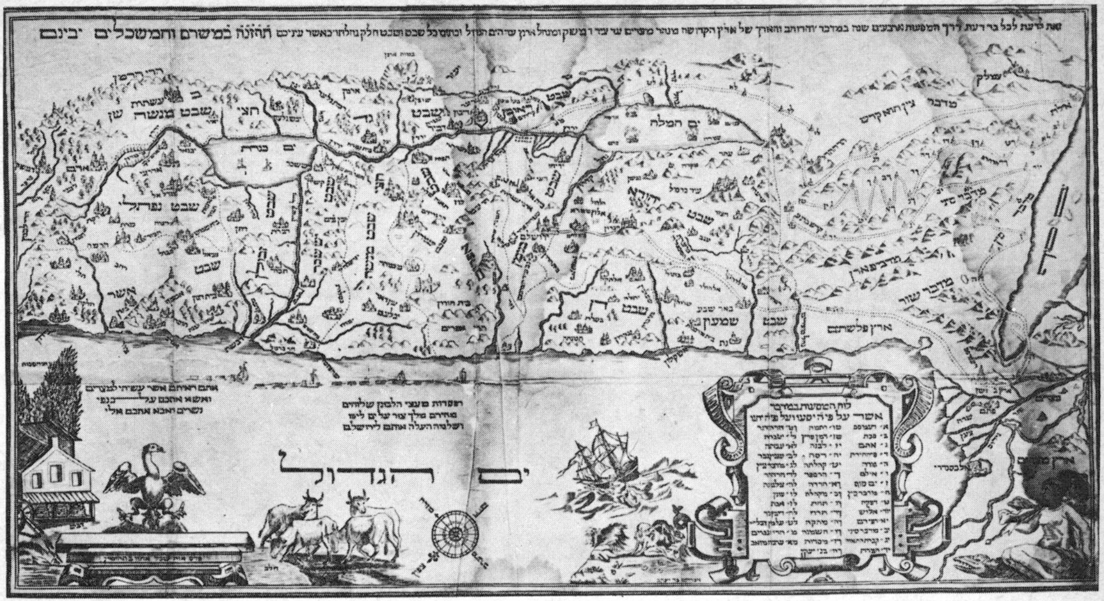

The first map printed in Hebrew. Made by Abraham ben Jacob, it appears in the *Amsterdam Haggadah*, 1695.

Israel based partly on topographical survey was made in connection with Napoleon's campaign in Egypt and Ereẓ Israel. The main result of this was a series of 47 maps of Egypt, Sinai, and Ereẓ Israel, named the Jacotin maps after their author (1810). Six of the maps depict parts of Ereẓ Israel, especially those parts through which the army passed on its invasion of the country. The scale is 1:100,000, and the maps show precise details of the areas where measurements were taken by means of the trigonometric methods that had developed in Europe by this time (based on the theodolite and the principle of triangulation). Thus, even the representation of relief on these maps was relatively exact and adequate. Relative differences in height and the diverse gradients of the slopes are shown by hachuring (i.e., expressing the gradient of the slope by discontinuous, proportionally dimensioned lines extending down from the summit to the base of the slope; the steeper the slope the shorter but thicker the hachure line and vice versa), and in general, the rest of the details shown on the maps, i.e., symbols and so on, are of a high standard. Some of the place-names are given in Arabic script, in addition to Latinized transcription. For a period of about 50 years these were the maps used in the exploration of the country.

Toward the end of the 18th century and in the first half of the 19th century, Ereẓ Israel became the subject of numerous exploratory voyages and expeditions, as though it was still "unknown territory." Although the emphasis was on the archaeological and historical aspects of the country, much attention was also paid to its natural conditions including its physiography. In particular, interest was centered on the Jordan Valley and the Dead Sea, because they formed the lowest depression on earth. The works produced by such itinerant scholars and explorers as Seetzen, Burckhardt, Buckingham, and Robinson generally included sketch maps of some areas and sites, and an overall map of the country. Outstanding among these maps is the one attached to Robinson's work, drawn by Kiepert, the well-known German cartographer. An American naval expedition, led by Lynch, executed a map survey of the Jordan River and the Dead Sea. All these works were summarized in *Erdkunde von Asien* ("Geography of Asia") the famous work by Ritter, which also contains a comprehensive list of all known maps of Ereẓ Israel, from ancient times up to the 19th century. A companion to Ritter's work, the atlas by Zimmermann, contains detailed maps of Ereẓ Israel, to the scale of 1:333,333. All the maps listed above were used as an important source for the study of the landscape of Ereẓ Israel in the first half of the 19th century. The final work of this period of individual research and mapping was the map of Van de Velde (scale 1:315,000), one of the most beautiful maps of Ereẓ Israel of this time.

In the second half of the 19th century, the existing maps were felt to be insufficient to meet the requirements of the growing interest in the country, especially for archaeological purposes. The Palestine Exploration Fund (PEF) was established in Britain to carry out a systematic survey of Ereẓ Israel "from Dan to Beer Sheba." The work of the fund was preceded by a survey of the coastline and the adjoining hinterland, ordered by the British Admiralty (1858–1862). They established not only the exact outline of the coastline but also a fixed number of points that were of great help in the survey that followed. An early project undertaken by the Fund was a survey of the Sinai Peninsula, aimed at establishing the route of the Exodus and the location of Mt. Sinai. The maps of Jebel Katerina (the presumed location of Mount Sinai) and Jebel Serbal, whose relief is expressed by form lines, are among the finest maps of the entire area. The first undertaking of the Fund in Ereẓ Israel proper was a survey of Jerusalem and its surroundings (1864), carried out with a precision hitherto not applied in the Near East. In the resulting maps the relief was presented by the hachuring method. In 1871 an expedition of the Fund, led by Conder and later on by Kitchener, embarked upon the main mapping project. The survey encompassed the entire country, from the Qasimiye River up to south of the Dead Sea, and resulted in a set of 26 sheets, made to the scale of 1:63,360 (inch to mile), as on the British topographical maps, and based on a precise triangulation (two base-lines), leveling (Acre-Sea of Galilee, Jaffa-Dead Sea), and altimetric measurements. The relief is represented by means of shading and tinting. In many instances the height is also given in figures; rivers and springs are shown in blue; the various kinds of vegetational cover are indicated by accordant symbols, as are also anthropogenic features. The maps are particularly accurate in the location of the many existing ruins of ancient places of settlement; much effort was also devoted to establishing the names of places and their proper transliteration. The Fund published its *Memoirs,* and they serve to this day as an important geographical and historical source.

"The Survey of Western Palestine" was followed by efforts to carry out a similar survey of Transjordan, which, however, failed for a variety of reasons. Only the Deutscher Palaestina Verein eventually carried out a survey of Gilead, executed to the same scale as the maps of PEF. The maps of the PEF and, to some extent, the German maps too, served as a basis for Ereẓ Israel maps that were produced up to the conquest of Palestine by the British. Among later maps based on those of the PEF, the most important was the Bartholemew map, in which the relief is expressed by contour lines and the subsequent altitude zones are also indicated by varying coloring. In World War I the existing maps were adapted to military requirements, with the help of aerial photography. The maps employed by the British army were made to a scale of 1:40,000, those of the German army to 1:50,000. Shortly before World War I a survey of the Sinai Peninsula was carried out by Newcombe, to a scale of 1:125,000; this included the Negev and the relief was represented by contour and form lines. Shortly after its establishment, the Mandatory government embarked upon a new survey of the country, using up-to-date methods. Two series of maps were printed, one a topo-cadastral set, made to a scale of 1:20,000, and the other a topographical set made to a scale of 1:100,000. This survey was also restricted to the area of Ereẓ Israel extending from the northern political boundary to somewhat south of Beersheba, and consisted of 16 sheets. In these maps the relief was presented by contour lines with a vertical interval of 25 meters. Agricultural areas appear in green and the hydrographic network in blue. The mapping was executed with comprehensive triangulation and fieldwork. Other maps produced by the Mandatory government were maps of the major cities and villages (scale 1:10,000) and a geographical map of the country (1:250,000). During the Mandatory period, efforts were also made to produce a Hebrew map of the country (Press, Brawer, Lief). These were necessarily adaptions of 19th-century maps and those issued by the government Survey Department but they made important contributions to the proper identification of localities, and the use of historical place-names and Hebrew transliteration. With the establishment of the state, "Survey of Israel" became one of its basic governmental institutions in view of the country's ever-expanding exigencies, in particular those connected with economic-demographic planning. These were met by extensive triangulation, leveling which also resulted in a dense altimetric network, new additions (Hebrew) of totally revised and updated map series 1:20,000 and 1:100,000, largely improved not only by the above-mentioned measurements but also by the thorough use of photogrammetric techniques. The 100,000 series is continuously supplemented by a far more comprehensive one at a scale of 1:50,000. The Israel atlas (Heb. 1956–64) and its English edition (1970)—the latest additions to the series of "National Atlases"—summarize both the history and the development of the cartographic representation of the country and its present state in all the fields given to cartographic expression.

BIBLIOGRAPHY

L. Lewysohn, *Zoologie des Talmuds* (1858).

A. Neubauer, *La géographie du Talmud* (1868).

C. R. Conder and H. H. Kitchener, *Survey of Western Palestine* (1881–83).

G. Le Strange, *Palestine under the Moslems* (1890).

P. Thomsen, *Loca Sancta* (1907).

F. M. Exner, *Zum Klima von Palaestina* (1910).

H. Klein, *Das Klima Palaestinas auf Grund alter hebraeischer Quellen* (1914).

G. A. Smith, *Historical Geography of the Holy Land* (1931[25]).

F.-M. Abel, *Géographie de la Palestine*, 2 vols. (1933–38).

M. G. Ionides, *Report on the Water Resources of Transjordan and their Development* (1940).

L. Picard, in: *Bulletin Geological Department Hebrew University Jerusalem*, 4(1943), 1–134.

I. Press, *Ereẓ-Yisrael, Enẓiklopedyah Topografit-Historit*, 4 vols. (1951–55).

D. Ashbel, *Aklim Ereẓ Yisrael le-Ezoreha* (1952).

A. M. Quennel, in: *Proceedings of the Geological Society London* (1954), 14–20.

M. Zohary, *Geobotanikah* (Heb., 1955).

Y. Karmon, *The Northern Huleh Valley* (1956).

F. S. Bodenheimer, *Animal and Man in Bible Lands* (1960).

K. O. Emery and D. Neev, in: *Bulletin Geological Survey of Israel*, 26 (1960), 1–13.

M. Avi-Yonah, *Ge'ografyah Historit shel Ereẓ Yisrael* (1962[3]).

J. Feliks, *The Animal World of the Bible* (1962).

I. Schattner, in: *Scripta Hierosolymitana*, 11 (1962), 1–123.

Rashut Shemurot ha-Teva, *Pirsumim* (1965–).

M. Avi-Yonah, *The Holy Land from the Persian to the Arab Conquest* (1966).

Y. Aharoni, *Land of the Bible* (1966).

E. Orni and E. Efrat, *Geography of Israel* (1971).

MAPS: J. E. Bailey, *Palestine Geography in the Seventeenth Century*, 4 (1872).
C. R. Conder, *Tent Work in Palestine* (1878).
K. Miller, *Weltkarte des Castorius, genannt die Peutinger'sche Tafel* (1888).
C. R. Beazley, *The Dawn of Modern Geography*, 3 vols. (1897–1906, repr. 1949).
D. Ashbel, *Bio-Climatic Atlas of Israel* (1948).
I. Schattner, *The Maps of Palestine and their History* (1951).
R. A. Skelton, *Decorative Printed Maps of the 15th to 18th Centuries* (1952).
The World Encompassed. An Exhibition of the History of Maps. Catalog. Baltimore, Md. (1952).
M. Avi-Yonah, *The Madaba Mosaic Map* (1954).
Y. Karmon, in: *Israel Exploration Journal*, 10 (1960), 155–73.
B. von Breydenbach, *Die Reise ins Heilige Land . . . 1485* (with repr. of Reuwich's woodcut map, 1961).
Old Maps of the Land of Israel. Exhibition. Maritime Museum, Haifa. Catalog by H. M. Z. Meyer (1963).
R. Roehricht, *Bibliotheca Geographica Palestinae* (enlarged and ed. by D. Amiran, 1963[2], Ger.).
L. Bagrow, *History of Cartography* (rev. and enlarged by R. A. *Skelton*, 1964; orig. Ger., 1951), index s.v. *Palestine*.
H. M. Z. Meyer, *The Holy Land in Ancient Maps* (1965[3]).
Z. Vilnay, *The Holy Land in Old Prints and Maps* (1965[2]).
idem, *Hebrew Maps of the Holy Land* (1968[2]).
Y. Aharoni and M. Avi-Yonah, *Macmillan Bible Atlas* (1968).
Y. Aharoni, *Carta Atlas of the Bible* (1968).
Atlas of Israel (1970).

ABBREVIATIONS

B.C.E.	Before Common Era (=B.C.)
C.E.	Common Era (=A.D.)
I (or II) Chron.	Chronicles, books I and II
Dan.	Daniel
Deut.	Deuteronomy
Eccles.	Ecclesiastes
Esth.	Esther
Ex.	Exodus
Ezek.	Ezekiel
G	Gadna
Gen.	Genesis
Git.	*Gittin* (talmudic tractate)
H	Histadrut
Ḥ	Ḥerut
Hab.	Habakkuk
Ḥal	*Ḥallah* (talmudic tractate)
HI	Hitaḥadut ha-Ikkarim
Hos.	Hosea
IḤ	Iḥud Ḥakla'i
IK	Iḥud ha-Kevuẓot ve-ha-Kibbutzim
Isa.	Isaiah
Jer.	Jeremiah
Jos., Wars	Josephus, *The Jewish Wars* (Loeb Classics ed.)
Josh.	Joshua
Judg.	Judges

KA	Ha-Kibbutz ha-Arẓi (Ha-Shomer ha-Ẓa'ir)
KD	Ha-Kibbutz ha-Dati
KM	Ha-Kibbutz ha-Me'uhad
Lam.	Lamentations
Lev.	Leviticus
m.	meter(s)
M	Mapam
I Macc.	Maccabees, I (Apocrypha)
Mal.	Malachi
mi.	mile(s)
Nah.	Nahum
Neh.	Nehemiah
Num.	Numbers
Obad	Obadiah
OẒ	Ha-Oved ha-Ẓiyyoni
PAI	Po'alei Agudat Israel
PM	Ha-Po'el ha-Mizrachi
Prov.	Proverbs
Ps.	Psalms
I and II Sam.	Samuel, books I and II
Shev.	*Shevi'it* (talmudic tractate)
Sif. Deut	Sifrei Deuteronomy
Song.	Song of Songs
Ter.	*Terumah* (talmudic tractate)
TJ	Jerusalem Talmud or Talmud Yerushalmi
TM	Tenu'at ha-Moshavim
Tosef.	Tosefta
Zech.	Zechariah
Zeph.	Zephaniah

ISRAEL PLACE LIST (1971)

PLACES OF JEWISH HABITATION

NOTES:

Geographical Region: The sign "67+" indicates a settlement beyond the pre-1967 borders.

Year of Founding: Where the year is not indicated, the settlement is ancient.

Where the year is given in brackets, the place was temporarily abandoned and resettled in the year given.

Form of Settlement: Only the present form of settlement is given.

Affiliation: Only the present affiliation is given.

Municipal Status. RC the settlement is represented in the regional council indicated.

(RC) the settlement belongs to the area of the regional council, but is not represented in it.

No. of Inhabitants: The sign . . indicates that the population figures are not available.

Name	Geographical Region	Year of Founding	Settlement Form	Affiliation	Municipal Status	No. of inhabitants 31 Dec 71
Acre (Akko)	Acre Plain	—	Town		municipality	34,2000 (thereof 8,950 non-Jews)
Adamit	Western Upper Galilee	1958	Kibbutz	KA	RC Sullam Zor	
Adanim	Southern Sharon	1950	Moshav	RC	RC Ha-Yarkon	199

Adderet	Judean Foothills (Adullam Region)	1961	Moshav	TM	RC Matteh Yehudah	265
Addirim	Jezreel Valley (Taanach Region)	1956	Moshav	TM	RC Ha-Gilboa	371
Afek	Acre Plain	1939	Kibbutz	KM	RC Na'aman	400
Afikim	Kinneret Valley	1932	Kibbutz	IK	RC Jordan Valley	1,350
Afulah (Ir Yizre'el)	Jezreel Valley	1925	Urban Settlement		local council	17,200
Agur	Southern Judean Foothills	1950	Moshav	TM	RC Matteh Yehudah	302
Aḥi'ezer	Coastal Plain (Lod Region)	1950	Moshav	PM	RC Lod Plain	890
Aḥihud	Acre Plain	1950	Moshav	TM	RC Na'aman	505
Aḥisamakh	Coastal Plain (Lod Region)	1950	Moshav	TM	RC Modi'im	670
Aḥituv	Central Sharon (Ḥefer Plain)	1951	Moshav	TM	RC Ḥefer Plain	560
Aḥuzzam	Southern Coastal Plain (Lachish Region)	1950	Moshav	OẒ	RC Lachish	510
Aḥuzzat Naftali	Eastern Lower Galilee	1949	Institution (Yeshivah)	PM	(RC) Lower Galilee	28
Allon Shevut	Hebron Hills; 67+	1971	Rural Center	PM		..
Allonei Abba	Southern Lower Galilee	1948	Moshav Shittufi	OẒ	RC Kishon	220

Name	Geographical Region	Year of Founding	Settlement Form	Affiliation	Municipal Status	No. of inhabitants 31 Dec 71
Allonei Yizḥak	Manasseh Hills	1949	Youth Village	OẒ	(RC) Manasseh	360
Allonim	Jezreel Valley	1938	Kibbutz	KM	RC Kishon	480
Almagor	Kinneret Valley	1961	Moshav	TM	RC Jordan Valley	70
Almah	Eastern Upper Galilee	1949	Moshav	PM	RC Merom ha-Galil	655
Alumim	Northwestern Negev (Besor Region)	1966	Kibbutz	KD	RC Azzatah	73
Alummah	Southern Coastal Plain (Malakhi Region)	1965	Rural Center		(RC) Shafir	150
Alummot (Bitanyah)	Kinneret Valley	1941	Kibbutz	IK	RC Jordan Valley	79
Amaẓyah	Lachish (Adoraim) Region	1955	Moshav Shittufi	Ḥ	RC Lachish	..
Amir	Ḥuleh Valley	1939	Kibbutz	KA	RC Ha-Galil ha-Elyon	411
Amirim	Eastern Upper Galilee	1950	Moshav	TM	RC Merom ha-Galil	148
Amkah	Acre Plain	1949	Moshav	TM	RC Ga'aton	595

Ammi'ad	Eastern Upper Galilee (Hazor Region)	1946	Kibbutz	IK	RC Ha-Galil ha-Elyon	252
Ammikam	Iron Hills (Northwestern Samaria)	1950	Moshav	Ḥ	RC Allonah	125
Amminadav	Jerusalem Hills	1950	Moshav	TM	RC Matteh Yehudah	265
Ammi'oz	Northwestern Negev (Besor Region)	1957	Moshav	TM	RC Eshkol	237
Arad	Northeastern Negev	1961	Urban Settlement	—	local council	5,450
Arbel	Eastern Lower Galilee	1949	Moshav	TM	RC Ha-Galil ha-Taḥton	163
Argaman	Lower Jordan Valley; 67 +	1968	Moshav(Kibbutz)	Ḥ		. .
Arugot	Southern Coastal Plain (Malakhi Region)	1949	Moshav	TM	RC Be'er Tuviyyah	241
Aseret	Coastal Plain, (Reḥovot Region)	1954	Rural Center	—	RC Gederot	510
Ashdod	Southern Coastal Plain	1955	City		Township	39,700
Ashdot Ya'akov	Kinneret Valley	1933	Kibbutz	IK	RC Jordan Valley	. .
Ashdot Ya'akov	Kinneret Valley	1933	Kibbutz	KM	RC Jordan Valley	. .
Ashkelon	Southern Coastal Plain	—	City		municipality	41,700

Name	Geographical Region	Year of Founding	Settlement Form	Affiliation	Municipal Status	No. of inhabitants 31 Dec 71
Athlit	Carmel Coast	1904	Urban Settlement		local council	410
Avdon	Western Upper Galilee	1952	Moshav	TM	RC Ma'aleh ha-Galil	278
Avi'el	Northern Sharon (Ḥaderah Region)	1949	Moshav	Ḥ	RC Allonah	219
Avi'ezer	Judean Foothills	1958	Moshav	PM	RC Matteh Yehudah	230
Avigedor	Southern Coastal Plain (Malakhi Region)	1950	Moshav	TM	RC Be'er Tuviyyah	316
Aviḥayil	Central Sharon	1932	Moshav	TM	RC Ḥefer Plain	590
Avital	Jezreel Valley (Taanach Region)	1953	Moshav	TM	RC Ha-Gilboa	380
Avivim	Eastern Upper Galilee	1960	Moshav	TM	RC Merom ha-Galil	
Ayanot	Coastal Plain (Rishon le-Zion Region)	1930	Agricultural School	—	—	300
Ayyelet ha-Shaḥar	Ḥuleh Valley	1918	Kibbutz	IK	Ha-Galil ha-Elyon	750
Azaryah	Judean Foothills	1949	Moshav	TM	RC Gezer	484

Azor	Coastal Plain (Tel Aviv Region)	1948	Urban Settlement	—	local council	5,200
Azri'el	Southern Sharon (Kefar Sava Region)	1951	Moshav	PM	RC Hadar ha-Sharon	490
Azrikam	Southern Coastal Plain (Malakhi Region)	1950	Moshav	TM	RC Be'er Tuviyyah	615
Baḥan	Central Sharon	1953	Kibbutz	IK	RC Ḥefer Plain	274
Balfouriyyah	Jezreel Valley	1922	Moshav	TM	RC Yizre'el	224
Barak	Jezreel Valley (Taanach Region)	1956	Moshav	TM	RC Ha-Gilboa	263
Baram	Eastern Upper Galilee	1949	Kibbutz	KA	RC Merom ha-Galil	328
Bareket	Coastal Plain (Petaḥ Tikvah Region)	1952	Moshav	PM	RC Modi'im	745
Bar Giora	Jerusalem Hills	1950	Moshav	Ḥ	RC Matteh Yehudah	210
Barkai	Iron Hills (Northwestern Samaria)	1949	Kibbutz	KA	RC Manasseh	325
Bat Shelomo	Manasseh Hills	1889	Moshav	HI	RC Ḥof ha-Karmel	161
Bat Yam	Coastal Plain (Tel Aviv Region)	1926	City		municipality	90,700
Be'eri	Northwestern Negev (Eshkol Region)	1946	Kibbutz	KH	RC Eshkol	487

Name	Geographical Region	Year of Founding	Settlement Form	Affiliation	Municipal Status	No. of inhabitants 31 Dec 71
Be'er Orah	Southern Arabah Valley	1950	Youth Camp	G	(RC) Ḥevel Eilot	. .
Be'erot Yizḥak	Coastal Plain (Petaḥ Tikvah Region)	1948	Kibbutz	PM	RC Modi'im	283
Be'erotayim	Coastal Plain (Ḥefer Plain)	1949	Moshav	TM	RC Ḥefer Plain	265
Beersheba (Be'er Sheva)	Northern Negev	(1948)	City		municipality	81,100
Be'er Tuviyyah	Southern Coastal Plain (Malakhi Region)	1930	Moshav	TM	RC Be'er Tuviyyah	655
Be'er Ya'akov	Coastal Plain (Lod Region)	1907	Urban Settlement		local council	4,120
Beko'a	Judean Foothills	1951	Moshav	TM	RC Matteh Yehudah	478
Ben Ammi	Acre Plain	1949	Moshav	TM	RC Ga'aton	294
Benayah	Southern Coastal Plain (Reḥovot Region)	1949	Moshav	TM	RC Brenner	270
Bene-Berak	Coastal Plain (Tel Aviv Region)	1924	City		municipality	74,200
Benei Atarot	Coastal Plain (Petaḥ Tikvah Region)	1948	Moshav	TM	RC Modi'im	282
Benei Ayish	Southern Coastal Plain (Reḥovot Region)	1958	Village	—	RC Ḥevel Yavneh	990

Benei Darom	Coastal Plain (Reḥovot Region)	1949	Moshav Shittufi	PM	RC Ḥevel Yavneh	199
Benei Deror	Southern Sharon	1946	Moshav Shittufi	TM	RC Hadar ha-Sharon	219
Benei Re'em	Coastal Plain (Reḥovot Region)	1949	Moshav	PAI	RC Naḥal Sorek	332
Benei Zion	Southern Sharon (Herzliyyah Region)	1947	Moshav	IḤ	RC Ḥof ha-Sharon	380
Ben Shemen	Coastal Plain (Lod Region)	1921	Youth Village		(RC) Modi'im	830
Ben Shemen	Coastal Plain (Lod Region)	1952	Moshav	TM	RC Modi'im	215
Ben Zakkai	Southern Coastal Plain (Reḥovot Region)	1950	Moshav	PM	RC Ḥevel Yavneh	620
Berekhyah	Southern Coastal Plain (Ashkelon Region)	1950	Moshav	TM	RC Ḥof Ashkelon	750
Berosh	Northern Negev (Gerar Region)	1953	Moshav	TM	RC Benei Shimon	350
Beror Ḥayil	Southern Coastal Plain (Ashkelon Region)	1948	Kibbutz	IK	RC Sha'ar ha-Negev	570
Bet Alfa	Harod Valley	1922	Kibbutz	KA	RC Ha-Gilboa	690
Bet Arif	Coastal Plain (Lod Region)	1951	Moshav	TM	RC Modi'im	540
Bet Berl	Southern Sharon	1947	Educational Center	H	(RC) Ha-Sharon ha-Tikhon	227
Bet Dagan	Coastal Plain (Lod Region)	1948	Urban Settlement		local council	2,720

Name	Geographical Region	Year of Founding	Settlement Form	Affiliation	Municipal Status	No. of inhabitants 31 Dec 71
Bet Elazari	Coastal Plain (Reḥovot Region)	1948	Moshav	TM	RC Brenner	459
Bet Ezra	Southern Coastal Plain (Malakhi Region)	1950	Moshav	TM	RC Be'er Tuviyyah	570
Bet Gamli'el	Coastal Plain (Reḥovot Region)	1949	Moshav	PM	RC Ḥevel Yavneh	380
Bet Guvrin	Southern Judean Foothills	1949	Kibbutz	KM	RC Yo'av	115
Bet ha-Emek	Acre Plain	1949	Kibbutz	IK	RC Ga'aton	315
Bet ha-Gaddi	Northern Negev (Gerar Region)	1949	Moshav	PM	RC Azzatah	650
Bet ha-Levi	Central Sharon (Ḥefer Plain)	1945	Moshav	TM	RC Ḥefer Plain	225
Bet ha-Shittah	Harod Valley	1935	Kibbutz	KM	RC Ha-Gilboa	910
Bet Ḥanan	Coastal Plain (Rishon le-Zion Region)	1930	Moshav	TM	RC Gan Raveh	367
Bet Ḥananyah	Northern Sharon (Ḥaderah Region)	1950	Moshav	TM	RC Hof ha-Karmel	260
Bet Ḥerut	Central Sharon (Ḥefer Plain)	1933	Moshav Shittufi	TM	RC Ḥefer Plain	299

Bet Ḥilkiyyah	Coastal Plain (Reḥovot Region)	1953	Moshav	PAI	RC Naḥal Sorek	263
Bet Hillel	Ḥuleh Valley	1940	Moshav	TM	RC Ha-Galil ha-Elyon	177
Beth-Shean	Beth-Shean Valley	—	Urban Settlement	—	local council	12,100
Beth-Shemesh (Formerly Hartuv)	Judean Foothills	1950	Urban Settlement	—	local council	10,600
Bet Kamah	Northern Negev (Gerar Region)	1949	Kibbutz	KA	RC Benei Shimon	258
Bet Keshet	Eastern Lower Galilee	1944	Kibbutz	KM	RC Ha-Galil ha-Taḥton'	278
Bet Leḥem ha-Gelilit	Southern Lower Galilee	1948	Moshav	TM	RC Kishon	274
Bet Me'ir	Judean Hills	1950	Moshav	PM	RC Matteh Yehudah	300
Bet Neḥemyah	Northern Judean Foothills (Lod Region)	1950	Moshav	OẒ	RC Modi'im	264
Bet Nekofah	Jerusalem Hills	1949	Moshav	TM	RC Matteh Yehudah	197
Bet Nir	Southern Coastal Plain (Lachish Region)	1955	Kibbutz	KA	RC Yo'av	187
Bet Oren	Mount Carmel	1939	Kibbutz	KM	RC Ḥof ha-Karmel	197
Bet Oved	Coastal Plain (Rishon le-Zion Region)	1933	Moshav	TM	RC Gan Raveh	217
Bet Rabban	Coastal Plain (Reḥovot Region)	1946	Yeshivah	KD	RC Ḥevel Yavneh	350

Name	Geographical Region	Year of Founding	Settlement Form	Affiliation	Municipal Status	No. of inhabitants 31 Dec 71
Bet She'arim	Jezreel Valley	1936	Moshav	TM	RC Kishon	308
Bet Shikmah	Southern Coastal Plain (Ashkelon Region)	1950	Moshav	TM	RC Ḥof Ashkelon	555
Bet Uzzi'el	Judean Foothills (Lod Region)	1956	Moshav	PM	RC Gezer	330
Bet Yannai	Central Sharon (Ḥefer Plain)	1933	Moshav	IḤ	RC Ḥefer Plain	234
Bet Yehoshu'a	Southern Sharon (Netanyah Region)	1938	Moshav	OẒ	RC Ḥof ha-Sharon	234
Bet Yiẓḥak	Central Sharon Ḥefer Plain)	1940	Rural Settlement	—	RC Ḥefer Plain	825
Bet Yosef	Beth-Shean Valley	1937	Moshav	TM	RC Beth-Shean Valley	320
Bet Zayit	Jerusalem Hills	1949	Moshav	TM	RC Matteh Yehudah	500
Bet Zera	Kinneret Valley	1927	Kibbutz	KA	RC Jordan Valley	640
Bet Ẓevi (Kefar Sitrin)	Carmel Coast	1953	Educational Institute	—	(RC) Ḥof ha-Karmel	350
Beẓet	Acre Plain	1949	Moshav	TM	RC Sullam Ẓor	239

Binyaminah	Northern Sharon (Ḥaderah Region)	1922	Urban Settlement	—	local council	2,560
Biranit	Western Upper Galilee	1964	Rural Settlement	—	(RC) Ma'aleh ha-Galil	
Biriyyah	Eastern Upper Galilee	1945	Rural Settlement	—	RC Merom ha-Galil	339
Bitan Aharon	Central Sharon (Ḥefer Plain)	1936	Moshav	IḤ	RC Ḥefer Plain	100
Bitḥah	Northwestern Negev (Besor Region)	1950	Moshav	TM	RC Merḥavim	710
Biẓẓaron	Southern Coastal Plain (Malakhi Region)	1935	Moshav	TM	RC Be'er Tuviyyah	425
Boẓrah	Southern Sharon (Kefar Sava Region)	1946	Moshav	IḤ	RC Ḥof ha-Sharon	410
Burgetah	Central Sharon (Ḥefer Plain)	1949	Moshav	TM	RC Ḥefer Plain	327
Bustan ha-Galil	Acre Plain	1948	Moshav	IḤ	RC Ga'aton	320
Dafnah	Ḥuleh Valley	1939	Kibbutz	KM	RC Ha-Galil ha-Elyon	570
Daliyyah	Manasseh Hills	1939	Kibbutz	KA	RC Megiddo	610
Dalton	Eastern Upper Galilee	1950	Moshav	PM	RC Merom ha-Galil	670
Dan	Ḥuleh Valley	1939	Kibbutz	KA	RC Ha-Galil ha-Elyon	430

Name	Geographical Region	Year of Founding	Settlement Form	Affiliation	Municipal Status	No. of inhabitants 31 Dec 71
Daverat	Jezreel Valley	1946	Kibbutz	IK	RC Yizre'el	293
Deganim (Merkaz Shapira)	Southern Coastal Plain (Malakhi Region)	1948	Rural Center	—	(RC) Shafir	510
Deganyah (Deganiyyah) Alef	Kinneret Valley	1909	Kibbutz	IK	RC Jordan Valley	442
Deganyah (Deganiyyah) Bet	Kinneret Valley	1920	Kibbutz	IK	RC Jordan Valley	545
Devirah	Northern Negev (Beersheba Region)	1951	Kibbutz	KA	RC Benei Shimon	190
Devorah	Jezreel Valley (Taanach Region)	1956	Moshav	TM	RC Ha-Gilboa	301
Dimonah	Negev Hills	1955	City	—	municipality	23,200
Dishon	Eastern Upper Galilee	1953	Moshav	OẒ	RC Ha-Galil ha-Elyon	..
Dor	Carmel Coast	1949	Moshav	TM	RC Ḥof ha-Karmel	167
Dorot	Southern Coastal Plain (Ashkelon Region)	1941	Kibbutz	IK	RC Sha'ar ha-Negev	411
Dovev	Eastern Upper Galilee	1963	Moshav	TM	RC Merom ha-Galil	..
Ein Ayyalah	Carmel Coast	1949	Moshav	TM	RC Ḥof ha-Karmel	297

Efal-Bet Avot	Coastal Plain (Tel Aviv Region)	1950	Aged People's Home	—	RC Ono	400
Efal-Merkaz Seminariyyonim	Coastal Plain (Tel Aviv Region)	1950	Educational Institute	—	RC Ono	62
Eilat (Elath)	Southern Negev	1951	Town	—	municipality	15,900
Eilon	Western Upper Galilee	1938	Kibbutz	KA	RC Sullam Ẓor	590
Eilot	Eilat Hills	1962	Kibbutz	KM	RC Ḥevel Eilot	..
Einat	Coastal Plain (Petaḥ Tikvah Region)	1925	Kibbutz	IK	RC Mifaloṭ Afek	480
Ein Ayyalah	Carmel Coast	1949	Moshav	TM	RC Ḥof ha-Karmel	302
Ein Gev	Kinneret Valley	1937	Kibbutz	IK	RC Jordan Valley	308
Ein ha-Emek	Manasseh Hills	1944	Rural Settlement	—	RC Megiddo	311
Ein ha-Ḥoresh	Central Sharon (Ḥefer Plain)	1931	Kibbutz	KA	RC Ḥefer Plain	610
Ein ha-Mifraẓ	Zebulun Valley	1938	Kibbutz	KA	RC Na'aman	620
Ein ha-Naẓiv	Beth-Shean Valley	1946	Kibbutz	KD	RC Beth-Shean Valley	378
Ein ha-Sheloshah	Northwestern Negev (Besor Region)	1950	Kibbutz	OẒ	RC Eshkol	270
Ein ha-Shofet	Manasseh Hills	1937	Kibbutz	KA	RC Megiddo	600

Name	Geographical Region	Year of Founding	Settlement Form	Affiliation	Municipal Status	No. of inhabitants 31 Dec 71
Ein Ḥaẓevah	Central Arabah Valley	1970	Moshav Shittufi	IH	(RC) Tamar	
Ein Hod	Mount Carmel	1954	Artists' Village	—	(RC) Ḥof ha-Karmel	37
Ein Iron	Northern Sharon (Ḥaderah Region)	1934	Moshav	TM	RC Manasseh	190
Ein Karmel	Carmel Coast	1947	Kibbutz	KM	RC Ḥof ha-Karmel	371
Ein Kerem	Jerusalem Hills	1952	Agricultural School	—	—	210
Ein Sarid	Southern Sharon (Kefar Sava Region)	1950	Rural Settlement	—	RC Hadar ha-Sharon	470
Ein Shemer	Northern Sharon (Ḥaderah Region)	1927	Kibbutz	KA	RC Manasseh	560
Ein Vered	Southern Sharon (Kefar Sava Region)	1930	Moshav	TM	RC Hadar ha-Sharon	520
Ein Ya'akov	Western Upper Galilee	1950	Moshav	TM	RC Ma'aleh ha-Galil	280
Ein Yahav	Central Arabah Valley	1951	Moshav	TM	RC Ḥevel Eilot	. .
Ein Zivan	Golan; 67+	1968	Kibbutz	KM	—	. .
Ein Ẓurim	Southern Coastal Plain (Shafir Region)	1949	Kibbutz	KD	RC Shafir	350
Eitan	Southern Coastal Plain (Lachish Region)	1955	Moshav	PM	RC Shafir	458

Eitanim	Jerusalem Hills	1952	Hospital	—	(RC) Matteh Yehudah	212
El Al (Ṇahal El Al)	Golan; 67+	1968	Moshav	TM	—	. .
Elifelet	Eastern Upper Galilee (Hazor Region)	1949	Moshav	TM	RC Ha-Galil ha-Elyon	372
Elishama	Southern Sharon	1951	Moshav	TM	RC Ha-Yarkon	560
Elkosh	Western Upper Galilee	1949	Moshav	TM	RC Ma'aleh ha-Galil	318
Elrom	Golan;67+	1971	Kibbutz	KM	—	. .
Elyakhin	Central Sharon (Ḥefer Plain)	1950	Rural Settlement	—	RC Ḥefer Plain	1,775
Elyakim	Manasseh Hills	1949	Moshav	TM	RC Megiddo	620
Elyashiv	Central Sharon (Ḥefer Plain) . .	1933	Moshav	HI	RC Ḥefer Plain	363
Emunim	Southern Coastal Plain (Malakhi Region)	1950	Moshav	TM	RC Be'er Tuviyyah	384
Enat	Coastal Plain (Petaḥ Tikvah Region)	1925	Kibbutz	IK	RC Mifalot Afek	490
En-Dor	Eastern Lower Galilee	1948	Kibbutz	KA	RC Yizre'el	555
En-Gedi	Dead Sea Region	1953	Kibbutz	IK	RC Tamar	. .
En-Harod	Harod Valley	1921	Kibbutz	IK	RC Ha-Gilboa	680
En-Harod	Harod Valley	1921	Kibbutz	KM	RC Ha-Gilboa	785

Name	Geographical Region	Year of Founding	Settlement Form	Affiliation	Municipal Status	No. of inhabitants 31 Dec 71
Erez	Southern Coastal Plain (Ashkelon Region)	1949	Kibbutz	IK	RC Sha'ar ha-Negev	203
Eshbol	Northern Negev (Gerar Region)	1955	Moshav	TM	RC Merḥavim	410
Eshel ha-Ṇasi	Northern Negev (Besor Region)	1952	Agricultural School	—	(RC) Merḥavim	280
Eshtaol	Judean Foothills	1949	Moshav	TM	RC Matteh Yehudah	344
Even Menaḥem	Western Upper Galilee	1960	Moshav	TM	RC Ma'aleh ha-Galil	313
Even Sappir	Jerusalem Hills	1950	Moshav	TM	RC Matteh Yehudah	440
Even Shemu'el	Southern Coastal Plain (Lachish Region)	1956	Rural Center	—	RC Shafir	230
Even Yehudah	Southern Sharon (Netanyah Region)	1932	Rural Settlement	—	local council	3,910
Even Yiẓḥak (Galed)	Manasseh Hills	1945	Kibbutz	IK	RC Megiddo	267
Evron	Acre Plain	1945	Kibbutz	KA	RC Ga'aton	440
Eyal	Southern Sharon (Kefar Sava Region)	1949	Kibbutz	KM	RC Ha-Sharon ha-Tikhon	112
Ezer	Southern Coastal Plain (Malakhi Region)	1966	Rural Center	—	(RC) Be'er Tuviyyah	47

Ga'ash	Southern Sharon (Herzliyyah Region)	1951	Kibbutz	KA	RC Ḥof ha-Sharon	412
Ga'aton	Western Upper Galilee	1948	Kibbutz	KA	RC Ga'aton	292
Gadish	Jezreel Valley (Taanach Region)	1956	Moshav	TM	RC Ha-Gilboa	470
Gadot	Eastern Upper Galilee (Hazor Region)	1949	Kibbutz	KM	RC Ha-Galil ha-Elyon	260
Galon	Southern Judean Foothills	1946	Kibbutz	KA	RC Yo'av	370
Gan ha-Darom	Coastal Plain (Reḥovot Region)	1953	Moshav	IḤ	RC Gederot	266
Gan ha-Shomron	Northern Sharon (Ḥaderah Region)	1934	Rural Settlement	—	RC Manasseh	320
Gan Ḥayyim	Southern Sharon (Kefar Sava Region)	1935	Moshav	TM	RC Ha-Sharon ha-Tikhon	220
Gannei Am	Southern Sharon (Kefar Sava Region)	1934	Moshav	—	RC Ha-Yarkon	179
Gannei Tikvah	Coastal Plain (Petaḥ Tikvah Region)	1953	Urban Settlement	—	local council	3,140
Gannei Yehudah	Coastal Plain (Petaḥ Tikvah Region)	1951	Moshav	IḤ	RC Mifalot Afek	630
Gannei Yoḥanan (Gannei Yonah)	Coastal Plain (Reḥovot Region)	1950	Moshav	TM	RC Gezer	279
Gannot	Coastal Plain (Lod Region)	1953	Moshav	IḤ	RC Emek Lod	292
Gannot Hadar	Southern Sharon (Netanyah Region)	1964	Rural Settlement	—	RC Ha-Sharon ha-Ẓefoni	80

Name	Geographical Region	Year of Founding	Settlement Form	Affiliation	Municipal Status	No. of inhabitants 31 Dec 71
Gan Shelomo (Kevuẓat Schiller)	Coastal Plain (Reḥovot Region)	1927	Kibbutz	IK	RC Brenner	277
Gan Shemu'el	Northern Sharon (Ḥaderah Region)	1913	Kibbutz	KA	RC Manasseh	750
Gan Sorek	Coastal Plain (Rishon le-Zion Region)	1950	Moshav	TM	RC Gan Raveh	120
Gan Yavneh	Coastal Plain (Reḥovot Region)	1931	Rural Settlement	—	local council	2,750
Gan Yoshiyyah	Central Sharon (Ḥefer Plain)	1949	Moshav	TM	RC Ḥefer Plain	203
Gat	Southern Coastal Plain (Lachish Region)	1942	Kibbutz	KA	RC Yo'av	462
Gat Rimmon	Coastal Plain (Petaḥ Tikvah Region)	1926	Rural Settlement	—	RC Mifalot Afek	177
Gazit	Southeastern Lower Galilee	1948	Kibbutz	KA	RC Yizre'el	446
Ge'ah	Southern Coastal Plain (Ashkelon Region)	1949	Moshav	TM	RC Ḥof Ashkelon	179
Ge'alyah	Coastal Plain (Reḥovot Region)	1948	Moshav	TM	RC Gan Raveh	380
Gederah	Coastal Plain (Reḥovot Region)	1884	Urban Settlement	—	local council	5,200
Gefen	Southern Judean Foothills	1955	Moshav	PM	RC Matteh Yehudah	374
Gelil Yam	Southern Sharon (Herzliyyah Region)	1943	Kibbutz	KM	RC Ḥof ha-Sharon	269

Gerofit	Southern Arabah Valley	1963	Kibbutz	IK	RC Ḥevel Eilot	. .
Gesher	Kinneret Valley	1939	Kibbutz	KM	RC Jordan Valley	. .
Gesher ha-Ziv	Acre Plain	1949	Kibbutz	IK	RC Sullam Ẓor	388
Ge'ulei Teiman	Central Sharon (Ḥefer Plain)	1947	Moshav	PM	RC Ḥefer Plain	185
Ge'ulei Teiman	Central Sharon (Ḥefer Plain)	1947	Rural Settlement	—	RC Ḥefer Plain	180
Ge'ulim	Southern Sharon	1945	Moshav	TM	RC Ḥefer Plain	515
Geva	Harod Valley	1921	Kibbutz	IK	RC Ha-Gilboa	515
Geva Karmel	Carmel Coast	1949	Moshav	TM	RC Ḥof ha-Karmel	395
Gevaram	Southern Coastal Plain (Ashkelon Region)	1942	Kibbutz	KM	RC Ḥof Ashkelon	220
Gevat	Jezreel Valley	1926	Kibbutz	KM	RC Kishon	640
Gevim	Southern Coastal Plain (Ashkelon Region)	1947	Kibbutz	IK	RC Sha'ar ha-Negev	255
Gevulot	Northwestern Negev (Besor Region)	1943	Kibbutz	KA	RC Eshkol	128
Gezer	Judean Foothills	1945	Institution	—	RC Gezer	20
Gibbethon	Coastal Plain (Reḥovot Region)	1933	Moshav	—	RC Brenner	159

Name	Geographical Region	Year of Founding	Settlement Form	Affiliation	Municipal Status	No. of inhabitants 31 Dec 71
Gidonah	Harod Valley	1949	Rural Settlement	—	RC Ha-Gilboa	149
Gilat	Northern Negev (Gerar Region)	1949	Moshav	TM	RC Merḥavim	580
Gimzo	Judean Foothills	1950	Moshav	PAI	RC Modi'im	156
Ginnat	Golan; 67 +	1971	Rural Settlement	—	—	..
Ginnaton	Coastal Plain (Lod Region)	1949	Moshav	TM	RC Modi'im	260
Ginnegar	Jezreel Valley	1922	Kibbutz	IK	RC Yizre'el	418
Ginnosar	Kinneret Valley	1937	Kibbutz	KM	RC Jordan Valley	400
Givat Adah	Northern Sharon (Ḥaderah Region)	1903	Rural Settlement	—	local council	1,410
Givatayim	Coastal Plain (Tel Aviv Region)	1922	City	—	municipality	47,600
Givat Brenner	Coastal Plain (Reḥovot Region)	1928	Kibbutz	KM	RC Brenner	1,525
Givat ha-Sheloshah	Coastal Plain (Petaḥ Tikvah Region)	1925	Kibbutz	KM	RC Mifalot Afek	440
Givat Ḥayyim	Central Sharon (Ḥefer Plain)	1932	Kibbutz	IK	RC Ḥefer Plain	690
Givat Ḥayyim	Central Sharon (Ḥefer Plain)	1932	Kibbutz	KM	RC Ḥefer Plain	720

Givat Ḥen	Southern Sharon	1933	Moshav	TM	RC Ha-Yarkon	225
Givat Ko'aḥ	Judean Foothills	1950	Moshav	TM	RC Modi'im	388
Givat Nili	Northwestern Iron Hills	1953	Moshav	Ḥ	RC Allonah	194
Givat Oz	Jezreel Valley	1949	Kibbutz	KA	RC Megiddo	385
Givat Shapira	Southern Sharon	1958	Moshav	IḤ	RC Ḥefer Plain	114
Givat Shemesh	Judean Foothills	1954	Educational Institution		(RC) Matteh Yehudah	106
Givat Shemu'el	Coastal Plain (Petaḥ Tikvah Region)	1942	Urban Settlement	—	local council	4,700
Givat Ye'arim	Jerusalem Hills	1950	Moshav	TM	RC Matteh Yehudah	530
Givat Yeshayahu	Judean Foothills (Adullam Region)	1958	Moshav	OẒ	RC Matteh Yehudah	114
Givat Yo'av	Golan; 67+	1968	Moshav	TM		..
Givati	Southern Coastal Plain (Malakhi Region)	1950	Moshav	TM	RC Be'er Tuviyyah	380
Givolim	Northern Negev (Gerar Region)	1952	Moshav	PM	RC Azzatah	210
Givot Zaid	Jezreel Valley	1943	Rural Settlement	—	(RC) Kishon	110
Gizo	Judean Foothills	1968	Rural Center	—	—	40
Gonen	Ḥuleh Valley	1951	Kibbutz	IK	RC Ha-Galil ha-Elyon	252

Name	Geographical Region	Year of Founding	Settlement Form	Affiliation	Municipal Status	No. of inhabitants 31 Dec 71
Goren	Western Upper Galilee	1950	Moshav	TM	RC Ma'aleh ha-Galil	338
Ha-Bonim	Carmel Coast	1949	Moshav Shittufi	TM	RC Ḥof ha-Karmel	170
Hadar Am	Central Sharon (Ḥefer Plain)	1933	Moshav	IḤ	RC Ḥefer Plain	168
Ḥaderah	Northern Sharon (Ḥaderah Region)	1890	Town	—	municipality	31,500
Ḥadid	Northern Judean Foothills	1950	Moshav	PM	RC Modi'im	414
Ḥafeẓ Ḥayyim	Southern Coastal Plain (Reḥovot Region)	1944	Kibbutz	PAI	RC Naḥal Sorek	330
Ḥagor	Southern Sharon (Kefar Sava Region)	1949	Moshav	TM	RC Mifalot Afek	306
Ha-Gosherim	Ḥuleh Valley	1949	Kibbutz	KM	RC Ha-Galil ha-Elyon	410
Ha-Ḥoterim	Carmel Coast	1948	Kibbutz	KM	RC Ḥof ha-Karmel	354
Haifa	Mt. Carmel and Zebulun Valley	—	City	—	municipality	219,200 thereof 13,500 non-Jews
Ḥamadyah	Beth-Shean Valley	1942	Kibbutz	IK	RC Beth-Shean	

Ha-Ma'pil	Northern Sharon	1945	Kibbutz	KA	RC Ḥefer Plain	446
Ḥamrah	Lower Jordan Valley; 67 +	1971	Moshav Shittufi	—	OẒ	. .
Ḥanitah	Western Upper Galilee	1938	Kibbutz	IK	RC Sullam Ẓor	. .
Ḥanni'el	Central Sharon (Ḥefer Plain)	1950	Moshav	TM	RC Ḥefer Plain	275
Ha-Ogen	Central Sharon (Ḥefer Valley)	1947	Kibbutz	KA	RC Ḥefer Plain	486
Ha-On	Kinneret Valley	1949	Kibbutz	IK	RC Jordan Valley	156
Harel	Judean Foothills	1948	Kibbutz	KA	RC Matteh Yehudah	153
Ḥaruẓim	Southern Sharon	1951	Rural Settlement	—	RC Ḥof ha-Sharon	575
Ha-Solelim	Western Lower Galilee	1949	Kibbutz	OẒ	RC Kishon	176
Ḥavaẓẓelet ha-Sharon	Central Sharon (Ḥefer Plain)	1935	Moshav	IḤ	RC Ḥefer Plain	150
Ḥavvat ha-Shomer	Eastern Lower Galilee	1956	Educational Institute	—	(RC) Ha-Galil ha-Taḥton	250
Ha-Yogev	Jezreel Valley	1949	Moshav	TM	RC Yizre'el	352
Ḥaẓav	Southern Coastal Plain (Malakhi Region)	1949	Moshav	TM	RC Be'er Tuviyyah	760
Ḥaẓerim	Northern Negev (Beersheba Region)	1946	Kibbutz	IK	RC Benei Shimon	3,333

Name	Geographical Region	Year of Founding	Settlement Form	Affiliation	Municipal Status	No. of inhabitants 31 Dec 71
Ḥaẓevah	Central Arabah Valley	1965	Moshav	TM	RC Tamar	. .
Ḥazon	Eastern Lower Galilee	1969	Moshav	PM	RC Merom ha-Galil	135
Ḥaẓor Ashdod	Southern Coastal Plain (Malakhi Region)	1946	Kibbutz	KA	RC Be'er Tuviyyah	520
Ha-Zore'a	Jezreel Valley	1936	Kibbutz	KA	RC Megiddo	690
Ha-Zore'im	Eastern Lower Galilee	1939	Moshav	PM	RC Ha-Galil ha-Taḥton	310
Ḥaẓor ha-Gelilit	Eastern Upper Galilee (Hazor Region)	1953	Urban Settlement	—	local council	5,250
Ḥefẓi-Bah	Harod Valley	1922	Kibbutz	KM	RC Ha-Gilboa	473
Ḥeleẓ	Southern Coastal Plain (Ashkelon Region)	1950	Moshav	TM	RC Ḥof Ashkelon	565
Ḥemed	Coastal Plain (Lod Region)	1950	Moshav	PM	RC Emek Lod	510
Ḥerev le-Et	Central Sharon (Ḥefer Plain)	1947	Moshav	IḤ	RC Ḥefer Plain	215
Ḥerut	Southern Sharon (Kefar Sava Region)	1930	Moshav	TM	RC Hadar ha-Sharon	406
Herzliyyah	Southern Sharon	1924	City	—	municipality	40,100

Ḥever	Jezreel Valley (Taanach Region)	1958	Rural Center	—	(RC)	20
					Ha-Gilboa	
Ḥibbat Zion	Central Sharon (Ḥefer Plain)	1933	Moshav	HI	RC	281
					Ḥefer Plain	
Hod ha-Sharon	Southern Sharon (Kefar Sava Region)	1924	Urban Settlement	—	local council	13,000
Hodiyyah	Southern Coastal Plain (Ashkelon Region)	1949	Moshav	TM	RC	433
					Ḥof Ashkelon	
Ḥofit	Central Sharon (Ḥefer Plain)	1955	Rural Settlement	—	RC	420
					Ḥefer Plain	203
Ḥoglah	Central Sharon (Ḥefer Plain)	1933	Moshav	TM	RC	
					Ḥefer Plain	
Ḥolon	Coastal Plain (Tel Aviv Region)	1933	City	—	municipality	93,400
Ḥoreshim	Southern Sharon (Kefar Sava Region)	1955	Kibbutz	KA	RC	170
					Mifalot Afek	
Ḥosen	Western Upper Galilee	1949	Moshav	Ḥ	RC	243
					Ma'aleh ha-Galil	
Ḥukkok	Eastern Lower Galilee	1945	Kibbutz	KM	RC	200
					Jordan Valley	
Ḥulatah	Ḥuleh Valley	1937	Kibbutz	KM	RC	350
					Ha-Galil ha-Elyon	
Ḥuldah	Judean Foothills	1930	Kibbutz	IK	RC	274
					Gezer	
Ilaniyyah	Eastern Lower Galilee	1902	Moshav	IḤ	RC	190
					Ha-Galil ha-Taḥton	

Name	Geographical Region	Year of Founding	Settlement Form	Affiliation	Municipal Status	No. of inhabitants 31 Dec 71
Jerusalem	Jerusalem Hills	—	City	—	municipality	301,3000 thereof 79,100 non-Jews
Kabri	Acre Plain	1949	Kibbutz	KM	RC Ga'aton	540
Kadimah	Southern Sharon (Kefar Yonah Region)	1933	Urban Settlement	—	local council	3,970
Kadoorie	Eastern Lower Galilee	1931	Agricultural School	—	(RC) Ha-Galil ha-Taḥton	264
Kannot	Southern Coastal Plain (Malakhi Region)	1952	Agricultural School	—	(RC) Be'er Tuviyyah	304
Karmi'el	Western Lower Galilee	1964	Urban Settlement	—	local council	3,850
Karmiyyah	Southern Coastal Plain (Ashkelon Region)	1950	Kibbutz	KA	RC Ḥof Ashkelon	230
Kedmah	Southern Coastal Plain (Malakhi Region)	1946	Rural Settlement	—	(RC) Yo'av	—
Kefar Aḥim	Southern Coastal Plain (Malakhi Region)	1949	Moshav	TM	RC Be'er Tuviyyah	235
Kefar Aviv	Coastal Plain (Reḥovot Region)	1951	Moshav	IḤ	RC Gederot	258

Kefar Avodah	Southern Sharon (Herzliyyah Region)	1942	Educational Institution	—	(RC) Hadar ha-Sharon	. .
Kefar Azar	Coastal Plain (Tel Aviv Region)	1932	Moshav	TM	RC Ono	350
Kefar Azzah	Southern Coastal Plain (Ashkelon Region)	1951	Kibbutz	IK	RC Sha'ar ha-Negev	186
Kefar Barukh	Jezreel Valley	1926	Moshav	TM	RC Kishon	213
Kefar Bialik	Zebulun Valley (Haifa Bay Area)	1934	Moshav	IḤ	RC Zebulun	550
Kefar Bilu	Coastal Plain (Reḥovot Region)	1932	Moshav	TM	RC Gezer	368
Kefar Bin Nun	Judean Foothills	1952	Moshav	IḤ	RC Gezer	149
Kefar Blum	Ḥuleh Valley	1943	Kibbutz	IK	RC Ha-Galil ha-Elyon	530
Kefar Dani'el (Bet Ḥever)	Coastal Plain (Lod Region)	1949	Moshav Shittufi	TM	RC Modi'im	127
Kefar Darom	Gaza Strip; 67 +	1970	Kibbutz	KD	—	. .
Kefar Eẓyon	Hebron Hills; 67 +	1967	Kibbutz	KD		
Kefar Gallim	Carmel Coast	1952	Agricultural School	—	—	445
Kefar Gidon	Jezreel Valley	1923	Moshav	PAI	RC Yizre'el	134
Kefar Giladi	Ḥuleh Valley	1916	Kibbutz	IK	RC Ha-Galil ha-Elyon	635
Kefar Glickson	Northern Sharon (Ḥaderah Region)	1939	Kibbutz	OẒ	RC Manasseh	260

Name	Geographical Region	Year of Founding	Settlement Form	Affiliation	Municipal Status	No. of inhabitants 31 Dec 71
Kefar Ḥabad	Coastal Plain (Lod Region)	1949	Moshav		RC Emek Lod	1,620
Kefar ha-Ḥoresh	Southern Lower Galilee	1933	Kibbutz	IK	RC Kishon	234
Kefar ha-Makkabbi	Zebulun Valley (Haifa Bay Area)	1936	Kibbutz	IK	RC Zebulun	313
Kefar ha-Nagid	Coastal Plain (Rishon le-Zion area)	1949	Moshav	TM	RC Gan Raveh	340
Kefar ha-Nasi	Eastern Upper Galilee (Hazor Region)	1948	Kibbutz	IK	RC Ha-Galil ha-Elyon	417
Kefar ha-No'ar ha-Dati	Zebulun Valley (Haifa Bay area)	1937	Agricultural School	—	RC Zebulun	580
Kefar ha-Rif	Southern Coastal Plain (Malakhi Region)	1956	Moshav	IḤ	RC Yo'av	237
Kefar ha-Ro'eh	Central Sharon (Ḥefer Plain)	1934	Moshav	PM	RC Ḥefer Plain	860
Kefar Ḥasidim Alef	Zebulun Valley (Haifa Bay area)	1924	Moshav	—	RC Zebulun	380
Kefar Ḥasidim Bet	Zebulun Valley (Haifa Bay area)	1950	Rural Settlement	—	RC Zebulun	350
Kefar Ḥayyim	Central Sharon (Ḥefer Plain)	1933	Moshav	TM	RC Ḥefer Plain	340

Kefar Hess	Southern Sharon (Kefar Sava Region)	1933	Moshav	TM	RC Hadar ha-Sharon	420
Kefar Ḥittim	Eastern Lower Galilee	1936	Moshav Shittufi	TM	RC Ha-Galil ha-Taḥton	194
Kefar Jawitz	Southern Sharon (Kefar Sava Region)	1932	Moshav	PM	RC Hadar ha-Sharon	394
Kefar Kisch	Eastern Lower Galilee	1946	Moshav	TM	RC Ha-Galil ha-Taḥton	170
Kefar Maimon	Northern Negev (Gerar Region)	1959	Moshav	PM	RC Azzatah	260
Kefar Malal (formerly Ein Ḥai)	Southern Sharon (Kefar Sava Region)	1922	Moshav	TM	RC Ha-Yarkon	254
Kefar Masaryk	Zebulun Valley (Haifa Bay area)	1938	Kibbutz	KA	RC Na'aman	520
Kefar Menaḥem	Southern Coastal Plain (Malakhi Region)	1937	Kibbutz	KA	RC Yo'av	545
Kefar Monash	Central Sharon (Ḥefer Plain)	1946	Moshav	TM	RC Ḥefer Plain	307
Kefar Mordekhai	Coastal Plain (Reḥovot Region)	1950	Moshav	IḤ	RC Gederot	211
Kefar Netter	Southern Sharon	1939	Moshav	—	RC Ḥof ha-Sharon	240
Kefar Pines	Northern Sharon (Ḥaderah Region)	1933	Moshav	PM	RC Manasseh	405
Kefar Rosenwald (Zarit)	Western Upper Galilee	1967	Moshav	TM	(RC) Ma'aleh ha-Galil	. .
Kefar Rosh ha-Nikrah	Acre Plain	1949	Kibbutz	IK	RC Sullam Ẓor	. .

Name	Geographical Region	Year of Founding	Settlement Form	Affiliation	Municipal Status	No. of inhabitants 31 Dec 71
Kefar Ruppin	Beth-Shean Valley	1938	Kibbutz	IK	RC Beth-Shean Valley	
Kefar Sava	Southern Sharon	1903	Town	—	municipality	25,200
Kefar Shammai	Eastern Upper Galilee	1949	Moshav	PM	RC Meron, ha-Galil	275
Kefar Shemaryahu	Southern Sharon (Herzliyyah Region)	1937	Rural Settlement	—	local council	1,280
Kefar Shemu'el	Judean Foothills	1950	Moshav	OẒ	RC Gezer	234
Kefar Silver	Southern Coastal Plain (Ashkelon Region)	1957	Agricultural School	—	(RC) Ḥof Ashkelon	246
Kefar Syrkin	Coastal Plain (Petaḥ Tikvah Region)	1936	Rural Settlement	—	RC Mifalot Afek	540
Kefar Szold	Ḥuleh Valley	1942	Kibbutz	KM	RC Ha-Galil ha-Elyon	472
Kefar Tavor	Eastern Lower Galilee	1901	Rural Settlement	—	local council	300
Kefar Truman	Northern Judean Foothills	1949	Moshav	TM	RC Modi'im	277
Kefar Uriyyah	Judean Foothills	1944	Moshav	TM	RC Matteh Yehudah	265
Kefar Vitkin	Central Sharon (Ḥefer Plain)	1933	Moshav	TM	RC Ḥefer Plain	825
Kefar Warburg	Southern Coastal Plain (Malakhi Region)	1939	Moshav	TM	RC Be'er Tuviyyah	490

Kefar Yeḥezkel	Harod Valley	1921	Moshav	TM	RC Ha-Gilboa	437
Kefar Yehoshu'a	Jezreel Valley	1927	Moshav	TM	RC Kishon	650
Kefar Yonah	Southern Sharon	1932	Rural Settlement	—	local council	2,710
Kefar Zeitim	Eastern Lower Galilee	1950	Moshav	TM	RC Ha-Galil ha-Taḥton	261
Kelaḥim	Northern Negev (Gerar Region)	1954	Moshav	IḤ	RC Merḥavim	287
Kerem Ben Zimrah	Eastern Upper Galilee	1949	Moshav	PM	RC Merom ha-Galil	300
Kerem Maharal	Mount Carmel	1949	Moshav	TM	RC Ḥof ha-Karmel	210
Kerem Shalom	Northwestern Negev (Besor Region)	1956	Kibbutz	KA	RC Eshkol	..
Kerem Yavneh	Coastal Plain (Reḥovot Region)	1963	Educational Institution (Yeshivah)	PM	RC Ḥevel Yavneh	242
Kevuẓat Yavneh	Coastal Plain (Reḥovot Region)	1941	Kibbutz	KD	RC Ḥevel Yavneh	665
Kesalon	Judean Hills	1952	Moshav	IḤ	RC Matteh Yehudah	225
Kidron	Coastal Plain (Reḥovot Region)	1949	Moshav	TM	RC Brenner	570
Kinneret	Kinneret Valley	1908	Kibbutz	IK	RC Jordan Valley	660
Kinneret	Kinneret Valley	1909	Rural Settlement	—	local council	185
Kiryat Anavim	Jerusalem Hills	1920	Kibbutz	IK	RC Matteh Yehudah	327

Name	Geographical Region	Year of Founding	Settlement Form	Affiliation	Municipal Status	No. of inhabitants 31 Dec 71
Kiryat Ata	Zebulun Valley (Haifa Bay area)	1925	Town	—	municipality	26,700
Kiryat Bialik	Zebulun Valley (Haifa Bay area)	1934	Urban Settlement	—	local council	15,700
Kiryat Ekron	Coastal Plain (Reḥovot Region)	1948	Urban Settlement	—	local council	4,220
Kiryat Gat	Southern Coastal Plain (Lachish Region)	1954	Urban Settlement	—	local council	18,300
Kiryat Ḥaroshet	Zebulun Valley (Haifa Bay area)	1935	Rural Settlement	—	local council	231
Kiryat Malakhi	Southern Coastal Plain (Malakhi Region)	1951	Urban Settlement	—	local council	8,650
Kiryat Motzkin	Zebulun Valley (Haifa Bay area)	1934	Urban Settlement	—	local council	16,300
Kiryat Ono	Coastal Plain (Tel Aviv Region)	1939	Urban Settlement	—	local council	15,400
Kiryat Shemonah	Ḥuleh Valley	1950	Urban Settlement	—	local council	15,200
Kiryat Tivon	Southern Lower Galilee (Tivon Hills)	1937	Urban Settlement	—	local council	9,850
Kiryat Yam	Zebulun Valley (Haifa Bay area)	1946	Urban Settlement	—	local council	18,300
Kiryat Ye'arim	Jerusalem Hills	1952	Educational Institution	—	(RC) Matteh Yehudah	130
Kissufim	Northwestern Negev (Besor Region)	1951	Kibbutz	KM	RC Eshkol	261
Kokhav Mikha'el	Southern Coastal Plain (Ashkelon Region)	1950	Moshav	TM	RC Ḥof Ashkelon	319
Komemiyyut	Southern Coastal Plain (Malakhi Region)	1950	Moshav	PAI	RC Shafir	337

Lahav (Ẓiklag)	Northern Negev (Beersheba Region)	1952	Kibbutz	KA	RC Benei Shimon	212
Lahavot ha-Bashan	Ḥuleh Valley	1945	Kibbutz	KA	RC Ha-Galil ha-Elyon	457
Lahavot Ḥavivah	Northern Sharon (Ḥaderah Region)	1949	Kibbutz	KA	RC Manasseh	230
Lachish (Lakhish)	Southern Coastal Plain (Lachish Region)	1955	Moshav	TM	RC Lachish	225
Lavi	Eastern Lower Galilee	1949	Kibbutz	KD	RC Ha-Galil ha-Taḥton	500
Liman	Acre Plain	1949	Moshav	TM	RC Sullam Ẓor	250
Li On	Judean Foothills (Adullam Region)	1960	Rural Center	—	(RC) Matteh Yehudah	22
Lod (Lydda)	Coastal Plain (Lod Region)	—	Town	—	municipality	31,200 thereof 3,400 non-Jews
Loḥamei ha-Getta'ot	Acre Plain	1949	Kibbutz	KM	RC Ga'aton	341
Luzit	Southern Judean Foothills	1955	Moshav	TM	RC Matteh Yehudah	271
Ma'agan	Kinneret Valley	1949	Kibbutz	IK	RC Jordan Valley	266
Ma'agan Mikha'el	Carmel Coast	1949	Kibbutz	KM	RC Ḥof ha-Karmel	760

Name	Geographical Region	Year of Founding	Settlement Form	Affiliation	Municipal Status	No. of inhabitants 31 Dec 71
Ma'aleh Gilboa	Mt. Gilboa	1962	Kibbutz	KD	(RC) Beth-Shean Valley	
Ma'aleh ha-Ḥamishah	Jerusalem Hills	1938	Kibbutz	IK	RC Matteh Yehudah	273
Ma'alot-Tarshiḥa	Western Upper Galilee	(1957)	Urban Settlement	—	local council	5,200 thereof 1,850 non-Jews
Ma'anit	Northern Sharon (Ḥaderah Region)	1942	Kibbutz	KA	RC Manasseh	410
Ma'as	Coastal Plain (Petaḥ Tikvah Region)	1935	Moshav	TM	RC Mifalot Afek	424
Ma'barot	Central Sharon (Ḥefer Plain)	1933	Kibbutz	KA	RC Ḥefer Plain	550
Mabbu'im	Northern Negev (Gerar Region)	1958	Rural Center	—	RC Merḥavim	165
Ma'gallim	Northern Negev (Gerar Region)	1958	Rural Center	—	(RC) Azzatah	72
Magen	Northwestern Negev (Besor Region)	1949	Kibbutz	KA	RC Eshkol	216
Maggal	Northern Sharon (Ḥaderah Region)	1953	Kibbutz	IK	RC Manasseh	165

Magshimim	Coastal Plain (Petaḥ Tikvah Region)	1949	Moshav	IḤ	RC Mifalot Afek	392
Maḥanayim	Eastern Upper Galilee (Hazor Region)	(1939)	Kibbutz	KM	RC Ha-Galil ha-Elyon	303
Maḥáseyah	Judean Foothills	1950	Rural Settlement	—	RC Matteh Yehudah	198
Malkiyyah	Eastern Upper Galilee	1949	Kibbutz	KM	RC Ha-Galil ha-Elyon	..
Manarah	Eastern Upper Galilee	1943	Kibbutz	KM	RC Ha-Galil ha-Elyon	..
Ma'or	Northern Sharon (Ḥaderah Region)	1953	Moshav	TM	RC Manasseh	190
Ma'oz Ḥayyim	Beth-Shean Valley	1937	Kibbutz	KM	RC Beth-Shean Valley	..
Margaliyyot	Eastern Upper Galilee	1951	Moshav	TM	RC Ha-Galil ha-Elyon	..
Mashabbei Sadeh	Negev Hills	1949	Kibbutz	KM	RC Ramat ha-Negev	300
Mashen	Southern Coastal Plain (Ashkelon Region)	1950	Moshav	TM	RC Ḥof Ashkelon	705
Maslul	Northwestern Negev (Besor Region)	1950	Moshav	TM	RC Merḥavim	183
Massadah	Kinneret Region	1937	Kibbutz	IK	RC Jordan Valley	290
Massu'ot Yiẓḥak	Southern Coastal Plain (Malakhi Region)	1949	Moshav Shittufi	PM	RC Shafir	412
Matta	Judean Hills	1950	Moshav	TM	RC Matteh Yehudah	212

Name	Geographical Region	Year of Founding	Settlement From	Affiliation	Municipal Status	No. of inhabitants 31 Dec 71
Mavki'im	Southern Coastal Plain (Ashkelon Region)	1949	Moshav Shittufi	OẒ	RC Ḥof Ashkelon	140
Ma'yan Barukh	Ḥuleh Valley	1947	Kibbutz	IK	RC Ha-Galil ha-Elyon	. .
Ma'yan Ẓevi	Mt. Carmel	1938	Kibbutz	IK	RC Ḥof ha-Karmel	530
Mazkeret Batyah	Coastal Plain (Reḥovot Region)	1883	Rural Settlement	—	local council	980
Maẓli'aḥ	Coastal Plain (Lod Region)	1950	Moshav	TM	RC Gezer	665
Mazor	Coastal Plain (Petaḥ Tikvah Region)	1949	Moshav	TM	RC Modi'im	303
Maẓẓuvah	Western Upper Galilee	1940	Kibbutz	IK	RC Sullam Ẓor	353
Megadim	Carmel Coast	1949	Moshav	TM	RC Ḥof ha-Karmel	424
Mefallesim	Southern Coastal Plain (Ashkelon Region)	1949	Kibbutz	IK	RC Sha'ar ha-Negev	400
Megiddo	Jezreel Valley	1949	Kibbutz	KA	RC Megiddo	288
Meḥolah	Lower Jordan Valley; 67 +	1968	Moshav	PM	—	. .
Mei Ammi	Samaria (Iron Hills)	1963	Moshav Shittufi	OẒ	—	. .
Me'ir Shefeyah	Mt. Carmel	(1923)	Agricultural School	—	RC Ḥof ha-Karmel	500

Meishar	Coastal Plain (Reḥovot Region)	1950	Moshav	IḤ	RC Gederot	183
Meitav	Jezreel Valley (Taanach Region)	1954	Moshav	TM	RC Ha-Gilboa	485
Mele'ah	Jezreel Valley (Taanach Region)	1956	Moshav	TM	RC Ha-Gilboa	254
Melilot	Northern Negev (Gerar Region)	1953	Moshav	PM	RC Azzatah	356
Menaḥemiyyah	Eastern Lower Galilee	1902	Moshav	IḤ	local council	650
Menuḥah (Vardon)	Southern Coastal Plain (Malakhi Region)	1953	Moshav	TM	RC Lachish	565
Me'onah	Western Upper Galilee	1949	Moshav	TM	RC Ma'aleh ha-Galil	280
Merḥavyah	Harod Valley	1922	Moshav	TM	RC Yizre'el	227
Merḥavyah	Harod Valley	1911	Kibbutz	KA	RC Yizre'el	540
Merom Golan	Golan; 67 +	1967	Kibbutz	KM	—	. .
Meron	Eastern Upper Galilee	1949	Moshav	PM	RC Merom ha-Galil	260
Mesillat Zion	Judean Foothills	1950	Moshav	TM	RC Matteh Yehudah	221
Mesillot	Beth-Shean Valley	1938	Kibbutz	KA	RC Beth-Shean Valley	500
Metullah	Eastern Upper Galilee	1896	Rural Settlement	—	local council	360
Mevasseret Zion (Ẓiyyon)	Jerusalem Hills	1951	Urban Settlement	—	local council	4,500
Mevo Beitar	Jerusalem Hills	1950	Moshav Shittufi	Ḥ	RC Matteh Yehudah	203

Name	Geographical Region	Year of Founding	Settlement Form	Affiliation	Municipal Status	No. of inhabitants 31 Dec 71
Mevo Ḥammat	Golan; 67 +	1968	Kibbutz	IK	—	. .
Mevo Ḥoron	Judean Foothills; 67 +	1970	Kibbutz	PAI	—	. .
Mevo Modi'im	Judean Foothills	1964	Moshav	PAI	(RC) Modi'im	26
Meẓer	Northern Sharon (Ḥaderah Region)	1953	Kibbutz	KA	RC Manasseh	270
Midrakh Oz	Jezreel Valley	1952	Moshav	TM	RC Megiddo	452
Midreshet Ruppin	Central Sharon (Ḥefer Plain)	1948	Seminary	—	—	. .
Migdal	Kinneret Valley	1910	Rural Settlement	—	local council	525
Migdal ha-Emek	Southern Lower Galilee	1952	Urban Settlement	—	local council	9,500
Mikhmoret	Central Sharon (Ḥefer Plain)	1945	Moshav and Educational Institution	TM	RC Ḥefer Plain	740
Mikveh Yisrael	Coastal Plain (Tel Aviv Region)	1870	Agricultural School	—	—	1,000
Misgav Am	Eastern Upper Galilee	1945	Kibbutz	KM	RC Ha-Galil ha-Elyon	. .
Misgav Dov	Coastal Plain (Reḥovot Region)	1950	Moshav	Ḥ	RC Gederot	200
Mishmar Ayyalon	Judean Foothills	1949	Moshav	TM	RC Gezer	213
Mishmar David	Judean Foothills	1948	Kibbutz	IK	RC Gezer	80

Mishmar ha-Emek	Jezreel Valley	1926	Kibbuṭz	KA	RC Megiddo	715
Mishmar ha-Negev	Northern Negev (Gerar Region)	1946	Kibbutz	KM	RC Benei Shimon	500
Mishmar ha-Sharon	Central Sharon (Ḥefer Plain)	1933	Kibbutz	IK	RC Ḥefer Plain	380
Mishmar ha-Shivah	Central Coastal Plain (Lod Region)	1949	Moshav	—	RC Emek Lod	430
Mishmar ha-Yarden	Eastern Upper Galilee (Hazor Region)	(1949)	Moshav	Ḥ	RC Ha-Galil ha-Elyon	227
Mishmarot	Northern Sharon (Ḥaderah Region)	1933	Kibbutz	IK	RC Manasseh	220
Mishmeret	Southern Sharon (Kefar Sava Region)	1946	Moshav	TM	RC Hadar ha-Sharon	328
Mivtaḥim	Northwestern Negev (Besor Region)	1950	Moshav	TM	RC Eshkol	452
Mizra	Jezreel Valley	1923	Kibbutz	KA	RC Yizre'el	620
Miẓpeh	Eastern Lower Galilee	1908	Rural Settlement	—	RC Ha-Galil ha-Taḥton	38
Miẓpeh Ramon	Central Negev Hills	1954	Urban Settlement	—	local council	1,520
Miẓpeh Shalem	Dead Sea Region; 67 +	1970	Kibbutz	IK	—	..
Moledet (B'nai B'rith)	Southeastern Lower Galilee	1937	Moshav Shittufi	TM	RC Ha-Gilboa	419
Moẓa Illit	Jerusalem Hills	1933	Rural Settlement	—	RC Matteh Yehudah	406
Moẓa Taḥtit	Jerusalem Hills	1894	Rural Settlement	—	(RC) Matteh Yehudah	38

Name	Geographical Region	Year of Founding	Settlement Form	Affiliation	Municipal Status	No. of inhabitants 31 Dec 71
Na'an	Coastal Plain (Reḥovot Region)	1930	Kibbutz	KM	RC Gezer	875
Naḥalah	Southern Coastal Plain (Malakhi Region)	1953	Moshav	TM	RC Yo'av	400
Nahalal	Jezreel Valley	1921	Moshav	TM	RC	1,050
Naḥalat Yehudah	Coastal Plain (Rishon le-Zion Region)	1914	Rural Settlement	—	Kishon local council	2,350
Naḥal Diklah (Diklah)	Northeastern Sinai; 67 +	1969	Moshav	Ḥ	—	..
Naḥal Geshur	Golan; 67 +	1968	Kibbutz	KA	—	..
Naḥal Gilgal	Lower Jordan Valley; 67 +	1970	Kibbutz	KM	—	..
Naḥal Golan	Golan; 67 +	1967	Kibbutz	IK	—	..
Naḥal Kallia	Dead Sea Region; 67 +	1968	Kibbutz	—	—	..
Naḥal Keturah	Southern Arabah Valley	1970	Kibbutz	IK	RC Ḥevel Eilot	..
Naḥal Massu'ah	Lower Jordan Valley; 67 +	1969	Moshav	PM	—	..
Naḥal Na'aran	Lower Jordan Valley; 67 +	1970	Kibbutz	KM	—	..
Naḥal Oz	Northwestern Negev	1951	Kibbutz	IK	RC Sha'ar ha-Negev	279
Naḥal Paran	Southern Arabah Valley	1971	Moshav	—	(RC) Ḥevel Eilot	..
Naḥal Sinai	Northeastern Sinai; 67 +	1968	Kibbutz	IK	—	..
Naḥal Yam	Northwestern Sinai; 67 +	1967	Kibbutz	KM	—	..

Naḥal Ẓofar	Central Arabah Valley	1968	Kibbutz	KA	RC Ḥevel Eilot	..
Naḥam	Judean Foothills	1950	Moshav	PM	RC Matteh Yehudah	390
Nahariyyah	Acre Plain	1934	Town	—	municipality	23,000
Naḥsholim	Carmel Coast	1948	Kibbutz	KM	RC Ḥof ha-Karmel	245
Naḥshon	Judean Foothills	1950	Kibbutz	KA	RC Matteh Yehudah	260
Naḥshonim	Northern Judean Foothills	1949	Kibbutz	KA	RC Mifalot Afék	248
Naẓerat Illit	Southern Lower Galilee	1957	Urban Settlement	—	local council	15,800
Negbah	Southern Coastal Plain (Malakhi Region)	1939	Kibbutz	KA	RC Yo'av	412
Neḥalim	Coastal Plain (Petaḥ Tikvah Region)	1948	Moshav	PM	RC Modi'im	635
Nehorah	Coastal Plain (Lachish Region)	1956	Rural Center	—	RC Lachish	156
Ne'ot Golan	Golan; 67 +	1968	Moshav	HI	OẒ	..
Ne'ot ha-Kikkar	Northern Arabah Valley	1963	Moshav	IḤ	RC Tamar	..
Ne'ot Mordekhai	Ḥuleh Valley	1946	Kibbutz	IK	RC Ha-Galil ha-Elyon	630
Nes Harim	Jerusalem Hills	1950	Moshav	TM	RC Matteh Yehudah	371
Nesher	Zebulun Valley (Haifa Bay area)	1925	Urban Settlement	—	local council	9,650
Nes Ẓiyyonah	Coastal Plain (Rishon le-Zion Region)	1883	Urban Settlement	—	local council	12,200

Name	Geographical Region	Year of Founding	Settlement Form	Affiliation	Municipal Status	No. of inhabitants 31 Dec 71
Neta'im	Coastal Plain (Rishon le-Zion Region)	1932	Moshav	TM	RC Gan Raveh	205
Netanyah	Southern Sharon	1929	City	—	municipality	67,700
Netiv ha-Lamed He	Southern Judean Foothills	1949	Kibbutz	KM	RC Matteh Yehudah	280
Netiv ha-Shayyarah	Acre Plain	1950	Moshav	TM	RC Ga'aton	363
Netivot	Northwestern Negev (Gerar Region)	1956	Urban Settlement	—	local council	5,550
Netu'ah	Western Upper Galilee	1966	Moshav	TM	(RC) Ma'aleh ha-Galil	..
Ne'urim	Central Sharon (Ḥefer Plain)	1953	Educational Institution	—	(RC) Ḥefer Plain	550
Nevatim	Northern Negev (Beersheba Region)	1946	Moshav	TM	RC Benei Shimon	450
Neveh Avot	Northern Sharon (Ḥaderah Region)	1948	Aged People's Home	—	—	1,050
Neveh Efrayim (Monosson)	Coastal Plain (Petaḥ Tikvah Region)	1953	Rural Settlement	—	local council	1,140
Neveh Eitan	Beth-Shean Valley	1938	Kibbutz	IK	RC Beth-Shean Valley	245
Neveh Ilan	Jerusalem Hills	(1946)	—	—	(RC) Matteh Yehudah	..

Neveh Mivtaḥ	Southern Coastal Plain (Malakhi Region)	1950	Moshav	TM	RC Be'er Tuviyyah	210
Neveh Ur	Northern Beth-Shean Valley	1949	Kibbutz	KM	RC Beth-Shean Valley	..
Neveh Yam	Carmel Coast	1939	Kibbutz	IK	RC Ḥof ha-Karmel	137
Neveh Yamin	Southern Sharon (Kefar Sava Region)	1949	Moshav	TM	RC Ha-Sharon ha-Tikhon	560
Neveh Yarak	Southern Sharon (Herzliyyah Region)	1951	Moṣhav	TM	RC Ha-Yarkon	390
Neẓer Sereni	Coastal Plain (Rishon le-Zion Region)	1948	Kibbutz	IK	RC Gezer	515
Nir Akiva	Northern Negev (Gerar Region)	1953	Moshav	TM	RC Merḥavim	120
Nir Am	Southern Coastal Plain (Ashkelon Region)	1943	Kibbutz	IK	RC Sha'ar ha-Negev	267
Nir Banim	Southern Coastal Plain (Malakhi Region)	1954	Moshav	TM	RC Shafir	329
Nir David	Beth-Shean Valley	1936	Kibbutz	KA	RC Beth-Shean Valley	560
Nir Eliyahu	Southern Sharon (Kefar Sava Region)	1950	Kibbutz	IK	RC Ha-Sharon ha-Tikhon	220
Nir Eẓyon	Mt. Carmel	1950	Moshav Shittufi	PM	RC Ḥof ha-Karmel	478
Nir Gallim	Southern Coastal Plain (Yavneh Region)	1949	Moshav Shittufi	PM	RC Ḥevel Yavneh	413
Nir Ḥen	Southern Coastal Plain (Lachish Region)	1955	Moshav	TM	RC Lachish	110

Name	Geographical Region	Year of Founding	Settlement Form	Affiliation	Municipal Status	No. of inhabitants 31 Dec 71
Nirim	Northwestern Negev (Besor Region)	1949	Kibbutz	KA	RC Eshkol	280
Nir Moshe	Northern Negev (Gerar Region	1953	Moshav	TM	RC Merḥavim	185
Nir Oz	Northwestern Negev (Besor Region)	1955	Kibbutz	KA	RC Eshkol	200
Nir Yafeh	Jezreel Valley (Taanach Region)	1956	Moshav	TM	RC Ha-Gilboa	254
Nir Yisrael	Southern Coastal Plain (Ashkelon Region)	1949	Moshav	OẒ	RC Ḥof Ashkelon	230
Nir Yiẓḥak (formerly Nirim)	Northwestern Negev (Besor Region)	(1949)	Kibbutz	KA	RC Eshkol	257
Nir Ẓevi	Coastal Plain (Lod Region)	1954	Moshav	IḤ	RC Emek Lod	520
Niẓẓanei Oz	Southern Sharon (Kefar Yonah Region)	1951	Moshav	TM	RC Ha-Sharon ha-Ẓefoni	342
Niẓẓanim	Southern Coastal Plain (Ashkelon Region)	1943	Kibbutz	OẒ	RC Ḥof Ashkelon	250
Niẓẓanim (Kefar ha-No'ar)	Southern Coastal Plain (Ashkelon Region)	1949	Agricultural School	—	RC Ḥof Ashkelon	400
No'am	Southern Coastal Plain (Lachish Region)	1953	Moshav	PM	RC Shafir	500
Nofekh	Coastal Plain (Petaḥ Tikvah Region)	1949	Rural Settlement	—	RC Modi'im	210

Nogah	Southern Coastal Plain (Lachish Region)	1955	Moshav	TM	RC Lachish	535
Nordiyyah	Southern Sharon (Netanyah Region)	1948	Moshav Shittufi	Ḥ	RC Ha-Sharon ha-Ẓefoni	284
Ofakim	Northwestern Negev (Besor Region)	1955	Urban Settlement	—	local council	9,300
Ofer	Mount Carmel	1950	Moshav	TM	RC Ḥof ha-Karmel	238
Ofirah	Southern Sinai 67 +	1971	Rural Settlement	—	—	. .
Ohad	Northwestern Negev (Besor Region)	1969	Moshav	TM	RC Eshkol	152
Olesh	Central Sharon (Ḥefer Plain)	1949	Moshav	TM	RC Ḥefer Plain	295
Omen	Jezreel Valley (Taanach Region)	1958	Rural Center	—	(RC) Ha-Gilboa	20
Omer	Northern Negev (Beersheba Region)	1949	Rural Settlement	—	RC Benei Shimon	1,200
Omeẓ	Central Sharon (Ḥefer Plain)	1949	Moshav	TM	RC Ḥefer Plain	198
Orah	Jerusalem Hills	1950	Moshav	TM	RC Matteh Yehudah	295
Or Akiva	Northern Sharon (Ḥaderah Region)	1951	Urban Settlement	—	local council	6,400
Oranim	Southern Lower Galilee (Tivon Hills)	1951	Kibbutz Seminary	—	RC Zebulun	350

Name	Geographical Region	Year of Founding	Settlement Form	Affiliation	Municipal Status	No. of inhabitants 31 Dec 71
Or ha-Ner	Southern Coastal Plain (Ashkelon Region)	1957	Kibbutz	IK	RC Sha'ar ha-Negev	284
Orot	Southern Coastal Plain (Malakhi Region)	1952	Moshav	TM	RC Be'er Tuviyyah	248
Or Yehudah	Coastal Plain (Tel Aviv Region)	1950	Urban Settlement	—	local council	12,900
Oẓem	Southern Coastal Plain (Lachish Region)	1955	Moshav	TM	RC Lachish	640
Pa'amei Tashaz	Northern Negev (Gerar Region)	1953	Moshav	TM	RC Merḥavim	305
Palmaḥim	Coastal Plain (Rishon le-Zion Region)	1949	Kibbutz	KM	RC Gan Raveh	287
Pardes Ḥannah-Karkur	Northern Sharon (Ḥaderah Region)	(1913)	Urban Settlement	—	local council	13,800
Pardesiyyah	Southern Sharon	1942	Rural Settlement	—	local council	700
Parod	Eastern Upper Galilee	1949	Kibbutz	KM	RC Merom ha-Galil	214
Pattish	Northern Negev (Besor Region)	1950	Moshav	TM	RC Merḥavim	640
Pedayah	Judean Foothills	1951	Moshav	TM	RC Gezer	465

Peduyim	Northern Negev (Besor Region)	1950	Moshav	TM	RC Merḥavim	285
Peki'in Ḥadashah	Western Upper Galilee	1955	Moshav	TM	RC Ma'aleh ha-Galil	239
Perazon	Jezreel Valley (Taanach Region)	1953	Moshav	TM	RC Ha-Gilboa	510
Petaḥ Tikvah	Coastal Plain (Petaḥ Tikvah Region)	1878	City	—	municipality	87,200
Petaḥyah	Judean Foothills	1951	Moshav	OẒ	RC Gezer	437
Peẓa'el (Ma'aleh Efrayim)	Lower Jordan Valley; 67 +	1970	Moshav	TM	—	..
Porat	Southern Sharon (Kefar Sava Region)	1950	Moshav	PM	RC Hadar ha-Sharon	815
Poriyyah (Kefar Avodah)	Eastern Lower Galilee	1955	Moshav	—	RC Jordan Valley	110
Poriyyah (Neveh Oved)	Eastern Lower Galilee	1949	Rural Settlement	—	RC Jordan Valley	685
Ra'anannah	Southern Sharon (Herzliyyah Region)	1921	Urban Settlement	—	local council	13,600
Ramat David	Jezreel Valley	1926	Kibbutz	IK	RC Kishon	268
Ramat Efal	Coastal Plain (Tel Aviv Region)	1969	Rural Settlement	—	RC Ono	600
Ramat Gan	Coastal Plain (Tel Aviv Region)	1921	City	—	municipality	119,300
Ramat ha-Kovesh	Southern Sharon (Kefar Sava Region)	1932	Kibbutz	KM	RC Ha-Sharon ha-Tikhon	520

Name	Geographical Region	Year of Founding	Settlement Form	Affiliation	Municipal Status	No. of inhabitants 31 Dec 71
Ramat ha-Sharon	Southern Sharon (Herzliyyah Region)	1923	Urban Settlement	—	local council	18,500
Ramat ha-Shofet	Manasseh Hills	1941	Kibbutz	KA	RC Megiddo	540
Ramat Magshimim	Golan; 67 +	1968	Moshav	PM	—	..
Ramat Pinkas	Coastal Plain (Tel Aviv Region)	1952	Rural Settlement	—	RC Ono	745
Ramat Raḥel	Jerusalem Hills	1926	Kibbutz	IK	RC Matteh Yehudah	76
Ramat Raziel	Judean Hills	1948	Moshav	Ḥ	RC Matteh Yehudah	148
Ramat Yishai	Southern Lower Galilee (Tivon Hills)	1925	Rural Settlement	—	local council	800
Ramat Yoḥanan	Zebulun Valley (Haifa Bay area)	1932	Kibbutz	IK	RC Zebulun	520
Ramat Ẓevi	Southeastern Lower Galilee	1942	Moshav	TM	RC Ha-Gilboa	176
Ramleh	Coastal Plain (Lod Region)	—	City	—	municipality	32,600 thereof 4,000 non-Jews
Ram On	Jezreel Valley (Taanach Region)	1960	Moshav	TM	RC Ha–Gilboa	215

Ramot	Golan: 67 +	1970	Moshav	TM		. .
Ramot ha-Shavim	Southern Sharon (Kefar Sava Region)	1933	Moshav	IḤ	local council	465
Ramot Me'ir	Coastal Plain (Lod Region)	1949	Moshav Shittufi	TM	RC Gezer	220
Ramot Menasheh	Manasseh Hills	1948	Kibbutz	KA	RC Megiddo	483
Ramot Naftali	Eastern Upper Galilee	1945	Moshav	TM	RC Ha-Galil ha-Elyon	. .
Rannen	Northern Negev (Besor Region)	1950	Moshav	TM	RC Merḥavim	414
Regavim	Manasseh Hills	1948	Kibbutz	KM	RC Manasseh	290
Regbah	Acre Plain	1946	Moshav Shittufi	TM	RC Ga'aton	327
Reḥov	Beth-Shean Valley	1951	Moshav	PM	RC Beth-Shean Valley	345
Reḥovot	Coastal Plain (Reḥovot Region)	1890	City	—	municipality	37,900
Re'im	Northwestern Negev (Besor Region)	1949	Kibbutz	KM	RC Eshkol	200
Rekhasim	Zebulun Valley (Haifa Bay area)	1957	Urban Settlement	—	local council	2,570
Reshafim	Beth-Shean Valley	1948	Kibbutz	KA	RC Beth-Shean Valley	455
Revadim	Southern Coastal Plain (Malakhi Region)	1948	Kibbutz	KA	RC Yo'av	268
Revaḥah	Southern Coastal Plain (Lachish Region)	1953	Moshav	PM	RC Shafir	570
Revayah	Beth-Shean Valley	1952	Moshav	PM	RC Beth-Shean Valley	336

Name	Geographical Region	Year of Founding	Settlement Form	Affiliation	Municipal Status	No. of inhabitants 31 Dec 71
Revivim	Negev (southern Beersheba basin)	1943	Kibbutz	KM	RC Ramat ha-Negev	440
Rinnatyah	Coastal Plain (Lod Region)	1949	Moshav	TM	RC Modi'im	440
Rishon le-Zion	Coastal Plain (Rishon le-Zion Region)	1882	City	—	municipality	50,400
Rishpon	Southern Sharon (Herzliyyah Region)	1936	Moshav	TM	RC Ḥof ha-Sharon	442
Roglit	Judean Foothills (Adullam Region)	1958	Moshav	HI	RC Matteh Yehudah	269
Rosh ha-Ayin	Coastal Plain (Petaḥ Tikvah Region)	1950	Urban Settlement	—	local council	11,700
Rosh Pinnah	Eastern Upper Galilee (Hazor Region)	1882	Rural Settlement	—	local council	825
Rosh Ẓurim	Hebron Hills; 67 +	1969	Kibbutz	KD	—	..
Ruḥamah	Southern Coastal Plain (Ashkelon Region)	(1944)	Kibbutz	KA	RC Sha'ar ha-Negev	515
Sa'ad	Northwestern Negev (Gerar Region)	1947	Kibbutz	KD	RC Azzatah	540
Sa'ar	Acre Plain	1948	Kibbutz	KA	RC Ga'aton	226
Sadot	Northeastern Sinai	1971	Moshav	TM	—	..

Safed (Ẓefat)	Eastern Upper Galilee	—	Town	—	municipality	13,200
Sarid	Jezreel Valley	1926	Kibbutz	KA	RC Kishon	600
Sasa	Eastern Upper Galilee	1949	Kibbutz	KA	RC Merom ha-Galil	. .
Savyon	Coastal Plain (Tel Aviv Region)	1954	Rural Settlement	—	RC Mifalot Afek	1,760
Sedeh Boker	Central Negev Hills	1952	Kibbutz	IK	RC Ramat ha-Negev	. .
Sedeh Boker (Midrashah)	Central Negev Hills	1965	Educational Institution	—	RC Ramat ha-Negev	560
Sedeh David	Southern Coastal Plain (Lachish Region)	1955	Moshav	OẒ	RC Lachish	440
Sedeh Eli'ezer	Ḥuleh Valley	1952	Moshav	OẒ	RC Ha-Galil ha-Elyon	260
Sedeh Eliyahu	Beth-Shean Valley	1939	Kibbutz	KD	RC Beth-Shean Valley	405
Sedeh Ilan	Eastern Lower Galilee	1949	Moshav	PM	RC Ha-Galil ha-Taḥton	211
Sedeh Moshe	Southern Coastal Plain (Lachish Region)	1956	Moshav	TM	RC Lachish	295
Sedeh Naḥum	Beth-Shean Valley	1937	Kibbutz	KM	RC Beth-Shean Valley	277
Sedeh Neḥemyah	Ḥuleh Valley	1940	Kibbutz	IK	RC Ha-Galil ha-Elyon	313
Sedeh Uzziyyah	Southern Coastal Plain (Malakhi Region)	1950	Moshav	OẒ	RC Be'er Tuviyyah	800

Name	Geographical Region	Year of Founding	Settlemen. Form	Affiliation	Municipal Status	No. of inhabitants 31 Dec 71
Sedeh Warburg	Southern Sharon (Kefar Sava Region)	1938	Moshav	IḤ	RC Ha-Sharon ha-Tikhon	360
Sedeh Ya'akov	Jezreel Valley	1927	Moshav	PM	RC Kishon	530
Sedeh Yiẓḥak	Northern Sharon (Ḥaderah Region)	1952	Moshav	TM	RC Manasseh	152
Sedeh Yo'av	Southern Coastal Plain (Malakhi Region)	1956	Kibbutz	KA	RC Yo'av	73
Sedeh Ẓevi	Northern Negev (Gerar Region)	1953	Moshav	IḤ	RC Merḥavim	300
Sedei Ḥemed	Southern Sharon (Kefar Sava Region)	1952	Moshav	TM	RC Ha-Sharon ha-Tikhon	274
Sedei Terumot	Beth-Shean Valley	1951	Moshav	PM	RC Beth-Shean Valley	480
Sederot	Southern Coastal Plain (Ashkelon Region)	1951	Urban Settlement	—	local council	7,650
Sedom (Sodom)	Dead Sea Region	—	Industrial Site	—	—	..
Sedot Mikhah	Southern Judean Foothills	1955	Moshav	TM	RC Matteh Yehudah	290
Sedot Yam	Northern Sharon (Ḥaderah Region)	1940	Kibbutz	KM	RC Ḥof ha-Karmel	500
Segev	Western Lower Galilee	1953	Rural Settlement	—	—	162

Segullah	Southern Coastal Plain (Malakhi Region)	1953	Moshav	TM	RC Yo'av	235
Senir (Ramat Banias, Kefar Moshe Sharett)	Ḥuleh Valley; 67 +	1967	Kibbutz	KA	(RC) Ha–Galil ha–Elyon	
Shaalbim	Northern Judean Foothills	1951	Kibbutz	PAI	RC Gezer	300
Sha'ar Efrayim	Southern Sharon (Kefar Yonah Region)	1953	Moshav	TM	RC Ha-Sharon ha-Ẓefoni	491
Sha'arei Avraham	Coastal Plain (Reḥovot Region)	1958	Educational Institution	—	(RC) Naḥal Sorek	70
Sha'ar ha-Amakim	Southern Lower Galilee (Tivon Hills)	1935	Kibbutz	KA	RC Zebulun	570
Sha'ar ha-Golan	Kinneret Valley	1937	Kibbutz	KA	RC Jordan Valley	600
Sha'ar Ḥefer	Central Sharon (Ḥefer Plain)	1940	Moshav	IḤ	RC Ḥefer Plain	356
Sha'ar Menasheh	Northern Sharon (Ḥaderah Region)	1949	Institution (Aged People's Village)	—	(RC) Manasseh	400
Shadmot Devorah	Eastern Lower Galilee	1939	Moshav	TM	RC Ha-Galil ha-Taḥton	161
Shafir	Southern Coastal Plain (Malakhi Region)	1949	Moshav	PM	RC Shafir	241
Shaḥar	Southern Coastal Plain (Lachish Region)	1955	Moshav	TM	RC Lachish	355
Shalvah	Southern Coastal Plain (Lachish Region)	1952	Moshav	PM	RC Shafir	505

Name	Geographical Region	Year of Founding	Settlement Form	Affiliation	Municipal Status	No. of inhabitants 31 Dec 71
Shamir	Ḥuleh Valley	1944	Kibbutz	KA	RC Ha-Galil ha-Elyon	433
Sharonah	Eastern Lower Galilee	1938	Moshav	TM	RC Ha-Galil ha-Taḥton	190
Sharsheret	Northwestern Negev (Gerar Region)	1951	Moshav	PM	RC Azzatah	550
Shavei Zion	Acre Plain	1938	Moshav Shittufi	IḤ	local council	325
She'ar Yashuv	Ḥuleh Valley	1940	Moshav	OẒ	RC Ha-Galil ha-Elyon	..
Shedemah	Coastal Plain (Reḥovot Region)	1954	Moshav	IḤ	RC Gederot	161
Shefayim	Southern Sharon (Herzliyyah Region)	1935	Kibbutz	KM	RC Ḥof ha-Sharon	525
Shefer	Eastern Upper Galilee	1950	Moshav	TM	RC Merom ha-Galil	259
Shelomi	Acre Plain	1950	Rural Settlement	—	local council	2,010
Sheluḥot	Beth-Shean Valley	1948	Kibbutz	KD	RC Beth-Shean Valley	340
Shetulah	Western Upper Galilee	1969	Moshav	TM	RC Ma'aleh ha-Galil	..
Shetulim	Southern Coastal Plain (Malakhi Region)	1950	Moshav	TM	RC Be'er Tuviyyah	640

Shezor	Western Lower Galilee	1953	Moshav	TM	RC Merom ha-Galil	345
Shibbolim	Nort..western Negev (Gerar Region)	1952	Moshav	PM	RC Azzatah	402
Sho'evah	Judean Hills	1950	Moshav	IḤ	RC Matteh Yehudah	190
Shokedah	Northwestern Negev (Gerar Region)	1957	Moshav	PM	RC Azzatah	330
Shomerah	Northwestern Upper Galilee	1949	Moshav	TM	RC Ma'aleh ha-Galil	268
Shomrat	Acre Plain	1948	Kibbutz	KA	RC Ga'aton	316
Shoresh	Judean Hills	1948	Moshav Shittufi	OẒ	RC Matteh Yehudah	183
Shoshannat ha-Amakim	Central Sharon (Ḥefer Plain)	1951	Rural Settlement	—	(RC) Ḥefer Plain	360
Shoshannat ha-Amakim (Ammidar)	Central Sharon (Ḥefer Plain)	1956	Rural Settlement	—	RC Ḥefer Plain	226
Shoval	Northern Negev (Gerar Region)	1946	Kibbutz	KA	RC Benei Shimon	440
Shuvah	Northwestern Negev (Gerar Region)	1950	Moshav	PM	RC Azzatah	398
Sifsufah	Eastern Upper Galilee	1949	Moshav	TM	RC Merom ha-Galil	480
Sitriyyah	Coastal Plain (Reḥovot Region)	1949	Moshav	TM	RC Gezer	404

Name	Geographical Region	Year of Founding	Settlement Form	Affiliation	Municipal Status	No. of inhabitants 31 Dec 71
Tal Shaḥar	Judean Foothills	1948	Moshav	TM	RC Matteh Yehudah	401
Talmei Bilu	Northern Negev (Gerar Region)	1953	Moshav	HI	RC Merḥavim	270
Talmei Elazar	Northern Sharon (Ḥaderah Region)	1952	Moshav	HI	RC Manasseh	200
Talmei Eliyahu (Besor C)	Northwestern Negev (Besor Region)	1970	Moshav Shittufi	TM	RC Eshkol	55
Talmei Yafeh	Southern Coastal Plain (Ashkelon Region)	1950	Moshav Shittufi	OẒ	RC Ḥof Ashkelon	87
Talmei Yeḥi'el	Southern Coastal Plain (Malakhi Region)	1949	Moshav	TM	RC Be'er Tuviyyah	280
Ta'oz	Judean Foothills	1950	Moshav	PM	RC Matteh Yehudah	380
Tarum	Judean Foothills	1950	Moshav	PM	RC Matteh Yehudah	382
Te'ashur	Northern Negev (Gerar Region)	1953	Moshav	TM	RC Benei Shimon	184
Tekumah	Northwestern Negev (Gerar Region)	1949	Moshav	PM	RC Azzatah	234
Tel Adashim	Jezreel Valley	1923	Moshav	TM	RC Yizre'el	392

Telamim	Southern Coastal Plain (Lakhish Region)	1950	Moshav	TM	RC Lachish	570
Tel Aviv-Jaffa	Coastal Plain (Tel Aviv Region)	1909	City	—	municipality	383,200 thereof 7,400 non-Jews
Tel Kazir	Kinneret Region	1949	Kibbutz	IK	RC Jordan Valley	. .
Tel Mond	Southern Sharon (Kefar Sava Region)	1929	Rural Settlement	—	local council	3,040
Tel Yiẓḥak (includes Neveh Hadassah)	Southern Sharon (Netanyah Region)	1938	Kibbutz	OẒ	RC Ḥof ha-Sharon	545
Tel Yosef	Harod Valley	1921	Kibbutz	IK	RC Ha-Gilboa	520
Tenuvot	Southern Sharon	1952	Moshav	TM	RC Ha-Sharon ha-Ẓefoni	570
Tiberias (Teveryah)	Kinneret Valley	—	Town	—	municipality	24,200
Tidhar	Northern Negev (Gerar Region)	1953	Moshav	TM	RC Benei Shimon	375
Tifraḥ	Northern Negev (Besor Region)	1949	Moshav	PAI	RC Merḥavim	361
Timmurim	Southern Coastal Plain (Malakhi Region)	1954	Moshav Shittufi	OẒ	RC Be'er Tuviyyah	238
Tirat Karmel	Carmel Coast	1949	Urban Settlement		local council	13,800
Tirat Yehudah	Coastal Plain (Petaḥ Tikvah Region)	1949	Moshav	PM	RC Modi'im	330
Tirat Ẓevi	Beth-Shean Valley	1937	Kibbutz	KD	RC Beth-Shean Valley	. .

Name	Geographical Region	Year of Founding	Settlement Form	Affiliation	Municipal Status	No. of inhabitants 31 Dec 71
Tirosh	Southern Judean Foothills	1955	Moshav	PM	RC Matteh Yehudah	520
Toḥelet	Coastal Plain (Lod Region)	1951	Rural Settlement	—	RC Emek Lod	334
Tushiyyah	Northwestern Negev (Gerar Region)	1958	Rural Center	—	(RC) Azzatah	230
Udim	Southern Sharon (Netanyah Region)	1948	Moshav	IḤ	RC Ḥof ha-Sharon	367
Urim	Northwestern Negev (Besor Region)	1946	Kibbutz	IK	RC Merḥavim	398
Ushah	Zebulun Valley (Haifa Bay area)	1937	Kibbutz	IK	RC Zebulun	320
Uzzah	Southern Coastal Plain (Lachish Region)	1950	Moshav	PM	RC Shafir	715
Ya'arah	Western Upper Galilee	1950	Moshav	TM	RC Ma'aleh ha-Galil	270
Yad Binyamin	Coastal Plain (Reḥovot Region)	1949	Rural Center	—	RC Naḥal Sorek	196
Yad Ḥannah (Me'uḥad)	Central Sharon (Ḥefer Plain)	1950	Kibbutz	KM	RC Ḥefer Plain	..

Yad Ḥannah (Semol)	Central Sharon (Ḥefer Plain)	1950	Kibbutz	—	RC Ḥefer Plain	79
Yad Mordekhai	Southern Coastal Plain (Ashkelon Region)	1943	Kibbutz	KA	RC Ḥof Ashkelon	474
Yad Natan	Southern Coastal Plain (Lachish Region)	1953	Moshav	OẒ	RC Lachish	113
Yad Rambam	Coastal Plain (Lod Region)	1955	Moshav	PM	RC Gezer	565
Yagel	Coastal Plain (Lod Region)	1950	Moshav	TM	RC Emek Lod	377
Yagur	Zebulun Valley (Haifa Bay area)	1922	Kibbutz	KM	RC Zebulun	1,140
Yakhini	Northwestern Negev	1950	Moshav	TM	RC Sha'ar ha-Negev	550
Yakum	Southern Sharon (Herzliyyah Region)	1947	Kibbutz	KA	RC Ḥof ha-Sharon	340
Yanuv	Southern Sharon (Kefar Yonah Region)	1950	Moshav	TM	RC Ha-Sharon ha-Ẓefoni	535
Yardenah	Beth-Shean Valley	1952	Moshav	TM	RC Beth-Shean Valley	..
Yarḥiv	Southern Sharon (Kefar Sava Region)	1949	Moshav	TM	RC Ha-Sharon ha-Tikhon	520
Yarkonah	Southern Sharon (Kefar Sava Region)	1932	Moshav	TM	RC Ha-Yarkon	110
Yashresh	Coastal Plain (Lod Region)	1950	Moshav	TM	RC Gezer	410
Yas'ur	Zebulun Valley (Haifa Bay area)	1949	Kibbutz	KA	RC Na'aman	340
Yavne'el	Eastern Lower Galilee	1901	Rural Settlement	—	local council	1,490

Name	Geographical Region	Year of Founding	Settlement Form	Affiliation	Municipal Status	No. of inhabitants 31 Dec 71
Yavneh (Jabneh)	Coastal Plain (Reḥovot Region)	1949	Urban Settlement	—	local council	10,200
Yaziẓ	Coastal Plain (Lod Region)	1950	Moshav	TM	RC Gezer	605
Yedidah	Judean Hills	1964	Educational Institution	—	(RC) Matteh Yehudah	130
Yedidyah	Central Sharon (Ḥefer Plain)	1935	Moshav	TM	RC Ḥefer Plain	290
Yeḥi'am	Western Upper Galilee	1946	Kibbutz	KA	RC Ga'aton	440
Yehud	Coastal Plain (Petaḥ Tikvah Region)	(1948)	Urban Settlement	—	local council	8,750
Yeroḥam	Central Negev Hills	1951	Urban Settlement	—	local council	5,650
Yesha	Northwestern Negev (Besor Region)	1957	Moshav	TM	RC Eshkol	160
Yesodot	Judean Foothills	1948	Moshav Shittufi	PAI	RC Naḥal Sorek	288
Yesud ha-Ma'alah	Ḥuleh Valley	1883	Rural Settlement	—	local council	455
Yifat	Jezreel Valley	(1926)	Kibbutz	IK	RC Kishon	750
Yiftaḥ	Eastern Upper Galilee	1948	Kibbutz	IK	RC Ha-Galil ha-Elyon	. .
Yinnon	Southern Coastal Plain (Malakhi Region)	1952	Moshav	TM	RC Be'er Tuviyyah	615

Yiron	Eastern Upper Galilee	1949	Kibbutz	KM	RC Merom ha-Galil	. .
Yish'i	Judean Foothills	1950	Moshav	PM	RC Matteh Yehudah	510
Yizre'el	Mt. Gilboa	1948	Kibbutz	IK	RC Ha-Gilboa	290
Yodefat	Western Lower Galilee	1960	Kibbutz	—	RC Na'aman	59
Yokne'am	Jezreel Valley	1935	Rural Settlement	—	RC Megiddo	450
Yokne'am (Illit)	Jezreel Valley	1950	Urban Settlement	—	local council	3,650
Yoshivyah	Northwestern Negev (Besor Region)	1950	Moshav	PM	RC Azzatah	246
Yotvatah	Southern Arabah Valley	1951	Kibbutz	IK	RC Ḥevel Eilot	. .
Yuval	Ḥuleh Valley	1952	Moshav	TM	RC Ha-Galil ha-Elyon	. .
Ẓafririm	Southern Judean Foothills (Adullam Region)	1958	Moshav	TM	RC Matteh Yehudah	194
Ẓafriyyah	Coastal Plain (Lod Region)	1949	Moshav	PM	RC Emek Lod	307
Zano'aḥ	Judean Foothills	1950	Moshav	PAI	RC Matteh Yehudah	331
Zavdi'el	Southern Coastal Plain (Malakhi Region)	1950	Moshav	PAI	RC Shafir	411
Ẓe'elim	Northwestern Negev (Besor Region)	1947	Kibbutz	IK	RC Eshkol	193

Name	Geographical Region	Year of Founding	Settlement Form	Affiliation	Municipal Status	No. of inhabitants 31 Dec 71
Zeitan	Coastal Plain (Lod Region)	1950	Moshav	TM	RC Emek Lod	478
Zekharyah	Southern Judean Foothills	1950	Moshav	TM	RC Matteh Yehudah	585
Ẓelafon	Judean Foothills	1950	Moshav	TM	RC Matteh Yehudah	499
Zeraḥyah	Southern Coastal Plain (Malakhi Region)	1950	Moshav	PM	RC Shafir	46
Ẓerufah	Carmel Coast	1949	Moshav	TM	RC Ḥof ha-Karmel	430
Zeru'ah	Northwestern Negev (Gerar Region)	1953	Moshav	PM	RC Azzatah	294
Zikhron Ya'akov	Mt. Carmel	1882	Urban Settlement	—	local council	4,490
Zikim	Southern Coastal Plain (Ashkelon Region)	1949	Kibbutz	KA	RC Ḥof Ashkelon	227
Zimrat	Northwestern Negev (Gerar Region)	1957	Moshav	PM	RC Azzatah	412
Ẓippori	Western Lower Galilee	1949	Moshav	TM	RC Kishon	192
Ẓofit	Southern Sharon (Kefar Sava Region)	1933	Moshav	TM	RC Ha-Sharon ha-Tikhon	330
Ẓofiyyah	Coastal Plain (Reḥovot Region)	1955	Educational Institution	—	(RC) Ḥevel Yavneh	66

Zohar	Southern Coastal Plain (Lachish Region)	1956	Moshav	IḤ	RC Lachish	265
Ẓorah	Judean Foothills	1948	Kibbutz	IK	RC Matteh Yehudah	449
Ẓovah	Jerusalem Hills	1948	Kibbutz	KM	RC Matteh Yehudah	294
Ẓur Hadassah	Jerusalem Hills	1960	Rural Center	—	(RC) Matteh Yehudah	105
Ẓuri'el	Western Upper Galilee	1950	Moshav	PAI	RC Ma'aleh ha-Galil	210
Ẓur Moshe	Southern Sharon (Kefar Yonah Region)	1937	Moshav	TM	RC Ha-Sharon ha-Ẓefoni	415
Ẓur Natan	Southern Sharon	1966	Moshav Shittufi	Ḥ	(RC) Ha-Sharon ha-Tikhon	..

[E.O.]

ARAB, DRUZE AND OTHER SETTLEMENTS

Name	No. of inhabitants 31 Dec. 71	Geographical Region
Abū ʿAbdūn	326	Beersheba Region
Abu ʿAmār	266	,,
Abū ʿAmra	189	,,
Abū Balāl	595	,,
Abū Ghush	1,910	Hills of Judea
Abū Juwayʿid	1,670	Beersheba Region
Abū Quraināt	2,050	,,
Abū Rabīʿa	3,420	,,
Abū Raqāʿiq	4,390	,,
Abū Sinān	3,130	Plain of Acre
Abū Sraihān	284	Beersheba Region
Afeinīsh	525	,,
ʿAkbara	358	E. Upper Galilee
ʿAmariya	95	Haifa Region
ʿĀra	2,390	Mt. Alexander
ʿAr ara	3,190	,,
ʿArrāba (ʿArrābat al-Buṭṭūf)	6,200	W. Lower Galilee
Asad	488	Beersheba Region
Aʿsim	1,750	,,
ʿAtauna	800	,,
ʿAylabūn	1,500	E. Lower Galilee
ʿAyn al-Asad	371	W. Upper Galilee
ʿAyn al-Sahla	500	Mt Alexander
ʿAyn Māhil	3,330	Hills of Nazareth–Tivon
ʿAyn Rāfa	418	Hills of Judea
Baʿna	2,290	W. Lower Galilee

Name	No. of inhabitants 31 Dec. 71	Geographical Region
Bāqā al-Gharbiya	7,600	Hadera Region
Barṭa'a	785	Mt Alexander
Basmat Ṭab'ūn	930	Hills of Nazareth–Tivvon
Bayt Jann	4,590	W. Upper Galilee
Bayt Jimāl	58	Shefela Yehudah
Bīr al-Maksūr	2,130	W. Lower Galilee
Bīr al-Sikka	432	Sharon
Bittir	?	Hills of Judea
Biyāda	248	
(Khirbat al-Biyāda)		Mt Alexander
Bu'ayna	1,410	Hills of Nazareth–Tivon
Dabbūriyya	3,100	Hills of Nazareth–Tivon
(al-) Daḥī	207	Jezreel Valley
Dāliyat al-Karmil	6,050	Haifa Region
Dayr al-Asad	3,050	W. Lower Galilee
Dayr Ḥannā	2,870	,,
Dayr Rāfāt	?	Shefela Yehuda
Fassūṭa	1,560	W. Upper Galilee
Furaydīs	3,230	Carmel Coast
Ghazzālyn	35	Hills of Nazareth–Tivon
Ghurayfāt	360	,,
Ḥajājra	370	,,
Ḥalaf	580	,,
Hayb Abū Siyāḥ	415	,,
Hayb Baṭṭūf	423	,,
(Ramat Hibb)		
Ḥujayrāt (Dhahra)	545	W. Lower Galilee
Hurfaysh	1,790	W. Upper Galilee
Huzayyil	4,300	Beersheba Region
I'billīn	3,770	Western Lower Galilee
Ibtān	447	Sharon
Ibtīn	780	Haifa Region
Iksāl	3,630	Hills of Nazareth–Tivon
'Ilut	1,770	,,
'Isfiyā	4,260	Haifa Region
Jaljūliya	2,320	South Sharon
Janābib	294	Beersheba Region

Name	No. of inhabitants 31 Dec. 71	Geographical Region
Jatt	3,430	Hadera Region
Jatt	585	W. Upper Galilee
Jawāmīs	288	Hills of Nazareth–Tivon
Jish (Gush Ḥalav)	1,750	E. Upper Galilee
Jisr al-Zarqā	2,750	Hadera Region
Judayda	2,460	Plain of Acre
Jūlis	2,160	W. Upper Galilee
(Khirbat) Jurdayḥ	383	"
Ka'biya	850	Hills of Nazareth–Tivon
Kābūl	3,080	W. Lower Galilee
Kafr Barā	625	Petah Tikva Region
Kafr Kamā	1,330	E. Lower Galilee
Kafr Kanna	5,400	Hills of Nazareth–Tivon
Kafr Manda	3,880	W. Lower Galilee
Kafr Quari'	4,840	Mt. Alexander
Kafr Qāsim	4,550	Petah Tikva Region
Kafr Sumay'	880	W. Upper Galilee
Kafr Yāsīf	685	Kohav Heights
Kaukab	1,100	W. Lower Galilee
Khawālid	325	Hills of Nazareth–Tivon
Kisrā	1,090	W. Upper Galilee
Maghār	6,500	E. Lower Galilee
Majd al-Kurūm	4,120	W. Lower Galilee
(al-) Makr	2,390	Plain of Acre
(al-)Māqūra	60	Zihron Ya'acov Region
Marja	300	Sharon
Mashhad	2,080	Hills of Nazareth–Tivon
Mas'udiyīn al-'Azāzma	3,100	Beersheba Region
Maysar	470	Mt. Alexander
Mazr'a	1,640	Plain of Acre
Mi'ilya	1,510	W. Upper Galilee
Mu'āwiya	950	Mt. Alexander
Muqaybila	770	Jezreel Valley
Mushayrifa	965	Mt. Alexander
Mushayyikh Sa'adiya	166	Hills of Nazareth–Tivon
Muṣmuṣ	1,270	Mt. Alexander

Name	No. of inhabitants 31 Dec. 71	Geographical Region
Muzārib	645	Hills of Nazareth–Tivon
Naḥf	2,980	W. Lower Galilee
Najaydāt	700	Hills of Nazareth–Tivon
Nasāsira	675	Beersheba Region
Nāʻūra	555	Kohav Heights
Nayn	570	"
Nazareth	35,000	Hills of Nazareth–Tivon
Pekiʻin	2,260	W. Upper Galilee
Qalansuwa	4,900	Sharon
Qawāʻin	420	Beersheba Region
Qudayrāt al-Sani	1,750	Beersheba Region
Rāma	3,810	W. Lower Galilee
Rayna	3,930	Hills of Nazareth–Tivon
Rīhānīya	434	E. Upper Galilee
Rumat Hayb (Hayb-Baṭṭuf)	423	Hills of Nazareth–Tivon
Rummāna	198	Lydda Region
Saida	213	Hills of Nazareth–Tivon
Saida	460	"
Sājūr	980	W. Lower Galilee
Sakhnin	8,500	"
Sālim	282	Mt. Alexander
Samnia	190	W. Lower Galilee
Ṣandala	600	Harod Valley
Shaʻab	1,960	W. Lower Galilee
Shaykh Burayk	36	Carmel Coast
Shaykh Dannūn	840	W. Upper Galilee
Shefarʻam	11,500	W. Lower Galilee
Ṣubayḥ	1,100	E Lower Galilee
Sulam	800	Jezreel Valley
Suwāʻid (Kammana)	1,780	W. Lower Galilee
Suwāʻid (Shuwayki-Ḥamariya)	340	"
Ṭaʻbun	120	Haifa Region
Tamra	8,800	W. Lower Galilee
Tamra	405	Koḥav Heights
Tarābīn al–Ṣaniʻ	630	Beersheba Region
(al-) Ṭayyiba	12,000	Sharon

Name	No. of inhabitants 31 Dec. 71	Geographical Region
(al-) Ṭayyiba	470	Koḥav Heights
(al-) Tīra	8,000	Sharon
Ṭūba	1,570	Ḥaẓor Region
Ṭurʿān	3,780	Hills of Nazareth–Tivon
Um-al-Faḥm incl. Khirbat Biyār, ʿAyn Ibrahīm	12,700	Mt. Alexander
Umm al-Quṭūf	181	"
ʿUgbī	640	Beersheba Region
ʿUzayr	640	Hills of Nazareth–Tivon
Wadī Ḥamam	880	Kinneret
Yāfā (Yāfā al-Nāṣira)	4,430	Hills of Nazareth–Tivon
(Khirbat) Yamma	675	Sharon
Yānūḥ	1,140	W. Upper Galilee
Yirka	4,180	"
Zabārija	565	Beersheba Region
Zalafa	1,250	Mt. Alexander
Zubaydāt	450	Haifa Region

INDEX